Ripe Musings

Ripe Musings

Lucian Krukowski

RESOURCE *Publications* • Eugene, Oregon

RIPE MUSINGS

Copyright © 2011 Lucian Krukowski. All rights reserved. Except for brief quotations in critical publications or reviews, no part of this book may be reproduced in any manner without prior written permission from the publisher. Write: Permissions, Wipf and Stock Publishers, 199 W. 8th Ave., Suite 3, Eugene, OR 97401.

Resource Publications
An Imprint of Wipf and Stock Publishers
199 W. 8th Ave., Suite 3
Eugene, OR 97401
www.wipfandstock.com

ISBN 13: 978-1-61097-638-1

Manufactured in the U.S.A.

All scripture quotations, unless otherwise indicated, are taken from the Holy Bible, New International Version®, NIV®. Copyright ©1973, 1978, 1984 by Biblica, Inc.™ Used by permission of Zondervan. All rights reserved worldwide.

Contents

1   About Myself 1

2   Art and Life 77

3   Dying after Eighty 105

4   Place 147

5   Before Beginning and after Ending 185

6   Art and Brain 205

7   The Crooked and the Straight 245

1

About Myself

I

I want to write about myself; it's past time. But this time I must select what in particular I want to write about. I have the usual recourse of preferential memory, and I can embellish on the winey tales told by friends about our early frolics. But there also are the sober documents of past achievements that attest to the way I see myself when my selves are dusted-off and the cudos shine through to light the gloom. And then there are my dreams.

I have always slept a lot—perhaps a habit I developed when there was little in the waking world to embrace. The stronger images of my dreamng life have resisted the crossing-over from dream to waking. But some get through—otherwise, I would not be writng this. The dreams I best remember are the ones that come up just before the morning pee. They refer me back to the solipsistic nature of dreams—their indifference to the world we live in when we are awake. Yes, a dream can refer to the worldly contents of its dreaming, but not to dreams dreamt at other times by the same dreamer.

I pay little heed to daytime explanations of what my dreams are about. Instead, I retreat to the night-pictures I remember, the ones I could not have imagined when awake. The sequence of my dreams—the time-indifferent yet compelling transitions of their subjects—does not offer a strategy for living in life's time. I do notice, around mid-afternoon, that dreams, however susceptible to morning clarity in their recall, are gradually dimmed by day's passing—the mind being cleansed by late light in preparation for next night's dreaming. My best dreams come at night; they are free of the stubborn causality that infects even the choicest of my day-dreams.

Although my life is growing respectably long, my art has suffered from divagations and divertissements similar to those I remember in my dreams. An early premonition of good ideas no sooner grows some hair when it is confronted by a frizzy proponent of another good idea; then the straight and the curly both go to look for drinking buddies in the hope that a third head—parted in the middle but curly on the sides—will join them soon. Just two get lonely—or they fight (which is what always happens to dyadic pairs). But three that come together can proclaim an ever-changing new majority, a self-perpetuating dialectic of a finally free life. So I welcomed the third way—and yet, as happens in the waking memories of my dreams, I found only perplexity: Who are these people—and what do they want?

Still, I do not think that change, although unsettling, is a bad thing. But back then I was cautious: I kept diluting the brash new stuff by keeping the lively dead ones in. The past is like a candy store for kids—once inside, you must choose between the bonbons of drawing or of color, between pure austerity or saturated flesh, divine emptiness or expressive profligacy. So I imagined art (my take on life) as a buffet: I ate and ate—paying no attention to ambition or good taste.

But I knew all along, despite my feasting on the cadavers of old great art, that if I really wanted an opening to the out-there present, I would have to form tomorrow's loud and public noise, repeat it again and again, and hope that it is heard in the afternoon of today. I do not enjoy the notion of obsession (now in flower) and dislike the boredom of sameness (all the rage these days). Yet, I am not single-minded. As I grew older I saw, as in a dream, the faces of my gurus of the absolute—how they slowly became softer and more fleshy, while hiding to the death any hint of not believing in their images of finality. But did they not know (how could they not) that these final images, year by month by day, will be made by others into variant versions of the same-old absolute?

II

I get bored with the conflict between the parameters of change. To change or not to change may be the wrong way to think about life and art—but it is always settled in retrospect, when we are either the winners or the losers of the choice we have made:

They were my teachers—both the champions of the one and the advocates for the many—but this was long ago, when I was too young and callow for such either-or reflections. Mainly, I needed company to drink with and talk a lot of shit with, and to stay connected with life and art all through the night. Then, come morning, they would say to the rising sun as we stumbled through last-night's litter—that it's all alright, you could change or do the same old thing—it didn't really matter. And they also said that either way you do it—if you do it right—you will grow. "Growth" was a catchword then—it meant "Good Move." "To do it right," although I did not know it then, is harder.

As I understand growth now, it is a conjunction of Darwin's "evolution of the species" with Hegel's "evolution of spirit," given direction by the pull of Aristotle's "final cause." and made uncertain by Nietzsche's skepticism about "ends." But a good move was all I wanted back then, and I didn't care how it worked out later.

I am no longer interested in the endgame of growth: the discrediting of older traditions to where their demise becomes a reason for both aesthetic and social celebration. But I had once been interested in the notion that there is an inevitable process from "representation" to "abstraction"—the following of which, historically, has been touted as inevitable, and also, as a good move. The presumption here—at its conceptual peak—was that nothing containing even a friendly wave to older styles can count in the new post-historical land of art. This calls for a progressive "emptying-out" of pictorial strategies until pictorial essence is reached—thus achieving a last if not final style that comprises the sensually bare but conceptually replete components that justify the historical end of art .

Taking historical completion as both a stylistic and normative delineator in the history of art was a powerful idea through the early twentieth century. But it was already old as I grew older, and I see it now as trivialized by having turned its somber pronouncements into a growth industry, and so providing for ongoing variations on the chic images of less-ness. Representations of the end of pictorial reduction—images of less-ness—become competitive in trying to reveal the final image—that of "least-ness."

This has been a mission of purists for a century now. The older ones (like Malevich) who also worried about the end of the world, are heroes. Others, like Mondrian, took their heroics elsewhere, and subsumed the angst of getting too close to the end by dancing and painting the Boogie-Woogie—a true primordial response to the deadliness of least-ness. Ad Reinhardt, moved by Indian philosophies, painted (the same) black painting many times, so indicating that any of them will do because they are all one. Barney Newman painted leastness as mostness—hugh canvases that opted for intimations of the sublime—while denigrating his precursors—as a way of turning ending into a ongoing competition. More recent artists, like Stella and Judd, no longer took least-ness as an aesthetic or metaphysical task. They saw it, rather, as a cogent career move that tied in with advanced architecture and decor. This supported the idea that aesthetic emptying is not the least, but rather the best that one can do—given the failures of early (mostly European) modernism to support the promises of reduction to achieve a post-style.

III

I return now from my polemics to myself: Actually, I have never been away—just hiding behind old-age prejudices while engaged in good-saying to those I love, and bad-mouthing the artists I remember that I still don't like. I also worry about what I myself had failed to do, about what I should of course have done. I look harder now at classical paintings than I did when I needed to learn something quick about how paintings are made. Impatience was then a method. These days, an old-age intimacy occurs between what I do and what I look at. I prefer to look at old art, at master-works in which my own inadequacies are suggested, but then (let me brag) are resolved in ways mostly personal, often metaphysical, and sometimes even good.

Titian is my favorite artist for the pure succulence of his images. The painting of "Danae" with the shower of gold coins that Jove throws down to indicate his interest is among the greatest of painted nudes—and yet a trap for the salaciously ambitious. But the open arm-pit and the heavy thighs are beyond mere wanting. Celestial coins scatter over flesh and floor—with a few caught in the aprons of a servant. Sex between beast and beauty should be the next episode. But Titian made the fable into a timeless anticipation of divine and human coupling—an answer in paint to the skinny guilt of Adam and Eve, and the gonadically deprived Christian God. It is an affirmation of sexual power that, when made sacred, can also be understood as a historically fleeting conciliation between religious belief and self-love.

Van Eyck is my master for portraying divine cosmology here on concrete earth. "The Virgin and Chancellor Rolin" is in many of my worlds my favorite painting. It brings incompatibles into a unity that encompasses earthly power and heavenly scope. It exposes the intimacy between physical and spiritual within one pictorial moment—situated in the most exotic of interiors. The chancellor shows at once his fierce earthly face and his considered deference to divinity; the virgin acknowledges, by sitting there, her ecumenical mission brought back to earth, but not her enthusiasm. About the role of the infant Christ? When he is not on Mary's teat, only God knows what he is thinking. Then, looking through the central windows, a bridge can be seen which spans the river and allows the timid peasants to walk across and look back at their protected town—security for servitude has a long history. Further, in the distance, there is the untamed infinity of a forest—misty, vaguely demonic, but not overtly threatening—yet not a place where we would venture if we wish to safeguard our souls.

All these levels are in the painting—the sacred manifest on earth, the secular affinity with religious power, the faithful protected by an established communion, and the distant forests, the mists and mountains that are the unbounded realm of irrationality. The morality tale is strict; the principals join within one comprehensive scheme that incorporates faith, realism, power, fear, but not yet the seeds of non-belief.

I used to think about emulating such breadth in my paintings. It was just a matter of translating these ambitions into modern form. I think now how naïve I was—and I confess, still am in darker moments. But there were real hindrances to my ambitions that I did not see. For one, Pope Julius is dead. For two, the days that painting can better describe multiple realities than can, say, photography or film, are gone. For three—it doesn't hurt me now to say it—I am not that good.

Once, when I thought better of my powers, I schematized compositions for paintings based on a grid, and I mapped procedures that had forms move in calculated ways: "one up, two across; two up, four across" an infinite series expanding from the plane into a "cosmic" topology—all according to my belief that I could project my sequences wherever the grid could reach—across the room, the city, even the universe—if others would lend a hand. And if it happened that the gods would enjoy this late attempt at worship through the emulation of their passage—all the better.

Well, the others did not see it that way. So I abandoned my attempts to offer my logico-mathematico-cosmological constructions as a way to provide bracing insights for the benefit of modernist muddle-heads. I hate them all, of course! You should know too, that the unappreciative shits didn't see the enormity of my sacrifice—my rags and tatters, worn-out ruling pens, and conceptual suffering.

In truth, it didn't matter much—even then. I had become bored with all the picky attention to making cosmic grids and clean edges, and to self-loving thoughts of post-dimensional overreach. Yet someone here or there (where are you, Vasari, when I need you) can tell the story, however comical, of my singular vision. But it should not, at my venerable age, refer me back to the younger me. I happen now to disagree with that simple fellow—although, in truth, I am jealous that I was not young when he was! Still, given my seedy yet fecund past, there should be someone who will pull me into the sequence of "begats."—and give me a history.

But no one has volunteered, alas, to firm my place, and so I have to settle for myself—all the while fearing that without an adequate guide (where are you Virgil when I need you) I might trip and tumble down from the slopes of high ambition, slide past the village of modest comfort, and fall into the muttering pits of fire and ice (don't even mention the incessant winds that frustrate horny nakeds who lusted after nudes but didn't draw that well).

I am not, however, even as I scan the ruin of my deeper pretenses, a fallen hero. Those who are historically sympathetic to the downward path, will take my failures to be fashionably inevitable: "How sexy you look when you assume your final face." But I, obdurate rascal, even with all this longing in my dossier, will not undergo a death that is a saleable postlude to last-gasp celebration. I do not want to give even the carapaces of my life to someone's need for viewing a "good confession." Against the skinny sages who equate excess ambition with a miserable death, I say that living should be calculated within the longer distances—such as the time between those preliminaries that cause birthing—the frisky moments—to the celebration of the coming of light into the eyes of the new-born child—and following long- on, between joy and sorrow, to the waning that precedes dying.

In my early days, I was a good performer at the teat. I made the transition between diaper and potty in uncommon time, and survived the household screaming and the aggression in the streets by talking to myself. In this way, I found the self within myself, and henceforth used it as my protector. Later, I took some tests and got into a free college of New York's City University—an exemplary institution. I roamed those glorious years throughout the benign landscape of classrooms, gyms, and the ecumenical caferteria by tasting the privilege of learning to talk, and by sniffing after bright sweet-smelling girls, while writing poetry and doing art—pretty good as an introduction to a later life.

Concerning death: I do not, however long the time between my birthing and dying, want, at my death-bed, a ceremony of familiars. There are some few I now accept who can come and drink. But there also are those people happy to have outlived me who just might stop-by; and then there are the ones who will come even as they wonder what the fuss is all about. I can't keep them away—but you can.

Because I am present although dead in an event I would not have wanted when still alive, I will have no say about how the spare-ribs are done. They certainly will not be as crisp and yet chewy and hot as I would make them. But you should know that even dead, I am not dogmatic, and that given a bit more time I would have searched the ancient scrolls to find a canticle—a method first inscribed by a fat reclusive sage—through which I could influence the making of real-ribs—far better than those that have too-long languished in their smoky hell and so become impervious to the basting. Try a dry-rub of spices for a few hours before you start the coals.—and go gentle on the slather.

I now turn from the burping and farting I have always used as a companion to good spare-ribs and return to the scentless abstractions I once mistook for art. However bare their present bones, they still evoke the dream of chewing on the ample meat of older stuff. Could I mandate it, I would prefer, for future art, a strategy that is exemplified by the hot grumblings in my gut and the waning of my priapic interest in the new.

IV

To mark the case: I now bring collage together with my painted images and I make them to be neither of a piece nor separate. The wonderful panache of intruders who do not leave is what I'm after—especially those who assume, after the food and wine is gone, that their welcome still holds—both in mind and on canvas. They smile and wave even as they disturb, by their insouciance, the images I have reverentially painted by hand. But these are family quarrels—as between cousins with a secret lust for each other who have not recently said "hello" except on Sundays.

In these paintings, I extend hospitality to the old and the young, to the ill-sized and re-sized, to bottoms that do not acknowledge their sagging tops and have found no convenient face to sit on lately. What are the limits of ecumenicism, I wonder, before young and old and bottoms and tops, part company.

In the recent painted pieces I include writings, mostly by me but also by heavy-footed others, who are happy to canoodle with my paint and glue. What I write is to what I paint as is a tablet of sayings to one of showings. They had been lying quietly through the years, side by side—though never touching—until they were dug up and pieced together. The match is not inevitable, nor made in heaven, but it happens.

Sayings once had a broader and more elevated range than showings—but they have been diminished by the decline of reading. Yet they compete now, the little snippets, as quick as a ping-pong ball, flitting across the net to find lookers and readers who want to seem as nimble as they.

Words and images are never settled; they acquire meaning from the places where they stop to rest and eat. In a life, each place is distant from the other—a full day's drive—and the food is always different. Such places can be brought together, but not for the dull sake of continuity. Dead philosophers sometimes say that everything important in time occurs in places that are incommensurable with each other. But Miami beach and the Siberian Sea remain compatible—if only for the traveler who will visit both, and see the first as "she" and the second as "he."

V

The "her-story" is of the family—as separation myths have it—and is introduced on the potty. The his-story is of the world and it is taught in the wilderness. These myths are less prejudicial when they identify women as providers of nourishment, and men as factotums of survival. The distinction becomes less clear during such times when the trade-off skips across the gender line and rearranges roles to fit whim and pleasure as they compete with obligation. Why not the female huntress and the male philosopher joining forces to secure the family—if that is the best way they have?

The sequence of separations between your first waking and your later growing affects your eating, shitting, and masturbating, and so calibrates your alternations of pain and pleasure—what you can do that feels good and what feels bad, and what you must not do. Do nothing, I say, that feels worse than bad. This sequence lets you choose between, but will infect any subject you take on. If you choose the game of art and life—you will see that these memories—of good and bad, better or worse—define what it is you do until you die.

Dear old dying Moe (quite out of it, you know) was singing: "Buon giorno scungilli, calzone e gelato—tutti qui, tutti qui…(His name was once "Marcello," and one of his nieces is Italian). Moe migrated to the mid-west just after the first war, married a bouncy country girl, and forgot his Italian except when he got drunk and started singing. The local boys drank whisky, which he thought tastes terrible and gets you drunk more quickly than does the wine his father drank all day. Also, whiskey drinkers do not sing songs—they fight. Well, Moe tried to sing American songs but they just made no sense to his Italian ear— so, wanting to remain a good American, he stopped singing. But now that Moe is dying, he sees the opening to sing the songs once sung by uncles and cousins at the fests in Italy. He cannot any longer remember all the words, but no matter—he makes them up. Moe, my friend, is a collagist at heart—he enjoys mixing favorite foods with operatic heroes and heroines, which when brought together in a great repast, taste the same—yet different. The trick is to separate the sequence of your food, eat slowly, and between courses, roam around the tables –flirting outrageously with the old ladies, and engaging the men with loud toasts about the promise of equality and prosperity.

VI

Many stories about living and dying, and art and such, rely on "pap." You know what I mean: popular kitsch, mostly reverential, political, or sexual, manipulated by scoundrels, offered by the greedy purveyors of trivia, beloved of ambitious notables, and misunderstood by students. Reverential attitudes about art have often used pap as a source of subject—endemically now, but also to be found in master works that have accrued much historical fame. These, after all, share with us the task of adorning the beliefs and desires of our times.

Michaelangelo's "Pieta" is assuredly a great sculpture of mother and child, but he could not paint nor sculpt naked women—they turned out to be men with conical breasts. Titian, at about the same time, painted great female nudes. Venice, it seems, was more willing to accept the coupling of myth, religion, and sex than was Florence. But real "pap" has little to do with either repressed or communally warranted images unless they are trivially art that aim at maximal titillation. The problem comes up when the greatness of art is weighed against its titillation. The "Apotheosis of Napoleon" by Ingres is a borderline case—but not his "Grand Odalisque." Boucher's "Mme. Morphy," Fragonard's ephemoral yet concupiscient novices, cross the border into Pap-land" as do many of Bierstadt's western idylls. But all these are good art as well—and there's the rub, or perhaps the strategy for a parlor game. Dekooning's ferocious "Woman," are not pap—unless feminine ferocity becomes modish.

The fear of pap in art is a modern phenomenon—an issue of academic uncertainty. It is now difficult, to identify any specific art-work as "pap" because this (perversely) becomes a provocation to return it to art: "Paint by the Numbers" kits and soft-porn posters are examples. Judgments against pap do not issue from those who can efficiently separate their public from their private tastes. Rather, pap is a confirmation, through its confectionary allure, of the modest titillations that aestheticize the great middle—eager to belong but quite innocent of irony—that may easily be accepted, if one stays around, as the major symbols of our collective life.

Pap is not a sweetener of aesthetic experience. Rather, it is an opiate through which ever-clever powers maintain control and thereby further their own interests. The historical antagonist to pap is purity—emptying life of everything the compliant privileged classes might enjoy. Here, class warfare finds a new battleground in modern art: Let us take out all things ingratiating, titillating, obfuscating and socially conforming—all those things that encourage pap. What must then be left is either nothing or art's true content. If not nothing, what is left will emerge as a Platonic form, or as a witness to the soul's dark night—or as good reason for brooding way past bedtime. But this move, as with the search for hidden sin, is never final: Critical probing may uncover low pap masquerading as high art—or high art, in extremis, offering itself as pap so as to be admired.

Yet, I cannot entirely agree with this take on what can make good art bad: Purity and reduction, in comparison to pap, have served art poorly. These austere doctrines winnow the needed nutrients and sap the vital juices necessary for simmering the meat together with its vegetables and spices, and so do not create the anticipated daube replete with the invitation to hearty dining. Purity often breaks down because it cannot countenance reheating its dry roast in the same charred pan without, at least, the addition of a little wine. But by this time, it is too late—a failed attempt at repackaging when its art has already been reduced to a willow-wisp –which is certainly not worth the eating.

Avoid pap, the elders say, as you would any intemperate jollity—such as thick paint, skewed shapes, unseemly naked nudes, like the very plague. Such vigilance is necessary, but as elders may admit before they die, impossible. The varieties of pap, like the cockroach, are eternal, and their adversaries are dwindled because of the waning power of the concept of progress.

But there is a more benign take on progress—one that might keep it going: Change can occur without specific goal or reason, but some changes happen, that for the purposes of their clientele, are better than others. The enjoyment of pap in art is a contender in art's making—as in preferring Bacon and Warhol to Pollock and Dekooning. It is also a defence against the end of art.

Predicting the world's end through fire and brimstone, given the span of time invoked, is a matter of theological politics. The images of that charred mess ascending to the heavens and there being cleansed by assistant-angels so as to restore the promise of its origins, is pap. Also pap are the images that strive to convince you that the end of you will not happen in your lifetime, and that anyway—if you watch the dancing-girls, believe in immortality, and buy our products—you will live forever.

VII

I am not dying; I now live in the Mid-West; and I do not like the local music (although I occasionally get the hots for a country alto who sings about how badly she's been treated). I write a lot, as this shows, and I send out my efforts on occasion, but they usually are not returned. I paint too, still insisting on this ancient mode, for reasons not so much of age but of increasing allegiance to that which was before what got me here. The size of my works is no longer architectural—the paintings do not compete with, nor want to enhance, the space of buildings. (I did paint a few monsters, on large swathes of canvas and even designed some for the sides of buildings. I threw the biggest canvases into the dumpster every time I moved; and the building walls—there were two—were painted over by moron developers when the buildings were sold).

Well, we must all, most all of us, do something new: Break the chains of style, turn our backs on the enticements, meager as they are, of success as measured by all the criteria on which we were once spoon-fed. So I say: Stop making art—or if you are too far gone, find some lovely scruffles and muffins in your fantasies—but not the ones that neutralize your propensity for shapely limbs. Paint the paint out, paint in the limbs, and have a show. There must, as is usual, be a big party at the opening: I will (I am invited too, no?) drink some wine, and I will sing (as did old Moe) " Buona notte padrone, e buon giorno a tutti belli giovanetti." Then, after the voice gives out, your Italian is compromised, and they still let you stay, you will have found the proper balance, Lucian, between your ancient paths and the ones now pressing you to find some place to hang your hat.

The Brooklyn blocks where I lived as a child offered a continuing festival of small events in which stoop-ball and stick-ball were punctuated by sacred holidays duly celebrated by mostly male outpourings of beer and whiskey from late afternoon till early morning.

In the hung-over grey gatherings of the sunday morning after the night before, women, as was the custom, would leave their foul-smelling snoring husbands and go to church—to the six-o-clock mass where the gentle Father Fleming would tell them, in a soft voice, how their earthly trials increased their heavenly reward. Some women came for the homily, for the comfort of prayers, chimes and incense. Others, the younger ones, came to hear something, beneath the droning, that would help them believe anything, other than what was whispered in the alleys after dark.

Privacy of imagination, they said, is the umbrella sin that requires public recanting—I did not think that Father Fleming would have wanted to hear that. But what, I asked, after all that confessing, could I save of the flesh-infected, sin-infested privacy that was my best early weapon against the snoopy prying of the outside world? They said: God knows everything you're thinking—and so does the Virgin. What? What? The celestial mother of us all is watching me jerk-off? And then they said: The Archangel Michael was told by God to cast down Lucifer—and he did. What do you think he'd make of you?

Despite all the years of piety that have washed over me with the view to cleansing me before I had a real chance to sin, and before I first came to know about the class struggle and the ascendancy of the proletariat (the girls at those meetings had hairy legs). In my dreams I continued to be interested in the infernal couplings of licentiousness and purity, sin and disobedience, ecstasy and agony. I did not, in those young years, see anything of such goings on—except for Jeanette being threatened by Indians at Saturday matinees until stolid Nelson saved her by singing "Give Me Some Men." But what was the threat? What would those infernal Indians—I wanted to see it all—have done to her? What do the frolics, when the innocent and wanting meet the damned and knowing, look like as they all come together?

Years later, I found, in a perfectly proper high-school library, an edition of Dante's Divine Comedy with illustrations by Gustave Dore. Wow! There it all was: Supplicant maidens blown by the winds of hell into graphic stills that bring together unrequited lust and eternal despair. Hoo! I am here, I cried. I am Lucian from Brooklyn by way of the Russo-Polish controversy. What you need, girls, I will provide.

VIII

Before you, dear readers, think of leaving, I have more stories to tell you—if you are willing to stay around. And why should you not? I continue to write this paean to our recent intimacy, to the moment you, unaware, opened this writing as you were lolling on the summer beach in—is it Fire Island? Yes, the same place where drunk O'Hara was squashed like a turtle into the night sands by a beach taxi and then immortalized by Leslie and others into an apotheosis of the artist's unkind fate. But it's a good place for you to read this because it's about me and not O'Hara. Without his heavy breathing, I can continue to write about myself. It's not a large topic and you won't have to read it all. Swim between sections but stay within the buoys.

I was saved from the rough early roads by an intercession that kept me from going to sea—the only job I then thought might fit. Those fellows at the docks knew my story—they had heard it many times—so when I went looking for a ship, they asked to see my seaman's papers, and when I went to apply for the papers, they asked what ship I'm hiring on. So you slink off, relieved, with your Murray friend as crazy then as you, and we went to donate blood at the bank two blocks away—the rate was ten dollars for a pint. Afterwards, woozy and hungry, we went to nearby Chinatown and spent our riches on sub-gum fried rice, shrimp in lobster sauce, and Chinese vegetables. Then, with our bellies now beatifically full, we wandered out to the midday sun to walk the downtown streets. We came to agree that we really didn't want to go to sea at all. But we could only give blood once a month. (Anyhow, those were pretty grim scenes: short-arm inspections, needles in the vein—and no way to entice the needle-wielders into a discussion even when my bright red blood was dribbling into a bottle hanging beside them on a hook). So we went back to school.

CUNY, the City University of New York, was then an institution that embraced the smarter children of recent immigrants and showed them a world that was receptive to talent and intelligence. It took a lot of doing, and there were stumbles—more for the invested adults than for the transient students. I remember the time when the president of my (Brooklyn) college, called a public meeting in which he denounced the radical faculty within our midst, and declared his intention to "scrape the barnacles from the ship." Not good poetry—as should befit a leader of intellectuals—but the point was made. All sorts of faculty folk were fired, and although we students protested, it was not enough to sway the controversy. Unlike the later opposition to the Vietnamese war, we were arguing a foreign issue—the ascendancy of the proletariat—which we didn't really understand, and which could not possibly come about—although we didn't think that far—in the country where we were born and suckled. But we marched, nonetheless—with placards in the pouring rain ; the poster paints the messages were written in ran down the placards and turned our pants into puddles of color. The campus police watched all this wondering whether they should beat up on bonified students even though they were acting like commies.

So what did I do next? Well, I was close to flunking out. I left the classes I had enrolled in because they bored or bewildered me. I didn't read much then. Murray, The friend of our blood-donating past, told me about a class he had enrolled in, called Design something, whose instructor spoke in riddles about why the map is not the territory. It was too late to register but I went anyway, and the instructor, my later mentor Harry, said you are welcome as long as you do the work. But there was no work to be done, unless you took his allusions, as I did, to show (paint, draw) the difference between what you see and what you make—the latter (the map) those days being preferable. So at the age of nineteen I became an abstract artist, much coddled by the "Design Department" (which I must explain was so named because "design" had Bauhaus vibes of integration of art, theory, and business. Design—but not "art"—was allowed into the college.)

No one in the department taught design in any of its commercial senses. But it was not the college mandate they were failing; it was the quiet but deep belief among the faculty (who were largely saving their own asses through teaching) that design was a commercial cop-out, while the life and times of advanced art gave a sufficient curriculum to expand the needs of the post-war, aesthetically challenged generation. The pedagogy was largely a matter of bringing the good news of the "New Art" to their benighted, deeply parochial, students.

I was a prime receptacle for good news. I was painfully poor but not benighted, and I had nothing to be complacent about. In that short span, I irrevocably changed my interests and my nature. I didn't think about a vocation—I didn't really know what that meant. Free from the concern of success, I learned the catechism quickly: The European contingent of Bauhaus, Mondrian, Kandinsky et al, was the radical source that provided ways of learning and living—and this belongs to a history that, just a few months ago, I didn't know existed.

IX

Enlightenment didn't happen right away. I was drafted into the Marine Corps. This was during the war in Korea. MacArthur was on the loose and the Chinese were threatening to cross the Yalu river and join the fight in order to thwart an American invasion of China. It was not a paranoid fear, and it resulted in the all-volunteer Marine-Corps, happily fighting the North Koreans, having to face a much more serious enemy—the Chinese. To achieve adequate numbers, the Marines had to resort to the draft. So when I went to the draft board for my swearing-in, I found that I was the "three" of a one-two-three sequence,—the first two go to the army, the third becomes a Marine.

I would have had a great career in the army, where I might have been sent to Germany or France –languages I spoke well enough for military purposes. And then there were all those sleek and hungry women I would have met and loved while furthering my language skills and convincing them I am not like the others.

Instead, I spent two years in North Carolina. No, they didn't ship me to Korea, although I had no say in the matter. Instead, I spent my time teaching people how to shoot the current weapons, (we were still using the M-1—a sturdy heavy rifle, accurate enough, but particularly good for bludgeoning and bayoneting). When I could escape the guns, which was mostly on weekends, I worked as a lifeguard at a nearby beach. As part of the job I rented floats and supported my tan. I looked good against the ocean, and so attracted local girls who could not imagine, for all my talk, that my real ambition was to return to New York and become an artist. What a queer idea! It was not that I didn't like the sandy-crotch, mosquito-infested lovings on the twilight beach, but the girls—imagine—considered these rituals as rites of passage, necessarily undergone so as to reach the place of verdant lawns and the large connected family that they wanted.

But it wasn't so bad. The camp was by the North Carolina coast, and I swam and swam with a new-found buddy who was interested in Jean Cousteau. We bought fins, and filled some discarded air tanks at a filling station—60 lbs pressure max—and we could not get them down below the surface of the water. So we attached hoses and sat on the bottom of the inland waterway—about eight feet down—sipping air and watching the little fishes swim past our masks. We did a lot of that and then swam for miles, with flippers, in the open ocean. Bill, my friend, had become obsessed by the then new mystique of scuba-diving. Eventually—although he hated military discipline—he reenlisted on the stipulation that he would be sent to UDT school and spend the rest of his life underwater. I was discharged soon after, and I don't know what became of him—although I realized that becoming a military diver-warrior was more important than anything he could see to do on the outside.

Before he left, Bill introduced me to Marianna, who was enrolled in a religious college about two hours drive from the base, and had once been his girlfriend. But Bill became enamored of a schoolmate that Marianna invited to sleep over at her parents' seaside cottage. I sensed the beginnings of a great adventure: Marianna was not unhappy that she had lost her lover—this freed her to attend to me. I think she wanted things she thought I had—east coast smarts, a slanted attitude towards sex, and the promise of a future that would free her from Christian rural North Carolina. We tried, but it didn't work—that joining of her needs and mine—not because I didn't like her but because I was sure she wouldn't fit into the New York art world—the world where I, carrying two years of pent-up ambition, wanted so much to go back to.

I think of Marianna more often than I thought I would. Even among the New York festivities, I retained that image of a simpler life, corn-fed, fueled by big tobacco, adorned by country cottages, and filled with daily intimacy of a quietly repetitive kind.

No, No! Get thee behind me! I could not have stood it then; it would have been the death—the rummage sale of my soul. But I could stand it now, if I were twenty-one and Marianna still nineteen, with her freckles, upturned nose, and rosy thighs.

Why, Marianna said to me, should these dreams of silly fame be important to you—what with my father's tobacco fields and the houses we will inherit. I know you think that I'm only a southern country-girl, soon to become as fat as my gracious mother, and not prepared at-all to care about the world beyond North Carolina's northern borders. Well let me tell you something, you late version of a carpetbagger: I have always wanted a boyfriend who has a family like mine, landed, settled, and modestly successful. But you—you Polack from Manhattan—have no family, no income, an uncertain future, and you have a circumcised pecker, which I don't really mind, but which is not much appreciated in these parts.

I am willing, she said, to forgive all this, and work it through to our own sense of a happy life—in the now condition of where we are—here in verdant Carolina, not there in smelly New York bars which only collect the residue of ambition and the rot of failure. She did not say it quite that way—but close.

It is one of my many faults that I do not appreciate a woman's hidden wants when we have an affair. Look at this one: We would get married in a country ceremony with sweet-smelling ladies and scrubbed upright men in uneasy attendance: "Let me know if there is anything we can do to help you kids—anything that you might need, my boy, to compensate for your coming from that New York with no money or real-world skills. But then, no question, you became a Marine—a defender of our country, and we do understand that they didn't happen to send you over there: Some fight and some teach the others to fight—no problem."

Then what happens? I work for Pappa in the tobacco fields, and return at night to play at impregnating Marianna, and then we spend the year (by this time I'm working in the office) planning for next year's crops, and for the caring of the to-be inheritor of the great estate.

How is it, Marianna, that you—you crimped-up vessel who had been reserving herself for the delectation of a perfect mate, how come you chose private first class me—from New York? Me perfect in any way? No way that matters! I did not then appreciate that Marianna too was diagonal—much more so than all the surrealist tales had prepared me for. Marianna, my sweetheart of the chubby thighs, were you, in your little crib already hiding from what the elders of your tribe would want for a fair young maiden of an impeccable family? Yes you were, because you also hid from me—although you seemed practiced in the way you pulled down your shorts that summer evening in the back seat of your parents' car. But you wanted to get the sex thing done—as an obligation that must be met for a real relationship to continue. It was all too fast for my contemplative pecker. I was put off by your unwillingness to play, to find a way for just the two of us to just get along.

In the supercharged male aura that surrounds a military base, there are few chances to find a love—the aura is too aggressive, too congested, and too vulgar. Marianna thought I was not like that, and I did not recognize the weight she gave to her decision. Although not vulgar, I was a will-of-the-wisp, giving her no sense that I knew (or cared about) the depths at which her needs were to be found. This is what I saw: Marianna actually lived in that North Carolina, was being given a Christian education, and had a father who prospered on tobacco. And she used sex, so I thought, as a grainy prelude to marriage. But I was wrong about this last part. Her affirmation, however partial, of the flesh, was much more difficult for her than was my escape from the strictures of Brooklyn Catholicism. There was no rote expiation in her beliefs—no formal confession—only ongoing guilt. Then too, she knew I had the "Big City" to escape to—so it was easy for me, just a matter of time. She would have nothing then but wayward Marines, faculty lesbians, and tobacco executives with which to focus a life that was barely begun.

I'm sorry now that I did the slippery dance around her wanting, but I could not have done what she really needed. I think now, being eighty, that I should have—were we now transported back to our young unblemished selves, I could have—with my accrued wisdom of the flesh providing a string of hallelujahs to our copulation.

Marianna and her family—in the early flush of celebration—would have tolerated me. But I was leery of those good-old-boys who cooked the barbeque, looked at me crooked, and roared around in pick-up trucks on summer nights. So I ran back to the safety of the New York Art World, that most benign of institutions—back to the mean-streets of Brooklyn and Manhattan where, even in extremis, there was pastrami to eat.

I make too much of the tale of Marianna. It didn't last all that long, not much past when her mother, a pleasant but suspicious woman, spotted me kissing the neck of a master-sergeant's wife on a seaside bench where she came for some attention because her husband, after all, had been away a year or so. It was just a nibble, that kiss, and I didn't return for the later, moonlight meeting that she offered. But Mamma Marianna, peering across the dunes, saw it all and, I'm sure, told her daughter that this foreigner, deviant Christian, sexual profligate, possible atheist, is not a suitable mate. Thanks mom.

X

When I was discharged, I went roaring back to Manhattan, and I celebrated my arrival, in the wee morning hours, with a glass of drambuie—the most exotic drink I could think of—in the Times-Square "Crossroads Café" that was open all night for prodigals and pilgrims. But soon the glow faded, and the city road of little praise and much blame began. That concrete road seems in retrospect more dreary that the dirt roads leading to the beach in North Carolina. The ocean did not demand that you sink or swim—it was up to your legs and shoulders how you would do. I never feared the currents or the sharks.

Actually, once, I did meet a shark; I saw it through my faceplate. It was just curious—but it came close enough for me to kick it with my fins before it left. It was so lithe as it circled me—so girlish and hesitant. Then, just a few feet away, she turned full face and swam, oh so slowly towards me. Her eyes were far out on the sides of her face, and her mouth was a large semicircle open downwards as if she were drooling—just enough to show the beginning of her rows of teeth. But then, for her own reasons, she fast-flipped back over the reef and disappeared into the murk.

I'm sure they saw me swimming back, those sag-bellies sitting on the beach. But I did not die for them—I kicked the sweet shark, said good-by, and surfed the waves till dusk. Perhaps it was the same self-serving impulse that later kept me from being a famous painter. Talent aside, I was too wary to accept the public demand for image: "This is the painter who was eaten by a shark—you can see his forebodings in the dark-red strokes and the jagged edges of his last works."

But, then, all the artists I knew and admired were being eaten by something—heart-attacks while fucking, slitting wrists when despairing, liver problems after decades of drinking, and just plain-old ways of disgruntled dying. I wanted their fame but not their lives—not even their third or fourth young wives.

Teaching art was a way to pursue my own ideas. I was good at it. How could students know anything about art unless I convinced them that my consecutive assignments, each more demanding than the last, would give them the first secrets to making art. My pedagogy, of course, could not compete in the historical task. I was a young, unknown, perhaps delusional formulator of a new academy. But I did teach my kiddies something—better than the nothing they got elsewhere—and my histrionics assured them that they were connected to art in a way that was new, even though they were still across the river in decaying Brooklyn in the sixties.

Learning about art through problem solving sounds terrible, doesn't it? But what if Tiepolo offered to teach you perspective drawing—you cack-handed scribbler? Would you decline—citing reasons of personal expression? I thought of my tutorial sequence as a modern revision of academic training. This gave me leeway to expound on art's historical changes—a continuing version of the academic verities of anatomy, composition, light and shadow, and the like. I made the sequence of changes just vague enough to keep the experience juicy and unsettled.

Such teaching once played its role within the practices of art-making. In my academic replay, however, they became ironic—compendia of fits and starts and heavy disbelief culled from Whitney annuals and art-history texts with no stylistic imperative to authenticate them.

I was old-time serious, but the students came to love the irony I did not then see—the self-imposed rigor, and the sense of accomplishment in doing something they could not have thought of six months earlier. Now, with my impress of talk and gesture, they could bring these arcane thoughts into their fullest fantasy. But given the short life of ungirded belief, they had to face, after leaving the cloister of my class, the task of finding other practices that are justified by different beliefs—or they could stop listening to the fugue between art-acts and life-ironies altogether, and go on to other occupations.

I also used my pedagogical imperatives for my own art—not the specific sequences of problems, but the general idea that each painting had to both change and enlarge upon the theme and means of its predecessors: Hegel's notion of progress instantiated in paint by Lucian in Brooklyn! But isn't that what modern art is all about? No, you fool—it's not if you want to be successful. The old walruses of note found a rock on which to weather the changing seasons; they stabilized it, smoothed out its bumps, and chased away intruders. And every season they showed it forth again—as that eternal rock you can bet your future on.

When they taught—and God bless that I was there to "study" with them rather than face a smart ass such as I became who would present me with "foundational tasks." My dear walrus mentors showed me that being an artist is a good thing, directed me to the shows I should see, and to which bars are best for making art-talk. Also, unlike other professors, they didn't seem at all annoyed when I sniffed around the pretty girls; rather, they seemed pleased that something closer to their preferred way of life had made its way into the classroom.

XI

The art-world, even in those days of low enrollment did not much notice me, but I was happily back, and soon joined the line of supplicants for the role of promising young artist—spending a good portion of my unemployment checks on beer in the artist bars. There, nightly, we played the scenes of pontificating, chest-puffering, and some real controversy about who is slated to be better than the rest. But, however much beer I drank, I was never a contender—not someone to be included in the decade's list of comers. I did have some shows, but they did not enter into that awful assessment of instant recognition.

In North Carolina, I had no doubts about my decision to return to New York where I could again take up being an artist—the only identity that did not assault me with remembered places and unwelcome beliefs. Just as well that I came back, my memories tell me—returning was a faith in which I categorically believed. Its denial, through the offices of sweet Marianna and her portent of a life of sex and tobacco, would have turned me into a psychotic exile—or, who knows, into a successful tobacco farmer. Admittedly, in the sober examination of my prospects, and in the still-fresh memory of those chubby rosy thighs, my belief in furthering my eastern ambitions became fragile. But the thought of staying was too scary. Despite all the good Christian talk, those folks seemed more like delegates of an up-tight Devil. So, to save my soul I went back east, to where they thought and sounded and even looked like me.

But New York, when I got there, was strangely empty. I had no base, as I once had in Brooklyn College. My teachers were all moribund or dead, and my friends, those classmates of some years back, were interested in their own thrusts at success. They didn't want me around to over-salt the porridge they were making. So I left again and went to Yale, as a teaching assistant to the sculptor Jose DeRivera. There, in New Haven, we hammered molten steel into the morning hours, fortified by swigs of gin, and then we went to the Italian section where there were good cheap restaurants and no concern about our loud unsteadiness. I couldn't figure Jose; he'd order a split filet, which was all he could afford, but which could not have fed a cat, while there were large dishes of spaghetti and meatballs on the menu for one-third the price. But artists are poseurs—not to the world as such, but to themselves and to their place in the chronicles of art- history. There was show-biz in this: You are known by what you do—and if you are to be successful, you must act your act accordingly—even if in the short term for only a few. Never mind that the unfathomable long term is not watching—all of that happens later. So after drinking three beefeater martinis,—up and with a twist of lemon—we take a cab to Tony's Trattoria, and have another martini. Then Jose orders his split filet—not much meat, but it does come with salad and potatoes and lots of Italian bread. I opt for the spaghetti and meatballs, which also comes with lots of bread.

Looking back, my separation from all this posing was far too slow. I didn't distinguish it from belief. I suspect now that successful posing can become belief and as such, needs a feast of followers to substantiate it. I had to battle through Jose's dogma to see where I could be. I began to rid myself of the seductions of pure-form, and the titillations of beyond form, and I tried—painfully I assure you, to get (back?) to stories—to where my vagrant heart has ever been. Now I paint narratives of dream images as they continue into daylight, and combine them with photographic images which I cut and paste, thus evoking the love-hate relationship between them and my painted images with which they, like new dogs in the old dog's house, are confronted. I had no teacher who spoke about such matters, so I scratched at them myself, and soon found out that nobody in this our present of progressive minimalism and pedantic formalism was interested. What a bummer; I could have stayed with Marianna.

Marianna would not have cared about Mondrian's reductions or Duchamp's destructions, and she would wonder what on earth there is about such things that would make them matter to me. The tobacco fields are there each morning. (I still smoked then) Daddy is a careful but amiable man, and Mommy is her usual combination of charm and deep suspicion. It would not have been easy, Lucian, but if you had abandoned your interest in the end of art, you could have done it. You could show Dad that you're up to figuring out the harvest protocol; and Mom would eventually come to understand—through our red-cheeked appearance in the morning—that her daughter is better off than she was earlier.

XII

When I was discharged, I left quickly, and drove east, with five other newly anointed civilians. We dropped some off in New Jersey but I went on to Times Square where I took the subway to Brooklyn. But rather than go right on to my aunt's house, where for a time I would have to live—and where that sweet unhappy lady wanted to feed me good Polish food, I went to find Marilyn who was staying, as she wrote me, at her mother's small apartment in a large building in a neighborhood (Bay Parkway and 86 Street) where, even then in 1954, the ethnic tensions were being redefined—the appetizing stores with their sidewalk barrels of sour pickles were just a storefront away from new boutiques that catered to the habits of the emerging Beats and Latinos.

I knew the address and apartment number, but the name was not listed on the bells, so I pushed all the buttons (it was four in the morning) hoping that someone would let me in. One bantam-man, followed by his fearful wife, came out of his first-floor apartment, and threatened big-young-me with mayhem while I tried to assure him, pointing to my duffle-bag, that I was just an ex-serviceman hoping to get laid. They retreated in an aura of Yiddish curses, but they had opened the door and I was in. I climbed five flights and found the apartment where Marilyn had spread a quilt on the living-room floor. There was no polite chatter. This was a serious moment and it required a focused meeting—although I smelled of two days on the road—that would help make two years of "yes sir-no sir" just fade away.

New York did not recognize the returning prodigal—at least not with fanfare and job offers—so I left again, this time to Yale, as assistant to De Rivera who was visiting artist in sculpture. The Yale agreement for my coming was that I didn't pay tuition—but my only money was a Korean-war stipend of 110 dollars per month. I found an apartment in the Italian section, behind the churches that mark the border between Yale and the downside of New Haven, for 30 dollars a month—no heat no hot water and a toilet in the hall. There was enough money for some food but for nothing else. Marilyn said she would join me there—but only if we got married. I think she wanted to marry to erase her first debacle—or maybe as a defense against Yale propriety. So here I was, a goy, an artist-type, penniless, brighter than most she knew, and not bad-looking when all stretched out. She settled for it—as Marianna would have.

My degree from Yale got me a job at Pratt Institute in Brooklyn. They thought I would give them a bit of Ivy class to counter-balance New York's identity as a receptacle for the new unruly style. Abstract-expressionism did not fit the culture of mendicant design and illustration with which the Pratt art school had long been identified, but the curriculum had become boring, new students were needed but had to be enticed. Also needed was a change in the faculty. I was one such. My rise in the ranks—instructor to professor to department chair was swift, abetted by a new dean who, beleaguered by the extant factions among the faculty, needed to find advocates of both "expressive art" and of "cutting edge" design. He was happy to leave the expressive side to me. There was no trouble finding artists who (for the short term) were happy to teach. Some (as with me) found that expounding their ideas three times a week, and greeting admiring students at their occasional shows was soul-food enough. Advanced design was harder. Christ-Janer, the new dean, was good at finding sterling designer-practitioners who liked the prestige of an academic appointment. But the salary was laughable; they had good jobs; so they showed up every so often, pontificated a bit, and left.

The student unrest of the sixties broke all this up. The ferment was largely in the art-school: "Fine Art" is not an academic pursuit, the students said—it is a personal and a social calling. Therefore, we want no assignments, no class times, no grades. Instead, we demand open studios, models on demand, and faculty by invitation only.

I was upset by all this. I have never liked hot breath and invective thrown in my face. I felt that teaching art is imparting knowledge of its particular subject—not finding a solution to social problems. But the encouragement to student activism did not come from the art faculty. It came from some misfits in the liberal arts component, at that time a service area for the studio programs. Disgruntled radicals, unhinged psychologists, unappreciated authors—this was a chance to get back at the school which gave them only the shitty job they have.

I remember one meeting at the height of student unrest where a faculty member, a psychologist, harangued the assembled students—with arms waving and spittle spraying—for a cause that was never clear. He had lost members of his family in the Nazi camps—but now he addressed the students with the same stridency as did the Nazi manipulators of the masses. There was a palpable image he projected—of a monstrous edifice that must be destroyed. And schools—his school—much more vulnerable than corporations or government institutions—became the target—not of choice but of possibility. So our students set about to destroy their own educational sources, egged on by those whose neurotic problems found a nesting place in the perversion of adolescent dreams.

And then, to make matters worse, the community, representatives of Bedford-Stuyvesant, sensing weakness, came and demanded that Pratt become a school for all the people, and their assets be reallocated into the community cause. These visits, by large men with close-cropped hair and dark glasses (no women), were directed at the President's office. They marched through the open doors en-masse, and presented demands that neither they, nor their quaking targets, really could fulfill.

In retrospect, I can find no cause, no issue, to justify the rowdiness and frivolity that marked the protests over national policies that the kids in the sixties were mounting. After a while, generational change and an increase in living standards deflated this (the Viet-Nam protests were still in the future) and the questions then raised—of participation and social control—became diffuse and irrelevant.

The beliefs that held up my teaching suffered during that time. No longer were students eager to leap into the opaque yet demanding "problems" which I earlier was able to assure them led to timeless art. They wanted to express themselves "here and now"—but not within the terms of studio-classes that still reeked of the strictures and control they remembered wanting to abolish. Between the assaults by errant students and neighborhood aggressors, there was no one left in the school to direct the response: The generals had disguised themselves as privates and fled to the hills at the first sign of attack. What remained were the logistics of the clean up. But there was little teaching and no art—only residual nastiness. I couldn't find another job in New York, so I accepted a deanship at an art-school in Saint Louis.

XIII

Washington University in Saint Louis—so named as to distinguish itself from the academic "Washingtons" in other places—needed a dean for their art-school. And I was the one they wanted. Their reasons were the usual academic mix of needing new ideas and not having much money to spend. My lower class origins and my middle class salary, sprinkled with New York and Yale, must have seemed to them a perfect solution to their desired amalgam of ambition and penury.

The faculty I encountered was a mix of old folks who had spent their lives as "Mid-West Artist-Teachers." They wanted to protect that. Sulking in the corners was the younger faculty who wanted to replicate the glamour of New York by introducing the recalcitrant Saint Louis millionaires into the joys of collecting (them). The elders wanted nothing more than to be left alone to splash a bit more in the varying depths of their beliefs. The young ones wanted an active sign—a local display—that would substitute for the east-coast recognition they did not have. That they could have it here before they got it there was fine with them—and the coming of the impresario from New York showed them how the world is shrinking.

I agreed with their ambitions—they were mine, too. But soon we all had to face the fact that appreciating and buying art are indeed mid-west pastimes—but not for art made in Saint Louis. The real collectors got their stuff direct from Janis and Castelli in New York. They did invite a few of us to their parties, but I could not get any of them to buy good student work at year-end shows—even for the price of a good cigar.

This parade of disappointed ambition was instructive for my mid-western re-habitation. The faculty and their desires provided a mirror for viewing the crimp in my own reasons for coming to Saint Louis. But the daytime urgencies were fewer and did not seem as painful: Success and failure in art was not as consequentially global or historical there as it was in that other world at which, with often bloody fingernails, I had been scratching.

I remember a scene in a chic New England art-school where I once went as a candidate for an administrative position. We, the "head of painting" and I, walked through the buildings, commenting on the various resources—collections of preserved flora and fauna, old photographs that compare natural and architectural forms, and inventories of ancient art-materials—all good stuff. We then wandered into a large studio that was completely empty except for a pale model, dusted with freckles and with just glorious light-red pubic hair. She sat, reading, with her legs casually apart. But when she sensed me looking, she gave me the practiced angry look that wards-off insistently horny students. She had been hired for posing—nominally for those who want to learn to draw. There was no one there—so what? But her job certainly did not include a visiting dignitary's look and leer. Whether students drew or not, she didn't care; she was putting in her time. I intruded, and then stopped and looked at her, hiding my desire under a lowered academic brow. She did not respond until she felt my looking, but then she looked back, and without closing her legs, countered my lust with her loathing. I was a suit who demeaned her vocation by entering the otherwise innocent preserve of her posing for a life-class. She could handle the students and the faculty through soft gestures of disapproval, but I had upped the ante. I, a no doubt lascivious foreigner, offered a game she would not play. Her lover (as I imagine that brutish young man whom she supported) didn't mind her posing naked in front of all these young unlettered eyes—but there would have been hell to pay if she had fucked me—under the stairs, say, that lead to the administrative offices.

There she was that day in all her naked finery (I still think of her light red pubic hair) with no students around to draw or even look. (Can you imagine?) This was their life-class, as stated in the curriculum, but no one told them that they were there to learn to draw, or (heavens forbid) would show them how. Also, no one told them why it is important to look upon this mound of flesh and make it into something special—draw first, then inherit the world.

What a lousy place—they didn't seem to care about all that, and they wouldn't pay me enough anyway—so I didn't take the job.

I came to feel that I didn't like art-schools. "Artists shouldn't teach," one oracle says; "teaching saps your vital juices" says another. When I began to teach back some fifty years ago, there seemed no other alternative for an anxious artist who wanted to become noticed. But if success in art is to be made on your own time, it means selling work—or, at least, getting people to write about you as a prelude to selling work. But this presented another morass—worse, I still think, than teaching—of catering to all those super-sensitive critics, dealers, curators, collectors, who have power over the reception of your work. It is a lot to ask of the indifferent world and of your quivering self, whether you want to go through all of this. Insisting on an answer can lead to an untimely death.

Whether professors of art live longer than untrammeled geniuses is a question that may change the current notion of what it is to be an artist. Keats and Shelley each died in their thirties—good for us but not for them. There is a satisfaction—a variant of Schadenfreude—when the art-star born at the same time you were born dies while you remain alive. This is a consolation of old age that does not mollify your jealousy, or the limits of your own accomplishments—but it does raise the existential banner: I am alive and living while he, that overrated shit, alas is dead.

Being famous not only results from what one is able to do, with all the strength and belief that can be mustered, it is also a circumstance of history—the style and the aptitude you have to fit with what is then required. But importantly, attaining fame needs a sponsor, whether Pope Julius or Clement Greenberg, to present you, artist, as exemplar of a harbinger of great art. The competition is incredibly fierce, given the conflicting seductions of present success, future acclaim, and eternal value. It is difficult to balance a life against such ambitions. So one gnashes, pontificates and postures, and then digs deep to find that beginning channel for the way of getting there.

A friend, a considerable painter, once said that he wanted immortality in his lifetime. Seemed sensible at the time—what with all the geniuses being acclaimed just after they had miserably died: No sacrifice, expiation, or resignation, he said—I want my due, and my money too, now, when I can still enjoy it. But I have come to think that this hubris, this in your face assertion, masks a hidden fear: I will die before I know. And no matter what they tell me now, the question of whether I indeed am historical will be in the hands of people not yet born.

I, myself, do not have that fear I say (oh, maybe I do in the wee morning hours.) But I was never so enraptured with myself as to want future guarantees in the present. I do not, for example, want young artists to emulate what I do. Actually, I was upset, when teaching, that on occasion students—even the beautiful Natasha—tried to paint like me.

I was even more upset when other teachers—all prophets of individual expression—actually coerced students into painting as they did.

I have few regrets about a life of teaching. The mix of institutional discipline and time for personal dreams is not adversarial. There is the joy of bright young things that have an agenda of finding out what you—and they by extraction—are all about. They, as you did and still do, want to find out how one should be in the world when one is away from parents and facing the indifferent yet calculating regard of others. Teachers are surrogates of protection, no doubt—but without the damper of blood ties, they also become guides to the dark places near where your parents have unwittingly left you.

"Professor, can I ask you about something that's been bothering me?" "Of course my dear—ask away." Professors are confessors with varying degrees of insight (depending on the course) but without the mandate to scold (which is different from admonish) but they should all have full bags of advice. They often become friends with those students who are energized by exuberance as manifest in cheap Chinese restaurants and shady jazz-joints: Chopsticks function like pincers not fork-lifts, I say to them, and don't flirt with the vocalist, she's with the drummer who is well-connected. I became a chopstick whiz (a necessary New York pedagogical skill). But I do remember thinking that the tawny golden singer would have found a refuge—she clearly needed one—in some student's undemanding arms, or if that failed, in mine. I'm still good at chopsticks—but that singer (she was so fine) is by now an ancient gourd, while I am an old stick with no juice left who seeks solace mainly in my dreams.

Treacly isn't it, my regression to fried rice and once-wet dreams—but hey, don't you dig treacle? It's better when you're high than just mixing dry bread-crumbs and Crisco. Treacle supplies the juice—the "what the hell" that counters style and prohibition. My appetite is for the lower middle, the food that sustains isolation but is frowned upon by those who still think they have a shot at fame. While waiting, one has to live and eat, and despite the current strictures, to enjoy both. Such enjoyment counters the belief that it is better, if you really are an artist, to die sooner than later.

No, no. I will eat fried rice so as to live longer; and on a cool September morning, I may yet find my ancient singer feeding pigeons in the park. I will say: Don't you remember me—the kid who made a grab at your ass, oh so long ago, when you had just finished your last encore? They hustled me out and I thought that you would leave my life forever. Well, you know, you never touched my life—but don't you remember the bit of froth that crawled beneath your frock that night? When was it? I don't remember either. I was all decked out in primary colors, as if God Mondrian—that skinny celibate who danced a mean Lindy—would help you recognize the young crown prince from Brooklyn who was just starting to overcome his own conflict between purity and prurience. Of course you don't remember—but I continue to. How? Through the power of dry daydreams and sweaty nightmares which, when they evoke the same person, put aside their differences and come together. I have a dry yet sweaty image of you sitting with me feeding pigeons on a bench in Central Park. I hate pigeons, but you, you baggy remnant of what you were, now with rheumy eyes and a clitoris that has long been rubbed to a nub, you have come, no wonder, to like pigeons more than people. They are always young and hungry, scatter at the least threat, but return to eat your peanuts, knowing that some will die so that others may live. I know why you once preferred your drummer to me; but I do not understand why now, notwithstanding my shrunken scrawny legs, gnarled feet, hairy ears, long drippy nose, and uncertain gait, you prefer the pigeons to me.

XIV

But I have overstepped myself. At last recall, I had gotten my first teaching job. Art schools at that time were engaged in teaching fundamentals rather than asking the question as to whether making art is a profession or a calling or just a pleasant ride. The days of artistic sublimity have long been over. Our shadows of ambition, the art-teachers, do not have the ateliers of Titian or Rubens where apprentices develop skills by filling in the more mundane passages of the master's commissions, and if they are good with drapery and lucky in studio politics, may be assigned a peripheral nude or two.

We are a historical distance from masters informing apprentices—when art was a profession for the few. We now can only encourage many indifferent students to dream their dreams—because, who knows, a calling can morph into a profession—and anyway, what will future-art call for in the matter of skills and talents? I became interested in the shifts in justification of studio practices—and I became an administrator of changes. Managing the teaching of art was indeed a way of staying with the times. Alternatives to the old academy and its base in patronage gave way to the market-place—the "mosh-pit" of fame and fortune. It took a sensitive eye to recognize when the practices taught in art schools were no longer relevant to the art being celebrated in the market—and a sensitive nose to adjudicate between the newest claimants to fame and fortune. I have both, said I.

But teaching art had become a perilous course: Seeking new direction, it left the art-school, and began to invade the polyglot streets, or looked for crisper identities through interaction with other arts. For the time that I was a dean of an art-school, I was mostly a benevolent opener of possibilities. When I first came, protecting students from the moribund strictures which some faculty thought constituted real teaching, was a high priority—and then telling these same faculty that they could hold on till retirement (only if you're not dumb about how you treat the students who pay your way). In my public persona, I whooped, pontificated, and waved my arms, telling students that art is not a profession but a calling. If done well, arting may gain you grace, love, some pain, and perhaps wisdom. The students took this message as an aphrodisiac—the good times came first, the rest in due course.

Eventually, I became disgruntled by the continuing demands of local art-lovers (potential patrons who wanted invitations to art-school parties), and of underfed faculty (who wanted less teaching and more praise). So I made the most ridiculous life-swerve that I could have imagined—I began to study philosophy. I was encouraged, indeed guided in this by an esteemed professor, Richard Rudner, who had the notion (by way of his own mentor, Nelson Goodman) that art and philosophy can be circumscribed within a framework of linguistic verities—not the act itself (although maybe in time) but the work's structure, context and value—these could be made knowable through descriptions that would translate the symbols which characterize the various arts, into their adherence to or differentiation from the symbols of formal discursive language.

The idea was not so much to correct the blather of linguistically innocent art criticism and history—although it was that too—but to create a new field for philosophical inquiry, namely, the possible convergence between linguistic and non-linguistic symbol systems. But what was needed in-situ for this wedding was sophistication in the value structures of both fields—what, in the art-world, is up, what down, and what are the reasons given. I was not an ideal candidate for that merger—I am at base too skittish to profess or probe—but I was the best around; and so I snuck eight years of studying philosophy into my life while continuing to dean away—and I found that my decreasing commitment to the job of running an art school actually made me better at that job—disinterestedness provides clarity. But my interests had moved elsewhere.

I was warned by New York art-types that the mid-west is no place to further an art career (they were right). But I had been shuffling through the dregs of Brooklyn for some years. My inability to further my early promise was basted with the glee of sometime friends, and the flavor was enhanced by general dismay at the abomination art I was then making (which I still make, but better). All this made the move out of New York not a matter of loss and foreboding, but a rebirth—with my early sins, commissions and omissions, blurred by geography and distance. The university we were joining was good to us—people quickly learned our names and invited us to parties. No one really knew what to make of us nor we of them. But universities are like that—this one, being more fragile at the time than others, was quicker to accept us.

We came in good faith; there were three of us, I the hero, my wife, hoping to find a place for her own work—which had sort of been promised her—and our daughter, for whom the dislocations of moving were a strain (even though on arrival I made good on promises of providing her with a pussy-cat and a puppy-dog—the grumpy Gretel and the great protector Hansel). Samantha had a hard time coping with the overt nastiness of the landed daughters of old Saint Louis. But then, I too had to cope with the ingratiating nastiness of the art-lovers of new Saint Louis, who wanted their collections to be admired and their personal daubs of art-making praised. We learned a good deal about coping—lessons that came from the heart of the country into which we arrived like immigrants, but with the attitude of Czarist émigrés, namely, that in such a place, there were no real lessons to be learned from the locals. We, of course, were wrong.

There was not much of an art-world in Saint Louis from which I could cull the latest aesthetic strategies of disobedience and dissemblance, and then demonstrate to enthralled art students that they—in principle—were being too placid and too obedient for survival in both the inner and the outer world. This was an incitement bordering on Bolshevism to mid-western seventeen year olds. But with my aura still fresh upon me, I said to them:

"Break your fetters and you will be glory bound. But before you leave, practice this: Become an irritant in your locale—use your body to incite your spirit to appear. But it is not enough to appear loudly on the runway. You must show your aura in the darker corners so that all will believe that, night or day, you are the same. If you had once engaged in the dumb-play of appearances (to keep you a step ahead of childhood goons) you must now go further. Innate swiftness may have given you the start you need, but now you must slow down, and like a brooding hen, settle into your image—that by which you shall be known. But, still, especially in the springtime, do look outside and watch the horny birds and the early blooms. Images are hard to make, and most made are hard to believe in. But the achievement of your own image is in the depths beneath the river's muddy surface. You are in Huck-Finn country you know. "

XV

During beery nighttimes, I said other things to them: "If you do go to New York (and don't guilt me with tales of how hard it is to live there) you will find that the images of less-than-nothing are currently all the rage—we didn't teach you this. Then, if you stay, it may be that you will need do nothing but point at something, call it art, and make some noise—better, a lot of noise. If you insist on making things, however, make them oppressive in their sameness—with no hint of change—so that they pass the tests of consistency and eternity. You must also do your street-work, and make sure that your images find vacancies in the changing carrousel of style. Don't ask me how—I don't know how."

My need to be a savior—to have my students enlarge our lives together became a fading dream. Each year that passed lessened the urgency of the message I had brought; and I began to forget what it was I so desperately wanted to tell them. Then again, the pervasive dream of the New York art world was fading for us all. Most students did not want to go anywhere else than where they came from—maybe teach some art courses in a junior college, but then go back and help the folks work the family farm.

This is the way it is out here: When I came, I was not only an intruder, but a subversive. In retrospect I got off light—but only because very few went east, and those few did not complain. Some actually put me up in their big-city hovels when I came traveling to New York for my annual fix of how it is back there. The others, the ones who stayed in the mid-west, thanked me at graduation for the fantasies I had offered them—most enlightening, they said, and I'll never be the same—but I didn't hear from them again.

Art schools have a way of attracting students who are sensually precocious and who pride themselves in wanting to be wilder than those other people. Students who did not like to read chose wildness (attractive misbehavior) because it is, they argued, universally attested to in art and song as a source of creativity. But most of the art students in my school were women and most of the art teachers were men. This is an ungodly mix. In our case, it was not until women artists became faculty did this scene begin to improve.

There is a site the university was offered which is located in the Ozark countryside. It was an abandoned army munitions storage site.

There were acres studded with empty concrete bunkers and warehouses and lined with rusty railroad tracks that had connected the needs of old wars. With new wars having different operational needs, the university would be given the site for educational purposes—for free—if it could document the new pacific uses. But what academic purposes could be fulfilled in an Ozark forest, in unheated buildings overgrown with all manner of weeds and bushes, without facilities, thirty miles from the campus at Saint Louis?

Art to the rescue! This Tyson Valley place became the center of our new graduate program—a place of ticks and chicks and rattlesnakes, and much more room for art and the probing for real talent than could occur in our mausoleum of the arts in the city. It was a fantasy, often funny, periodically merging on catastrophe—a mixture that is not likely to occur again.

We faculty (some of us) were as enthusiastic as the students about making art in the wilderness. It fit with that time of social disengagement and nature worship. I gathered artists who came from the big-city art-worlds, or had at least been there, and who were looking for a new place, more innocent, and not as dangerous for them to teach in and do their own work.

But Tyson Valley was not the bucolic country of Impressionism. It was a wild Ozark backland. We drank beer with the kids come late afternoon, and in the mornings gave lessons about how to make a cast, or glaze a rock and then chain it high to sway from tree to tree. Some made paper that was better art than the print imposed on it. Others splashed paint with more vigor than they thought they had, or made a deeply felt straight line despite last night's unsteady hand. A few just sat quietly until a vine would come to wrap around and announce that you and it are art.

This was good stuff for the first six years or so—as long as leaving civilization continued to be understood as an aesthetic virtue. But eventually, the gnawing of a coming reality began to show. Wilderness, once identified as guiltless godlessness and continuing fecundity, was being brought to ground (pavement) through lack of funding and the threat of real-estate development. More important—students began to take on a new-style distaste for all those creeping and biting bugs, days-old body smells, latrines in back of logs—and the snakes, oh my. Did you know that you should not jog at dusk because snakes find the residual warmth of paved paths more comforting for their cold-blooded selves than are the fast-dampening woods? Other students, attuned despite our efforts, to the majority world, found the promises of profession in our general syllabus more compatible with Madison Avenue than with the Missouri woods. Thoreau, they said, spent only two years at Walden Pond—and then went back to Boston. And no one, they also said, would come to see their work in the Ozarks boondocks.

I don't blame the kids, after the juices of infatuation had dried, for how they came to think about the littleness of art—especially when isolated from its ordinary market through a crazy ideology. They must have wondered what I was doing there, a Brooklyn boy in the midwestern woods spouting all this nonsense about nature as a fount for purity and expression. If I really knew better, as they came to suspect, why had I had come to preach in the hinterlands? So we began the next phase by just talking with each other—confessing more as equals—until it was later than late afternoon. After that, after the sun had set and the snakes were out, we talked some more, less pointed this time, about possible art-worlds that need no actuality for them or for me. In this sense I had succeeded as a teacher of my own beliefs. We had become closer to the way it counts for thinking about making art. My students came to believe that thinking is not a problem for making because I was there with them—an itinerant sophist—to lecture about the reciprocity of purity and excess, to commiserate with their difficulties, and to fabricate mostly useless but encompassing solutions. They soon ceased to believe me, but they remained kind.

The early ones in the program graduated with aplomb, having been given the top of the best bottle we could offer. Later ones, the ones who came after the decline of woodland aesthetics, showed the anxiety of ordinary student needs—but all we could give them then was the old advice. This bored the students and bored me too—the heroic age was over. Making art wasn't a profession and, except for a few, not even a calling. I felt embarrassed by the combination of criticism and hucksterism that I had been projecting for now too many years.

XVI

So I shifted my energies into the perspective (as I understood it) of philosophical studies and scratched away for about eight years. A kind-hearted vice-chancellor, who approved (I guess) of my traverse—and who anyway was leaving—gave me a year off to complete my dissertation. My early flirtation with philosophy had grown too intense over time—much like a runaway extra-marital romance—to relinquish for the grind of teaching art in the trenches. I was relieved when the philosophers, my often bemused mentors, asked me to join with them—on the supposition that my skewed sense of things might enliven their own dull grind of tending to the rationalist-empiricist controversy, and thereby save the department from irrelevancy.

One would think that artists are territorial and self-protective until one encounters an academically captive tribe of philosophers: There was the Kantian rabbi who couldn't stomach Hegel and revered Hermann Cohen for bringing traditional Judaism and enlightenment rationality together. And then there was the secular, although Jewish, philosopher of culture for whom Hegel was a link to Marxism and Modernism, and who thought that Kant, especially in his ethics, was quite mad, and that Whitehead was the way to go. But these were outriders. The center was a whirling cadre of those who disavowed, in the tradition of Carnap, Ayer and Quine, any theories that were not quantifiable in strict extensional terms. For them, the soft inquiries of history, aesthetics, sociology, were tolerable only because of antiquated curriculum requirements—although they were pleasant fodder to play language-games with over cocktails.

Moving in the other direction was ethics, newly energized by feminist, racial, and environmental issues that came largely from social concerns of the time. For these concerns, the historical disputes over language and its applications were so ideologically laden with their derivation from formal languages, that they could not be adequate instruments with which to face present ethical dilemmas.

Science infatuated philosophy, variously called Logical Positivism or Logical Empiricism, was to many of the out-riders, a philosophical cop-out. It did not offer the clarifications that scientists purportedly needed—a regimented and logically transparent language that is adequate to the variety of scientific assertions and their sometime interactions. Yet it insisted, by default, on demeaning other forms of language more appropriate to non-quantifiable concerns. Through this neo-scholastic attempt, the world of philosophical thought became impoverished by distinguishing what could or could not be cogently spoken about, and what in "ordinary" language—and its fields of attention—needed discarding before obscure subject and adequate description could come into equilibrium.

Thus, not only language, but its designated worlds, became victims of high-minded reductionism. Wittgenstein well understood this danger when he called for "language-games" that are appropriate to different "forms of life."

XVII

I left my position in the art school to join the philosophy faculty just a year after I had finished there as a student. A Surreal experience—and yet, imagine further: Within another year, I became chair of the department. Here was a bare-faced administrative ploy: I was given this position because the powers thought that as I was practiced in such situations—whatever their venues—a change, what with my newly found erudition, should pose few problems. But I was not told—nor did the powers know—what this change would amount to. An administrative background clings to you like dog-shit on a blanket. It is the mark of Cain, stipulating that the solitary ambitions you once nurtured in the trenches, are not relevant to your new position—even if in cocktail parties you dredge them up. But despite your past foibles, said the powers, we need you now to get the juices flowing in that stale department, to make peace between the factions, regulate the few new hires, and proclaim what it is that you-all have really been doing all these years. As of now you do not even have a good turf war to bring the department into focus.

Well, institutional administration is a living, so I began the most bizarre episode of my life—chairing a department where I just recently had been a student—to shape them into something other than they are. And I, along with most of them, was beyond the age of fifty. Were the faculty, my dear once mentors, amenable to this? I don't know. Some must have feared retaliation for their outlandish views on some issue of concern—or their lack of publications. But they did not want me to tamper with their dreams—or their politics. I did not. For others, my appointment provoked a territorial response. Did I know enough to accept the triumph of logic and language over the messiness of speculative metaphysics? They had a point—but why should philosophy be immune to messiness? I have always sought a kinship—distant friends if nothing more—with the learned romantics who sought concordance with the non-logical world—the world that endures, they claim, despite language—or, at least, in the spaces between everything that, at any given time, language can allude to. I had learned a lot about parsing the world through philosophical distinctions between reality and its descriptions, between connotation and denotation, extensional and intensional predicates, the struggle between the unruly varieties of conditioned truths and their demanding father who wants a single mode of definition. But I felt constricted with this—much as I was with formalist abstraction.

The new wave came shortly before I retired—the brain-mind scanners who don't much care about definition but are after explanation. They want the subjects of hard theory: the empirical sciences, much of medicine, as well as the subjects of soft theory: ethics, aesthetics, to be approached through the explanatory apparatus of neurological mapping. The aim here is to invade the physiological arena of decision-making, where judgments of all kinds—empirical, ethical, aesthetic—can be shown to characteristically stimulate areas of the brain in specific and hopefully predictable ways. Then we will be able, they argue, to make the causal claims between brain phenomena and soft-behavior less mysterious, the workings of moral choice and political action more transparent, and even artistic genius less transcendent.

But there are also inverse factors here—as old as the dawn of inquiry: Explanation makes the explanandum simpler than it was before it became the object of analysis. The best explanation (somebody said this first) is that which overrides the puzzles and presumptions surrounding its subject. It would be nice if neuro-mapping could be codified and then applied to show, say, lesser artists how to make good art—better, how to identify a promising artist at birth, so that precocious creativity is not mistaken for unruliness. Also valuable would be to show disturbed persons the neural patterns that cause the discomfort they feel, how these can be modified—and so relieve that person from the guilt and pain of living.

But such variables—art, artist, creativity, genius, the angelic and the diabolic, just and unjust, sane and crazy, are deeply permeated by social preferences and historical position. How social development interacts with genetic predisposition (predictable before the behavioral fact) is as yet a fuzzy issue.

All is not lost, said my successor chair. Teams of experts could be formed to see if anything new can be learned by bringing the array of warring beliefs, styles and cultures, together with the findings of the latest science. To begin with, it takes a committee (all such ventures do). This committee should include neuro-scientists, art-historians, philosophers, artists, writers, anthropologists, theologians, radical and religious sceptics—all predominant in their areas (it wouldn't do to begin with pretenders) and who are willing to defend their own language and beliefs against the strangeness of other such. There cannot be a philosopher-king to rule the roost—no one believes in that anymore; yet there should be some muscle that encourages the softer heads to leave.

But what then do we have—after all this fine ecumenical effort? At the least, a consensus of bright minds that produces findings to which no one of its members completely subscribes. The questions asked are both dignified and timely. They include the prejudices of earlier inquiry into the designated subjects which, by discarding accumulated dross, can be made to fit present concerns. But this task becomes difficult when projected into the future: Is poking into the brain the final, albeit evolving, way of understanding the world? Are there no separate ways of knowing—intuition, introspection, ecstatic vision—that are adequate to (some parts) of the rich content of the world?

Such questions bring up the larger philosophical question of the nature of belief—the battle between eternal and transient verities. Many methods, from drowsy seminars to brutal wars, have been used—if not to resolve, then at least to map—ways of answering them. My fear is that the neuro-philosophical method can become another way of relieving us of the always messy, often hostile, ways of "believing that." Referring difficult problems upwards, to an empirically neutral and thus conceptually immaculate source for answers can be deeply misleading. I well-remember the hubris of Logical Positivism, through such tomes as Ayer's "Language Truth and Logic," in its conviction that speculative philosophy is at an end thanks to the method of analysis which separates the meaningful from the meaningless. Yet, we are surrounded by consumers of all sorts of "meaningless meaning."

XVIII

There are many questions concerning the "end" of art—so many as to elicit a favorite undergraduate dictum: "Der Konflikt zwischen Kunst und Leben." In those early neo-Spenglerian days, the conflict was viewed as never-ending but its playing out was all downhill—a pessimistic counter to Hegelian optimism, but a fertile subject for Mann and Hesse.

Yet, there were small optimistic insights to be found in post-war New York about art's, however contradictory, historical march: The notion of "expression" for one, contained a nostalgia for the wild and lawless heritage of the American west (although the great historical painters of that landscape, such as Bierstadt, Cole, and Moran, relied largely on European models}. Another notion was "form"—the search for an uncontaminated image of art-reality—which found its reductive passage though still-lifes and small French mountains.

These virtues, despite their often acrimonious passage through the interplay between expressionist abstraction and geometric formalism, projected a message of artistic liberation: Art has to do with both attitude and place; the "city" superceded the "country" as the place, and the attitudes were to be learned in the watering holes of openings and down-town bars. Such learning—as contrasted with the rigors of the academy—or the enticements of pleine-aire—was not meant to diminish individuality and self-expression. And who isn't in favor of that? As a consequence, there were more artist-candidates than the society could sustain. But oh it was a lot of fun—especially for the young.

In the fifties, the end of the second world war needed celebrating—the period of grim reality and kitschy patriotism was over, and images of what was newly important needed making. The first of the post-war artists found this transition hardest. They drank too much and died too young or went dithering into their senescence . But this mattered only to them—to the rest, they became culture heroes. They had achieved the tutti-frutti topping that gave them entry into the crowded antechambers of art-history. What more could be asked by later multitudes of seekers for a real fame-topped identity?

The hopefuls came to New York from all over: The California contingent, ripe as ever for serious competition with the east, and then the lads and lassies, family brutalized and historically impoverished, from Montana, Mississippi, Missouri, Maine and such, who had heard of a forward world planted with art and life and love and maybe money, that was germinating in New York, a city which by all accounts had become the victor over Paris for the role of art-center-of-the-world. New York was a good place –the only place to be for young artists who had become artists just a little while ago.

If you are serious, said Professor James, the studio teacher at Rosedale-West Community College in Tennessee, go to New York and scratch till you find your way-to-go. You might make it—sure you will. I would like to go back with you, but I've been there and now I'm here—you know, personal problems. Then again, loft living is not easy; it can be cold-hot and dangerous-expensive. The dealers want to see if you can withstand that craziness—they only want the genius who is barely whelped, but who will do wild things non-stop, or who can (him, her, it, them) fully coincide with their art-work.

But why would you, Professor Asshole James, want to steer your students into that mosh-pit of pain and failure, knowing, as you do, that artists are daily turned into aesthetic hamburger so that their patrons can eat? Does this sound severe? Remember that once, not long ago, art was regarded as both a psychic and social revelation—a way of understanding hidden parameters of the soul. It was also a sometime window onto oppression. But it may be, that even then, too many artists subscribed to that notion—only to find, belatedly, that the new art (which they in fact were making) was not about criticism or belief, but discrete and selective consumption.

I left New York because the art I was then doing—timid ugly shit—was not being recognized—and the place where I was teaching had been crumbling. So I left—a move subsequently described by me and others as "the great mistake"—but at that time, it was more like "le grand adventure." Anyway, we moved to Saint Louis, where I saw that my new position, and my art, were of sufficient interest to the wealthy folks such that, could I have finessed it, would have been a boon to all our expectations.

But I'm really no good at such stuff. There was nothing I could think to offer but my unsung paintings, a dilapidated art-school, and some skill at rhetoric. Yes, we had talented students, and the faculty, given the mid-western malaise, wasn't bad. But I found that the monies for art schools do not come from philanthropists but from collectors who want admiration for their adventurous tastes. I once suggested, in an early "friends" lecture, that they buy, each year, a student work from the annual year end show—for fifty bucks or so—and then discard it if they no longer like it come next May. A good move, I said, for collectors who are philanthropic and who have been made anxious by missing out on the millions a Rothko or Pollock now cost.

But then one friend said to me: How can this bright and fanciful collage-construction made by one Lester Porcupine from Hollow Hills Arkansas—a most talented student for sure—be mounted in my mansion whose competitive walls sport Rothkos and Pollocks? Well! This is high-stakes warfare I had blundered into, one that tramples the soft-hearts who confute art with beneficence. Soft-hearts, it has been whispered, cannot be sufficiently hardened—perhaps a deficiency in their surrogate—to be trusted with economic decisions. I had not faced any such decisions in New York; Instead, I roamed the Village streets, nosing around with my no-good friends, pleasing myself, but vague about the demands of my calling.

So there I was, by God, in Saint Louis, at the age of forty—a long–time native of New York, with the reputation for knowing the innards of the scene. That must have been what intrigued them, and also that we were the most (and cheapest) that they could get to come to Saint-Louis in the mutual hour of need. And so we went.

There was a wealthy widow who didn't much talk about how her money had been made—but she was a brooder about large things, and had a great desire to not be left behind in what really matters. Such a conscience is hard enough to find in hip New York; but we're talking Missouri here. During a trip to the boon-docks of Tyson Valley—she had put on boots and a slicker—we wandered through the studio-quonset huts, and I showed her what the students were doing. She did buy some Porcupines. It could be that she just liked Lester's work—or that she just wanted to help—but she did say to me, over cocktails, that he and I might have a future.

XIX

One must have a stomach for such a life; I thought I did but I didn't. So, as if I had found a new downtown bar with different talkers, I began to study philosophy while still tending to art-school needs. I didn't especially hide this venture, but few believed it. My reasons had something to do with my increasing anxiety about educating artists—all those young sparkling faces who will face tuition loans and, after four quick years, an end to the empathy of faculty insisting that we're all in this together.

There were other, more central reasons for my philosophical studies. I had always thought, even in the drone of depression Brooklyn, that I was smarter than the rest. My mother told me this and I believed her. She died before she knew, but I continued to believe her—although it did me little good at first because I am not disposed to being powerful. It took many life scenarios, some focused and others chaotic, before I could think to leave New York and become an art-school dean in the Midwest. The invitation to study philosophy came soon after, from faculty with their own purposes—after all, becoming a prominent philosopher is even harder than being a successful artist.

But for me, the invitation was a way to be educated, and philosophy (with the old and the new—as in art—provocatively intermeshed) seemed the way to go. I wanted a real education—where I could talk about the ancients and moderns without bluffing. I stayed the course, and do not regret it—for I came to understand the world and myself by going through more tunnels and over more ridges than I had ever seen in Brooklyn. I also, I admit it, enjoyed becoming a "Doctor of Philosophy."

There are many more ways, I know, to satisfy ambition—like going out and making money. But by then, I had gotten to a place in mind that is good enough for me even now. (The notion of limit, in itself, provides an education). I have written some, painted much, and have found limits to my anxieties about being unheralded. This has to do with accepting that I am not as bright as I had previously thought—nor as talented. But I am better than many (hear me roar) and anyway, both the world and I are in no condition now to give me proper due. Maybe later.

The world is always in a precarious place, and art, mimicking the world, is there too. I marvel that the periodic wrecking of the world has historically been consonant with the production of great art. But what in the world is happening now, now that I am half-fulfilled and in my dotage? Great powers still vie with itinerant contenders, the stubbornness of the unequal conflict bemuse all those who believe in the efficacy of progress. And yet the arts play Mickey-Mouse with their allotted time. Glorifying the ways of virtue is not my aim—celebrating the wicked would be quite as good. Belief and cynicism are both goads for art. It has been said that art is connected to money through a golden vein—the effluences of beauty and of wealth commingle there. But the better reasons for patronage have been about the long-term uses of the work—the least of which being its entertainment value. The ideal reason for acquiring great art is to appoint ones-self (Kantian style) as custodian of its qualities for posterity.

Sounds sappy, doesn't it. The qualities of great works do indeed project their aesthetic virtues into social and theological beliefs. But they also testify to the importance, and good taste of patrons. Once, donors to major religious works were pictured with their families as witnesses to the transcendent event. So the longer is the artwork's influence in this history, the more valuable it (and the more noble its patrons) are taken to be. Truth—especially aesthetic truths about eternal truth—must be finessed by craft and guile so as to last for centuries.

From my perspective, the truths in question and their projection through these past centuries, are untruths: The depicted king, in fact, has a large growth on his nose—unpictured—because the courtiers who see him daily never make mention of his nose, and the multitudes ruled by him see him only at a distance. So the King's Queen and their royal children, all of whom have impeccable aquiline noses and sturdy calves given them by art, ignore their father's nose. The discomfort is left to the mistresses.

Landscapes, whether Ruisdale's or Bierstadt's, have no mosquitoes, horse-flies, snakes or leeches that would interrupt appreciation. Further, we must consider the contrast between beneficiaries of modern plumbing and the frequenters of out-houses as waystations on the path to ideality. The model for Michelangelo's "David" was not recorded as smelling bad; neither were any of Raphael's "Madonnas" nor their sacred offspring. Carravagio's "Putti" with their dirty feet did break the rule, but he suffered for it. The French panoply that depicted secular desirables: Ingres, Delacroix, Boucher, Fragonard, Courbet, Renoir, et al, did not include blemishes and smells in their depictions. But then, neither do our present porno-films or fashion ads. Shouldn't this be changed? I suggest that we add taste and touch and smell to sight and sound—an ecumenical challenge to the new artist. Sight, sound, smell, taste, and touch together, are the public extensions, as I see it—the subjects of the new art.

Concerts that have performers screaming and gyrating, and audiences coughing and whooping, sometimes bring distaff qualities together. "Togetherness," says the cynic, is just attenuated foreplay—but that is the verdict of the bifurcated. There is, in contrast, the smell of overheated audiences, the smoky float of incense, the saltiness of, say, arm-pits and potato-chips, and supporting this, the dank refulgence of an old uncared-for building. It may be a start—all these incommensurables hob-nobbing together—each contributing their prime ingredient to the communal stew. I hate Wagner—not only for his politics but for the boredom, between the good parts, that he imposes on his audience. But his notion of a total art, the "Gesamtkunstwerk" may, for my argument, be important.

When Titian's "Danae" opens her body to the gold coins of Jove's seduction, we are torn between her beauty and her willing prostitution. When Picasso's "Demoiselles D'Avignon" presents a spectrum of both cultural degradation and art-historical larceny, we struggle for the appreciative stance that we, as sophisticates of both worlds, should assume. On the other side, the monotony of repetition in Pollock and Rothko are as insistent and recognizable as are jingles selling products that require repetition to be noticed. We do notice them. And now we have the newest of new international artists, scheduled for a show somewhere but forgetting when, who arrives just in time to nail a used tissue to the gallery wall and then proffer it as a sufficient achievement, in fact his most advanced work to date.

XX

Where and when does art begin? I don't really know. The distinction between art and non-art is already well established in the pre-history of Lascaux and the Willendorf Venus. This was not a distinction made then, but it is one made now—an aesthetic distinction between symbol and reality that is purportedly of benefit to both. Much has been written on this. But the question more dear to me than beginnings is: Where and when does art end? Limiting the arena to the past hundred years will locate the modern trouble and the origins of anxiety—somewhere between Analytic Cubism and Warhol's antics. I contrast the early iconoclasts of the ideological end of art—Malevich, Mondrian—with the social frolickers waiting for the final party—unrepentant Dadaists, flaky Surrealists, manic Pop-ists. Once articulated, however, the "end of art" contagion spreads faster and wider than did the Black Death, and it threatens to go on as long as someone will pay to see the show.

The arch-villain in this story may be Hegel, whose philosophy dithers between necessity and freedom, and who gave art the imprimatur to be forever new, and quixotically, for history to devalue art when it was no longer consequential to the "evolution of spirit." In this sense, the Cubism of Picasso and Braque was a two-step affair: a reduction of natural form to geometric equivalents, and the reformulation of these equivalents into new, non-naturalistic arrays. Serious stuff, this—a competitor in seriousness to the Renaissance. But it bred, because of its flirtation with its own endgame, divergent streams of permissiveness that led to calling anything, made or thought, as "art."

There are many variations: Clement Greenberg, a Hegelian-manque critic, offered the notion of "flatness," the surface-enhancing disposition of painterly forms as a historical step beyond illusion. Badly executed attempts at flatness retained (to their unnoticed credit) intimations of space; more successful attempts attained the aesthetics of commercial wallpaper. I prefer craziness—the glorification of aesthetic failure—to this essentially decorative solution masquerading as metaphysical profundity. But craziness, although the frolics in question are fun when one is young, is not the answer to making the next decades' non-art connect to the grand post-art traditions of today. (Come on! Don't shudder at the term "tradition." With all the bad-mouthing about the past, artists still want to be compared to Michelangelo.)

Craziness as a strategy does not make distinctions that can be used to separate art from non-art. The provocations of my favorite pretenders to seriousness—Duchamp and Warhol—had critical access to the higher realms of taste and money. This is not craziness as such—as was skulking in the grime of the old-time bowery, or howling in the winter winds of Scandinavia. This is the new craziness which is usually marketed as the latest fashion. It is a very sane craziness. Art and non-art switch partners as the mores and markets dictate. One need not worry about the ephemerality of taste when there is no social or ideological pressure for continuity in taste.

History has gotten a bad rap through the fallout from failed ideologies of recent times, and its capitulations in defeat extend into the present through admission that the sacred marriage of "continuity and progress" has been annulled by the secular narcissism of the ongoing "now." We now live in the "eternal present." The idea that "old-master" art is better than "these days" art is only a given for the few who are inveterate sippers of the past. But we also know that this idea (given its parameters of theme, belief, and genius) is true.

That we cannot go back to what is better than our best, evokes a belief in historical insignificance—an inverse Hegelianism that results in the a-historical stance that we must protect our own, our slip-sliding present, from the encroachments of both past and future. In this sense, our present "not-as-good" is yet better than the old stuff because the advocates of "our best" need not bother with discontinuities between past values and current tastes: We know that the old stuff, in some old sense, is good, but why bother with "good." The past, through such rejections, becomes a victim of our present, and yet retains some force through its conservative insistence that one thing is better than another. In this way, the past gives us warning about our interest in the future—at least the future that we, without heeding evidence from the past, nevertheless want to own.

The past is irritating because it insists on being retrospective and won't go away to leave us to our living without the guilt that we have deviated from dimly remembered verities. The future, because it is so loose, can be terrifying through its way of giving us nothing dependably predictive that will tell us what it and we shall be. But that is our fault. We have forsworn the ideological glue of historicity and progress, and have thus suffered the loss of knowing what will become us after our own present becomes the past.

But then, why should we care, being patrons of the present, about whether before and after can be reified as past and future? Why cannot our temporal present take on the logical characteristics of the eternal present—where time and change have no impact upon the truth or falsity of belief? We would not have to worry then, in our Parmenidean salon, about where we come from or where we might be going—because, as the man said, movement, forward or backward, offered as prediction or remembrance, is illusory, the forlorn remnant of the physical experience of change—which we share with worms—but from which we, being somewhat brighter, have invented a past and future, and then denied it—to our present distress.

XXI

A recent theory about dreaming suggests that dreams are simply warm-up exercises, lubrications for the efforts of our waking minds. Earlier theories consider dreams as the hidden center of the self, and still other theories identify this self with underlying memories of the collective beginnings of self-hood. It is not a matter of whether such theories are true, but a matter of what is lost when we discard the fancies of Freud and Jung, and deny our guilt at not wanting to remember all those dreams we know we had—which could have made us better than we are if only we understood that they were about the us we did not want to know.

The old man asks: Are the kinks our dreams reveal so bad that we cannot face them in the transition to our outside selves? But no one can, it seems—although they often lie—describe the kinks they dream. And soon, with all the sanctioned buzz of falsifying, the fashions drift away from diving deep to snorkeling in the shallows. Safe from drowning, we flaunt our surface butterflies of rationality, and are surprised when the rational surface parts, and we tumble into the down deep where different criteria are used to sort out the larger nature of ending.

I think of Hell as a place where skepticism reigns, where the history of chants, parades, homilies, penances, exhortations of the faithful are viewed upon a giant screen, and enjoyed on weekends by the wicked as fictions that serve to illustrate the history of conflicts between them and the programs of Heaven. The history of art stops when art goes to hell—when belief in progress is undermined by infatuation with programs in the here and now. But think back and look around: When is now? And where is here? We accommodate our uncertainties about past and future to our desires for a concrete present—where the four horsemen who once signaled the end of life and hope appear again, bopping as they trot around the stage, making love to microphones, and loudly affirming that both art and life have (really, this time) ended—but never mind, we're all here enjoying it.

The issues the apocalyptic horsemen embody can be projected in post-demonic imagery: The old sins, now acceptable as ordinary practice, are the uses of art for financial speculation and for social aggrandizement. The new sins are more about sinners: artists who take on the role of entertainers, and critics who are mainly middle-men. Demons love this stuff—but remember, Socrates did warn us about it.

Despite age-old efforts at separating art from money and power, the angels never succeeded: Why should they have? Art has historically provided the documentation of success and the images of deception that encourage rationales for patriotic, ethical, and religious beliefs (are angels not part of this?) while providing delectation for private enjoyment . All this now seems uncontroversial. Artists (most of them) have looked to their patrons for their content: Battles, coronations, immolations, crucifixions, portraits of royals and popes, mythical stand-ins for objects-of-desire, are among their subjects.

Yes, there are exceptions. Genius often goes beyond the most sophisticated inquiries of appreciation and belief: The glowing eye of Titian's flayed satyr denies victory to Apollo; The anti-classical ugliness of Grüenewald's crucified Christ questions God's omnipotence; Goya's "Horrors of War" challenges the ways of empire; Manet's "Dejeuner sur l'Herbe" exposes the privileged separation between private vice and public virtue.

The arts of Modernism—say, from Cezanne on—began by radicalizing form at the expense of social content. The emphasis was on the direct and "unmediated" perception of nature. Such artists as Van Gogh, Seurat, Monet, did more than shift artistic attention to orchards, hills and trees; they used nature as an exemplar, a subject that evokes and justifies their own attempts at innocence. The artist emulates nature by taking on its purity, via an "unmediated perception" that translates into painterly process. But, following along through this gesture, the artist too becomes a work of art—diminishing the distance between the marks and the acts of creativity, so in effect forswearing the ills of the world for the intimate neutrality that nature provides. Conceptually, it is a considerable step (but historically not a long one) between the times when innocence before nature devolves into painterly innocence within the self. This marks the rise of abstract art.

Picasso brought Cezanne back into the cities by translating nature, with its changing light, undulating rhythms and deep spaces, into the hard city beat of analytic cubism and its battle between discrete subjects and the generalizing process. Although this peak did not sustain itself—it was too austere and impersonal—Braque and Picasso did join psyche and process in producing masterworks that pronounced the primacy of form over its representation. But Picasso's inclusion, in a late work of that period, of a label of "Suze"—the soft drink that changed art as radically as did Warhol's "Coca-Cola"—signaled the beginnings of synthetic cubism, and so split the ideology of progressive modernism into competing camps.

The camp which I title "form," invokes the value of impersonality, the value through which regimentation controls the indulgence of immediate feeling and the claim for verisimilitude. A formal aesthetic presumes (as a historically progressive mandate) to parse the elements of art-making—for the ideological reason that art is otherwise prone to vitiate its aesthetic responsibilities (given the laissez-faire seductions of populism) by turning into a beauty-contest. The formalist aesthetic denies seduction, as it warrants only those objects that not only delineate but also prescribe a proper response to the mission of art (Mondrian, Reinhardt, Judd). The formalist artist may be the eminence-grise behind the enterprise, but the attempt to explain the work through recourse to intention, does not reach the historical achievement—as the achievement is, by definition, impersonal.

The other camp, which I call "expression," begins with artistic immediacy, but then opens to an outside world that prefigures Pop-art through images that are topically rather than historically relevant, and through techniques such as collage that derive from commercial-art practices. Obviously, the arts of expression do not reject form as such. (There is no art-work, or anything else, without form). But the polemical difference is nevertheless categorical—between form as a descriptive term for the array of various uses, and form as a stylistic imperative which identifies abstract minimalist artworks as historically ascendant.

The aesthetics of form rests on dominant icons of past art—Classical architecture, Giotto, Piero, Palladio, Poussin. Cezanne. But note, that the developmental line offered here is itself dualistic: While it values the chosen icons of the past for their contributions, more potently, it treats their succession as a general sign of progress. In the center of this narrative of historical change, we also find the deeper claim of historical evolution. Its manifestation in art brings together historical awareness with the symbols of formal obligation.

Expressionism, even when taken as a historical style, gathers sustenance from Nietzsche's dim view of progress and stresses the irrationalities that vitiate sequential thinking, and so glorifies sensual immediacy. The art of expression, unlike that of form, is rooted in, indeed luxuriates in, it's moment. Expressionist art is not historically reductive nor is it thematically inevitable, and it is preferentially centered on critical or even hostile attitudes to a repressive society. Expressionists look for their inspirations in the late-Greek "Dying Gaul," the Roman frescos in the Villa of the Mysteries, the north European art of Grunewald, Breugel, Bosch, and the early modern works of Goya, Schiele, Van Gogh, Munch and Kandinsky. These are precursors of Pollock, Rothko, and DeKooning, Bacon and Kiefer.

The polemical split between the opposing styles of "form" and "expression" had force as long as its post-war American polemicists could keep the public interest. Indeed, the purchase of contemporary post-war art soon became a sign of sophistication and success. Clement Greenberg presented the orthodox stance of "inevitability"—that the best of future art must be abstract and reductive. Harold Rosenberg, in contrast, stressed the value of "novelty"—the best art being unpredictably new. Rosenberg offers radical individual action as opposed to Greenberg's collective radicalism. But for a time, both viewpoints in that hallowed period (1950-1980), fuelled with money, bedecked with images, and wanting to usurp European pre-war primacy, came together in a burgeoning of galleries, art- publications, and art-schools. Youngsters responded to this excitement by wanting to be part of it—to be artists. In response, institutions that had previously not entertained art as a subject, but only as cultural history—scrambled to offer classes in studio practice. The number of post-war, art-school trained artists, particularly in New York and the west coast, amounted to a new social class. "Being an artist" in the sixties was a rites of passage requiring little allegiance to either side of the form-expression debate.

Pop-art was the opening that destroyed the residues of both sides of high-minded modernism. Its program is as varied as an anti-ideological, success driven, program can encompass. Early moves incorporated the images and techniques of "commercial" art and design, and the use of large-scale printing, photography, and other reproductive techniques, to challenge the autonomy and singularity of the painted "picture plane." These moves also inferentially denied that there is a categorical difference between high-art and other forms of image-making. The prime mover in all this, its exemplar, is Warhol, who remains unfathomable in his attitude toward held values—toward present people as well as past-art. He was effectively outrageous in his bland rejection of the proprieties of "art-making"—the notion that a special artistic muscle is a requirement for ascribing the honorific of "art-work." onto an object.

This denial of the separation between public work and private making has now become a commonplace, especially for artists who identify "work" with "conception" rather than "making." But beyond that, Warhol exasperates through his aura of not caring about the historically durable "art–non-art" distinction, or about any other verity that had been counted on to maintain the distinction between lived life and created art. This elision gives Warhol the role of supreme post-modern practitioner of indifference. Such indifference does not deny interest in notions of before and after, high and low, good and bad, pain and pleasure, real or pictured—rather, it denies normative (critical) power to the ideologies that support any such distinctions. Characteristically, Warhol never made this notion of indifference explicit (he didn't write much). This, perhaps, is what leads Arthur Danto to consider Warhol the most philosophical of contemporary artists.

XXII

So what is to be done, after the idols of the temple have been displaced by the idols of the market-place, which in turn have been replaced by the idols of indifference? What can still be done with the occasions in art that claim the truth of manifest belief, the truth of disinterested (not to be confused with indifferent) representation, the truth of primary process, the truth of symbolic purification?

Do we discard them in the light—not of truer truths, but of more fashionable truths—so risking the wiles of pragmatism? It has been a short but painful journey from the ambitions of Kant, Schopenhauer and Hegel to the present indifference to art's autonomy such that a concept of artistic truth might provide. They weren't completely wrong, these sages, when they denied that art is not a vehicle for truth—but a good vehicle for conjecture.

The experience of art accrues to both the practiced and the naive—to those who dive deep into the universals of meaning and risk the bends, and to those who splash around in the shallows and get sand in their crotch. Neither experience of truth, of course, can be confirmed as being true unless the criteria for aesthetic truth—as with historical and moral truth—broaden beyond our present set of empirical-logical boundaries. The belief, (as in Carnap and Ayer) that discourse about meaningful issues, to be taken seriously, must be purified into logical utterances, is of a kind, it seems to me, with formalist (Greenbergian) stipulations on what needs discarding in order to allow that which must happen next to further art. And then, after all this, Warhol comes by to suggest it doesn't matter.

The faithful say in bad times—"wait it out." But what if the world of post-indifference and neo-language will not accept this faith in circularity? What if the world is just straight on? Shall we, nevertheless keep vigil for the return of our outmoded oracles—those idealists, conspirators, and romantics now hiding in the dark corners of our time? Few I know will wait; They do not know how to play the game of "eternal return."

Who is it then, that admonishes us to not wait? Well, lots of folks: There are docents, critics, connoisseurs self or otherwise appointed, dealers scrupulous or sneaky, the clever-clean and filthy-rich, and young companions of all the above.

About Myself 63

Then there are captains of industry and collectors with a nose for bargains, decorators and architects who really hate art, and pizza-parlor owners who need frescos on the peeling walls to glorify their pies. The waiting game is not popular now, and is only suited to those who anticipate an outcome—a historical winning or losing—that gives the waiting experience some purchase on the way things actually go.

Consider this contrast: Art is life made real through representation; life is art made actual through non-representation. There seems little way to bring the two together: Art lacks life's durational density, and life lacks art's forms of self-containment.

Art, unlike life, does not go on forever—it ends, that is, when it is discredited. Life goes on until it ends, and death is not a source of discreditation. Art ends when it never was art (our current take on fakes and forgeries) or when it transcends art (our current admiration for post-art gestures). There do remain questions about art-works made in places where they are never seen—except perhaps by wolves, or grandma and the kids.

The death of persons is different from the death of art-works. Art, unlike living things, can be reinterpreted. It is conceivable that the honorific 'art' can lose all discriminating power at some future time—and then we are left with a bunch of objects. But the question here shrinks from this eventuality. In a society where the notion of art still has currency, what can constitute the death of an art-work? Can the worst art-work ever cease being art, or just be a prime example of bad art? Does the acknowledged death of one art-work lead, inexorably—like the fatal virus—to postulating the death of all art?

Some folks, not too long ago, tired of transcendence, have tried to make life into art. A few of them succeeded. I admit I still am jealous: (All those parties—food by magic chefs, the finest companions with limbs and loins in fragrant disarray—perhaps not as fine as last week, but t'es passable—and someone to drive you home).

But we will all go a'moldering in our graves. Why not, then, demand of art that it transfer its presumption of immortality to us, and so help us to prolong our lives?

There is this, however: Art, when ended—destroyed, demeaned, forgotten—does not molder, as we do, at our end. Art, when it ends, evaporates the shape of its identity and joins the cosmic pool of non-historical entities—mere stuff. We, when we die, are inevitably, although often minimally, historical. We are remembered.

We cannot let this happen to art—to watch our investments, because of academic sophistry, so slide away. Hold on then, and through other tricks and trades, we will give rise to the notion of post-art art: things and events that are surely not the kind of art we have, but that can maintain the honorific "art" until it may suit us to discard it when it—and they—become too porous to contain value. So discarded, these post-art-art-things, by (our) agreement, become mere things again. Because the transformations have been so agreeable (no debate, no penalty for misrepresentation) post-art artifacts can be mollified for their loss of art-status (it was anyway hard to keep it going) by the hope that, in some more optimistic time it (this status) might yet return—and they (these objects) will again be art.

Why then, with its status become so nervous, is art still around—and more so now than ever? Actually, the world powers should give thanks: Arting has historically been a substitute (until things get really bad) for rebellion. The art-world should also acknowledge—and act upon—its under-remarked service to the status-quo.

"Bourgeois" is no longer a prejudicial term; it can now show how well it fits present day art-making. In the best entrepreneurial sense, art is now free of the academy, and is fast becoming free of the art-school. One good alternative is the neighborhood committee for art-life co-habitation—which feeds into city plans for increasing art-sophistication in the ghettos, which in turn nourishes the national mandate for cultural identity.

XXIII

The art-world remains with us, even though its scope and feeders will undeniably change. "Art" emerged from "artisan" just when it took on its battle between reality and transcendence. The irritation of living too long in such rarified air now leads art, after the ideological extravagances of modernism, back to 'artisan,' and so to rediscover itself, with the help of architects weavers and potters, in unlikely places. Unless they are nimble, museums and art-schools will lose out in the shuffle to show and help make art that is also "non-art." Museums will need to rethink their exclusiveness and their reliance on patrons who most admire "masterpieces." But this should not be too difficult: The acquisition of proto-neo-would-be-masterpieces—recent versions of historical contenders or the latest blasphemies—makes for a good party.

Art-schools will have it harder: Whether they are independent or embedded in colleges and universities, they no longer have the authority of the old rebellion—especially now, when the war-refugees who brought modern-art into this country are mostly dead, and the best of recent faculty, just out of college, chose—as I did—teaching in preference to histrionic starving in the market-place. All this need not be a problem. It turns out that art students these days shudder at the mention of the New York adventure—they want to teach their skills to kids and senior citizens, do their own quiet thing, and make a modest living. But if anything still needs doing in art schools, it is in vitalizing the sources of imagery and imagination .

To illustrate: Landscape was an important subject for the mystical German Renaissance, for the Impressionistic French, and for wilderness-infatuated Americans. The later transition from the rhythms of nature to the thrashings of psyche, transformed this subject into the action-paintings of Pollock and Dekooning, and the silent yet obsessive images of Rothko and Reinhardt. Alternatively, images of cityscapes had become documents of degradation, instigated by Cole in his "Ways of Empire," and followed by German and American socially minded artists between the wars—as with Bellows, George Grosz, and Edward Hopper.

With the treatment of nudes, we must tread lightly (although Picasso did not): Nude depictions are largely of naked females and so, are typically glorifications of male privilege. And yet the span of their allure seems as eternal as is sex. Accordingly, such works traverse between stylizations that accommodate moral strictures—the more sinful you are the more naked you will be—and yet the more mythical are your origins, your nudity will condone the juicy specificities that enliven the high-life imagination of the connoisseur. Within that tension—between the naked and the nude—great paintings have been made.

"What then is now to be done?" asks the troubled elder. Well, stay cool, say I, and do what you do—and if you want, lay onto others what you think is important about what you do, so that they should know. These days, of course, people seldom listen to old shit. But it doesn't much matter, after a while, how any of this is taken up or cast aside. Artists who believe in immortality wouldn't want, after death, to suffer for their failures more than they now suffer for their unsung attempts. Nor should you my friend, the committed artist who lives one flight above me, believe that some day your works will be dispersed like fecund art-seeds throughout the art-centers of the universe.

But, you know, it might happen. Rethink the naked and the nude.

XXIV

What about myself—the titular of this story? Oh, say I, I paint away, which is easier now than running away. I write some too—as you see—and I do other things, but I don't know whether I'll get to tell you about them until next time around.

Writing is more familiar than painting, yet is strangely harder to break through—it takes more time. Words are easier to spell than strokes, yet strokes are easier done, and can be seen all at once. This is an advantage for the museum-goer—more can be seen than what at the same time could be read. Also, there is no dictionary for strokes as there is for words, and making strokes into images requires rejecting the procedures of reading for the different ones of looking. Painted forms are linguistically vague; they are sensible and have a tradition but not a vocabulary. Verbal forms have both tradition and vocabulary—but their content has sensibility only through inference and imagination.

I have been asked by sometimes friends: Which are you more serious about—painting or writing? This is the pin-point ploy of friendly enemies: Define yourself, they say—are you butcher, baker, or candle-sticker—so that we can judge, dissect, praise, or merely gossip about what you do. But unless you tell us we can't know (unless we ask around). Well, I say, I am both. But I do not try to bring them so close together as to make one be about the other.

"Being about" is a controlling notion: Most art-works have made clear their obeisance to other art-works—this is how styles develop. The verbal "being about" can also be a style, but when questioned, it affirms itself as a mode of explanation that, because it promises to be more precise than say, resembling, will make clear, it promises, the latent content (if there is any worth considering) of what it is about. What paintings, through their representational force, are about can be shown, but not argued (at least not with the paintings). Argument here can only be about what, at different times, is said that paintings show.

In our critical age, writing is under great pressure to "be about." Its mandate is to explain, and thereby contain within propriety, all that stuff hunkering in galleries, floating down the river, walking the high tight-rope between Twin Towers, denouncing Jews or Muslims or illegal immigrants and capitalist pigs—or even exposing the inner quivers of such as you and I.

Once, in earlier times, when writing-about could get one burned at the stake, painting-about was the better way to go. An artist can put forth fanciful, irreverent, even blasphemous images that might indeed be-about forbidden thoughts and abhorrent appetites. But with images, unlike with words, one can never be sure what they are about. Images without words do not assert—and so the artist, unlike the philosopher, need not too much fear the fires of the Inquisition. Then again, there is the marvelous brushwork that delineates, for the delectation of preferred patrons, the bare bodice of a minor goddess—only remotely resembling your neighbor's wife. What more need one ask of art?

As for myself, they are both with me—painting and writing—but they are not about each other, nor (don't be so nosey) about me. We are all, as I say, together in the sense of "with." This relationship is more democratic than "about" and it ordinarily shows in peaceful ways, each member waiting its turn for the other's attention, and not anticipating rules that govern the priorities for consummating such attention.

I started writing when I was nearly seven (the writing was a way to test my outside world). I began to paint somewhat later—mostly by drawing images that showed back to me the extent of my precocious libido. After I drew the parts that really interested me (although, had I known about such things, I could have drawn the draperies and the dragons and the landscape too). I would burn the drawings or flush their shredded parts down the toilet. I certainly couldn't show them to my mother or to anyone at school!

It struck me then that there really are two worlds, my world and the outside world, and I could not, without great care, expose myself to that other world. The descendents of my young discovery are still with me. They are, as I am now, diminished by the limits of promise. But they are also sturdy enough, as I still am, to carry the weight of early promise grown old.

My paintings and my writings revert at times to competing demands for my affection. I love you both say I; you form my synthesis—the base of those most recent moves that promise to complete the journey. I have been recollecting the origins of my good fortune while sitting on the porch together with my love, sipping wine, and watching the Mississippi flow past, in Elsah, Illinois. Tonight there will be thunderstorms!

How many ways of "about-ness" are truly reciprocal—notwithstanding proclamations that people and their concerns can be equally about each other? Very few, I think. "With" is a benign alternative to "about"—and I will continue to use it. Although "with" is social and charismatic, it has no logical rigor; the distinctions it makes cannot be trusted to hold in a definition-obsessed context. "Withs," none-the-less, are charming. They also are a radical lot—known for concealing hidden strategies of a later take-over. "With" is more politically useful than "about." My words and paintings, as long as I have dominion over them, are with each other—they must (in my absence) avoid the politics of needing to explain, i.e., dominate each other. And they must be careful, especially when they are up and about, how often they are seen—in flagrante delicto—with each other.

This, I know, is hard. It has to do with the direction of preferred attention. We spend our days next to things we do not notice, and we pass people we do not know or care about. But sometimes, while sitting at an out-door diner, we see them—the ones we could, if tempted, come to care about. Look at them straight away I say, the ones who stride, with undulating bottoms and jiggly tops, and brush past the eyes and nose of memory.

XXV

Was this writing, Lucian, if I may interrupt, to be about you? Well yes. Its theme is a recitation of my ongoing. I am past eighty, as I tell all who come and ask. These writings are my Scheherazade—as long as they continue, I remain alive. But I know that there is nothing much of interest in tales of merely geriatric living. So be aware, sweet lady, that the Caliph is getting bored. Show him fragments of what memory has filtered out from the reconfigured pleasures he once knew. Old men's crotchets are more interesting when linked to memories that persist—he then can join his antecedents in dancing the intergenerational two-step.

I remember those times when art-openings, replete with Chinese food, and post-prandial sex, were weekly rituals—back then when we fed cheaply but well on illusions that art was mostly about making and loving.

My writings are often about such memories. I keep them close to my skin because, if let loose, others can take them as their own. Memory and philosophy make an unholy brew. The narcissism of artists is a historical given—their strength what with the few weapons at their disposal. But philosophy would be better if philosophers did not hide their memories beneath their arguments, as most do. I let mine dangle out—increasingly as the nights get longer.

Paintings are about paint, the art-scoundrel says. I do not agree. Paintings are also about memories—the ones long past which mingle with those now being made. Good paintings are better done by painters who remember memorable art than by those who will extemporize their wares to transient applause. I am good at remembering, but not so good at transcribing memories through what I see. (Tintoretto certainly did not paint his air-born Venus by hanging complaining ladies up by pulleys!) To compensate for my inability to fulfill all the particulars of my dreams in paint, I have recently pasted photographs onto my paintings—but only those that do not obscure my efforts at making howler-maidens and stormy landscapes come together. How do I make them fit? Well, in a way like the fit between my occasional philosophy and my discreet narcissism—with due respect for their autonomy but also with an eye to non-coercive joining—the "with" I just spoke about.

Sometimes, increasingly now, I include snippets of my writings in my paintings. This is a gesture toward my belief that however buffered by errant winds, I am still my own one. Of course, such a one is abstractly thinkable by encompassing contradictories in an ever-expanding balloon of "here I am and this is what I do." But this gives me little sustenance. Everyone has a balloon of being-me (haven't you seen them floating by?)

So my writing is divided, and my painting is divided, all in the enterprise (lente, lente, currite noctis equi) of filling them with what can be squeezed between the limit, after all, of the images that endure.

Painting and writing are divided until the times when they brave the burning sands and wade into the waters and thus come to splash or sink together. The old altarpieces did this readily. But we cannot fill the barrenness of our decorations with like belief. I think that, by now, abstract art has vitiated the potential of its early metaphysics of innocence. It has produced a false god; it has gone from the somber end of art to lots of happy post-art art. But I do not tout a strategy for "art of this time." Guts exposing, or God admonishing, or priapic celebrating, or evocative scaffolding, will be winnowed out.

As contestants, we have the enervated writer who offers accounts of the incestuous delicacies of a well-attended language; we have the tone-deaf composer who demands audience attention to the ear-drum assaults of his electronic way with volume; and we have the unwashed artist who cannot paint a goddess that does not smell like the odor of paint.

But, life-stories aside, no "now" is obligated to its "before," nor need it tremble or salivate (as the case may be) at the feet of its promised "after." I have hope that our "now" will attend to the need to destabilize each present by accepting its insufficiencies as measured by both its past and future. But this means a reigniting of passion with the past, and an increasing skepticism about the peddling of futures.

The Zen master, when asked by the novice what is the meaning of life, proceeds to beat him with a stick, thereby affirming the primacy of living in the present. This remains a good answer to those who desire a post-material infinity as a solution to their present infirmities. It also enlightens those who would live forever if only they could get the payments right. Further, it gives comfort to those who, while alive, are afraid of death.

But what about the others who want to engage the past—to find out where, in the grand sequence, they really belong—what peak or valley they now inhabit—and why their exemplary accomplishments have not gotten them further, to the better place they well deserve? But do they, those avaricious fuzz-heads, deserve anything at all, in that future where we do not know what deserving comes to?

Give them, I say, blossoms of the finest pot to smoke, on an early summer's afternoon, when commencement has come and gone, the children are all graduated, and the first intimations of real heat depress the leaves of trees and bushes. There is reason, now, to find a place to sit that does not notice ambition. Well, sensimilia is more comforting than a Zen beating, and it cures both cowering guilt and arrogant ambition—but only for a finite time. The past, as pot proposes it, expands, yet never is completed. It veers off into another version, equally plausible but not more real.

What, after all, was Saint Jerome doing in the desert? He was shitting, peeing, rooting for grubs to eat, expiating for his unfulfilled appetites, soliciting visions, and pontificating to the creatures that would listen. Why did our own literary ruffians, Ginsburg, Kerouack, Burroughs, blow their minds every chance they got? I think they wanted to get the crooked straight, as did the saint, before they started writing again.

I don't do that any more. I paint and write, and I find, to my occasional bemusement, that I go from one to the other and back without discomfiture, without the sense that I must leave one Lucian for a better other. I am a two-headed hydra, ill-equipped to compete in a trade-mark world, but happy (as I surprisingly am) to find, underneath the usual prejudices against divided selves (whether in art or love) what it is I can do to combine, without too much guilt, whichever two that come along.

I have a modest pension, and I am engaged in a surprisingly long life that I encounter in the mirror every morning. Quel brutto faccia. The monthly dole and the sagging face are the measures that give me time to tend my bifurcations on a daily basis. I suspect that bifurcation leads to longer life. After all, I have two time sequences to cope with, and they beat in different rhythms. All attempts at an agreement to a common beat have failed. Bifurcation, it is said, leads to an increase in anxiety but to a decrease of boredom. Like a crab, I scuttle between places when it is time to put down the wayward brush and form the telling sentence. "About-ness" is not any longer the issue between the two—they would love to be together with each other, after all these years, without further quarreling. But cold winds blow come winter, through windows that should have long ago been sealed. Sometimes, like Dante's wind-driven lovers, my two—my paintings and my writings—come very close and (although it is against the rules) they try to touch.

The images I use sometimes complain that the canvas does not give them room enough to show themselves as they deserve. So I have, at times, given them multiple canvases for the with-ness they had been promised. But while I have pasted my words upon my paintings, I have not yet tried to include my painted images in my books. Actually, the format I use is based on an old time prejudice that still lingers. In this electronic age, it would not be difficult to bring image and text together, whether in book form or on the canvas or across the walls of buildings. I suppose someone could devise a book so that the reader, with the pressing of some keys on a computer, could project my verbal and graphic entries onto a suitable receiver. But I can't yet.

For a time I made paintings of a geometric type whose elements—modules composed of bits and pieces of a schema—would spread across architectural space, and so deny the notion of an aesthetically isolating single "picture-plane." I maintained authority over the scatter through diagrams which show how all those modules conform to a central plan of distribution, and to a strategy which differentiates between those aspects of the diagram that are to be reified (made into painting-fragments) and those aspects that function solely to show the logic of progression connecting the discrete fragments with each other as this occurs within the larger scheme. When I exhibited this stuff, I also pinned the diagrams onto the wall—for those who might care about such things.

Well, nobody cared—except for a few graduate architects who admired the public extension format of my scheme; and there was a philosopher or two who liked the rational take on art-making. I did not push the issue then—but for anyone who wants a rational schema-on-a-wall, however large, I am happy to oblige.

XXVI

I retreated, after that, to what I do best—explaining my process to myself by writing, and expounding the necessity of the unattainable to a few still patient friends who would come around to look. When I think back, these gestures at failure are what I have always been good at.

Nevertheless, there is an objective dialectic here at work; I am only, as history says, its instrument. Now listen up, you who laugh behind your hands: To be an instrument for a good idea is not bad. Cosmic Objectivity has its benefits: it absolves you of the guilt that accompanies local failure.

So, after a painful time of staring, do what you can to make the wanting canvas better. Then believe that it has become (at least a little) better. But do not, at this point, question what counts as "better." Now you are on your way! If you are not to be historic, you'll never know—and believing that you will or won't be, may or may not make it so.

Consider this: You are not, sweet Polish boy from Brooklyn, a feral creature. You do not kill your enemies and eat your offspring. Killing enemies, in the original, is a time-honored custom—a fact of survival in the old country. It is also a directive to you, young aspirant to success, that you should bad-mouth and undercut your rivals.

Eating offspring, you know, is a metaphor for destroying competition. You also know, that all those retreats into the personal and contingent, all that doodling and canoodling that lets the satisfaction of small sensibility cloud the historic task, is yet another failure on your part. Yet, you prefer to avoid rather than kill your enemies.

To become historic is a wonderful happenstance—it has a swaggering there-ness to comfort those who putter in the here-ness while they seek the long-run. It also gives the assurance that your worth will be, in good time, duly measured by competent authorities. However, to be merely in your present without anxiety about the future can be pleasant. Presentness, abetted by its beneficiaries, confounds sequence by crouching in place; and even if forced to move, it proposes a circumspect movement—one so silent that you don't notice when things change. (Why change when you are having fun?)

So it does not help, my dear bifurcated one, to petition the unmoved mover and complain that the aspects of yourself should all have come closer together as time went on. The planners of the dialectic (there surely had to be a plan before the moving began) would respond—in good corporate fashion—that that's the way it all worked out.

Perhaps it is better, then, to rid myself of all these myths and stances that I once took on to damp down the fear of an inconsequential life. I cannot hope to sit upon supporting clouds and discourse with the greats over the wear and tear that art imposes—they are busy with their immortality. I cannot, either, expect the world parade to snatch up my ashes and carry them through the mean streets while singing "We love Lucian"—they have too many other ashes to carry as it is. But then, where do I go? The old guide suggests sunsets and a catfish fry on the Mississippi.

Art-book reproductions mostly suffice for images of great art. And who now can afford the trip to find good pastrami? Anyway, the memory of pastrami has lost its adolescent wonder; it has ceded its fatty primacy to a wood broiled filet (with roast potatoes, a good red wine, a complicated salad). But there usually is left, after gorging, the no-nonsense gnawing—not of pastrami—but of ambition. This assault comes most fiercely in the early-morning dreaming just before the need to pee. The best choice is to pee, return to bed and cajole your dreams to keep them directed towards resurrecting the delicate privates that evoke the smell of former loves.

Or, if that is not sufficiently robust for your wakening, get up early and lift some weights (breath as deeply as you can) and so force the circulating blood to wash away the clotting of ambition and the lingering smells of prurience. But then, how will you fill the rest of your day? Find two of you and put them with each other. Then let them work out which is ahead and which behind.

2

Art and Life

I

This is a study, primarily in the visual arts, of the interplay between art and life. Art has the broad features of aesthetic value and indeterminate duration, while life is characterized by indeterminate value and finite duration. Despite these formal distinctions, each realm has historically contested with the other for its own ends—art to confirm its completeness, and life to achieve historical newness.

From time to time, the visual arts have taken on the task—denied them by Plato—of offering critical rather than celebratory ways of representing the world. Plato, famously, considered the arts as imitations of imitations, and thus having no power to represent worldly reality—much less the reality of the Forms. Curiously, Western art, particularly that which models itself on neo-classic tenets, has been trying to represent, through the flow of refined imagination, and distaste for the accidental, the perfections that approximate the austerity of Plato's Forms. Less curiously, later (radical) movements in art—those preferring the personal to the universal and the immediate to the eternal, find Plato's stress on rationality too autocratic—and unfit for the revolutionary task of doing what must be done.

The waiting game of artistic fame is suited for those who anticipate an outcome, and so develop a strategic way of winning or losing that will give the waiting experience some purchase on the way things actually go. But this reveals a spoiler: if art is life configured, then life must be art let loose. Art lacks life's durational density, and life lacks art's self-commitment. Art, unlike life, goes on forever—that is, until a change in status washes over it. Life, even within the most restrictive ideologies, is never complete—but it always ends. The critics of enduring art, and the sages of life after death, find a common cause here—maintaining the reality of art and life as both transcendent and durational.

II

But what happens when we have grown tired of this schema? To further art and life beyond their categories—however advanced that may once have seemed—needs painful divestiture. Perhaps the give and take between these categories will soon become so frequent that the very distinction will cease to matter.

If there is critical work to be done here, it should not be presented though a philosophically austere language—which is apt to consider itself as impervious to the blandishments of sense, the distortions of desire, and the imperatives of history. After having been subject to such cleansings, there may be little left in such accounts for either art as opposed to life or life as indifferent to art.

At times, artists, even when not regarded as truth-bearers, are esteemed for their projection of other virtues—beauty, expression, form, and the like. These virtues, in some philosophical accounts, overlap with, or give material support to the logical functions of truth. But truth, even so authenticated, cannot of course become the "whole truth"—In many contexts, it is content to remain "belief."

Art's role, today, is anti-formal. It ignores alliances with classical systems and instead presents itself as the public representation of belief—and it becomes more persuasive as it feeds on the delimitations of what the general "we" like to know. Art now represents a variety of beliefs—indeed, a brimming basket of them—each centered in its own however disintegrating neighborhood. All these provide images that under-gird the dominant needs of those still interested in the patina of believing.

Patrons of the arts in artistically heady days (as ours recently were) are mostly rich and influential, and so do not countenance attacks upon their hard-won life-styles from the likes of disgruntled artists, co-op galleries, professors, exhibitionists, and street musicians. The popular arts (more public now than private) coat the messages of art's autonomy in more democratic guise and use the powers of publicity to make the case for denying what we all should know—how scruffy the world has become despite its progressive representations.

To illustrate this, go back awhile and watch the parade of nudes in art—their female or male representations, through different times and places—and trace their empowerment beyond the achievable desires if not the dreams, of mortals. Female power can be prohibitively revealed, as in Titian's Venuses and Courbet's Girlfriends. Which of us could make the move on them? Male nudes are more vulnerable and come earlier—skinny non-priapic saints in the forbiddingly fertile desert—until classic potency reasserts itself in Michaelangelo's Adam—whom only the Lord can lust after with equanimity.

Later, males of note are no longer exposed as in the classical gaze; but they remain covert, and proceed to their religious or carnal fate within the covering of style. (Was there ever a king who sat for a nude portrait?) Females of the lower class generally fared better than did males as artistic subjects—girls when stripped and washed can pass as nymphs or goddesses while males of the species are seldom naked unless they are saints—and even then their privates are hidden. Male nude fare better up north, where with all their musculature, they are pitted against wild boar (Rubens), or dance, cod-piece-in-place, with their strong women in the village square. (Breugel)

In the main, lower-class women did what was expected when artists told them to take off their clothes. This artistic privilege could conceivably have pictured a plateau in their growing-up, and confirmed a desire to be fictionally exhibited, "seen-as," for the spectator. In life, the rose-bud nakedness soon succumbs to the perils of childbirth and poverty; but in art the girls could be pictured as eternal playthings for universal delectation (as in Fragonard, Alma-Tadema, Courbet, and even Renoir).

It took Lautrec, George Grosz and Picasso to uglify the nude, and so abolish the separate anticipations of beauty and desire once reserved for each sex. Dekooning, with his ferocious "Women," did it so well for America that our fashion industry retreated en-masse to developing a taste for the female image of anorexia as a guide to buying expensive clothes.

III

After enjoying the times of combined belief, power, and seduction—as in the High Renaissance and Baroque—the world of art diminishes, and in defence begins to expand in social reach. But it took centuries for artists to move away from the privileged life of patronage, and opt instead to chant and sway upon the pure and misty mountain. The ancient oracle did it that way, most all her life, and with more belief than the artists who followed could muster. But those who must avoid uncertain heights can still howl and scold the world in basements and unheated lofts.

The new assaults upon artistic verities are, as Arthur Danto calls them, "arts of disturbation"—works which use shock to scold, mock, calumniate, and otherwise unsettle the advocates of present practices. But such artworks and their complicit artists do not really take on the challenge of Plato, or the risk of Socrates. Unlike the outcome of political strife, aesthetic misbehavior, especially in these secular days, only risks losing the role of becoming the next fashion. Art is now complicit in enhancing the very value structure it purports to criticize.

Goya's "Horrors of War," Picasso's "Guernica," and Serrano's "Piss-Christ" are trotted out as way stations on the creative-critical pilgrimage of art beyond aesthetics. Yet, they are highly regarded as commodities in the art-world. The crime of Socrates, in contrast, is in his approval of subversion; and his danger to the social weal was that he had an audience to subvert. Because he did not plead artistic immunity, he was sentenced to death. Plato's own fear of artistic subversion sounds a philosophical alarm, an attack on imagination– which quixotically, he had much of. The arts, Plato says, make people soft and wooly-headed—not equipped to be rational citizens of the state. But he does not seek to ban them—only to devalue their influence.

The notion of truth attaches to Modern Art because of its aura of freedom and social insight. But even this, these days, has limits. We now prefer our artistic truths to be low-keyed: We no longer want portraits of ascending saints, vainglorious kings triumphant, or saber-clad saviors of the commonweal. The precarious interplay between artistic genius and the needs of emperors and popes aspiring to immortality is now old history. In our time, portraits of our presidents (except maybe Stuart's "Washington") are not art—they are too full of virtue.

Yet, the beauties of form and the delights of imagination in the old depictive works continue to attract us—however reprehensible the history. Kings and their minions shine in portraits—whether by Velasquez or Van Dyck—where their regal heads are illuminated at the expense of all the rest –such as views of the village through a castle window which shows the residue of poverty and parlous times. This, if one lets it, grates.

It is also difficult to justify the appreciation of, say, a Fragonard nude to an advocate for sexual equality. The criticisms, for us, are more true, and have become more difficult to bypass than when the paintings were made. The paintings by the artist whom his young models called "Pappa Fraga," present a plateau of the beautiful in the female sex—hard to beat except by Titian. The female here is less degraded than in later presentation of the pudenda for the male leer. Modernism, looked at a-politically, was not sympathetic to the erotic. There was much flamboyance, exhibited in a panoply of formal kinks, but this was in the service of the denial of pleasure—an ideological requirement for the new politic of equality.

The forbidden has its own persuasions. It can be found in the domain of criticism that seeks to rescue art from its past enemies. (The Devil changes tactics in response to new beliefs). Form, taken as an independent and sufficient value, aspires to acerbic novelty and high-minded rejection. Its battle in Modernism has been to support the reductive allure of minimalism—that ideological counterpart of Occam's razor—and to flirt with the seduction of emptiness—an ideological bow to Nietzsche's disaffection with both life and literature. But this temptation to embrace nothing has become a media commonplace, and the popularity of formal abstraction (all those squares and squiggles on municipal and corporate walls) if you look skeptically, are rife with ingratiation.

The reductive ideology, of which Plato spoke, has become mainstream. Earlier, It flirted with the aesthetics of nullity—as in Malevich—but now seeks its appreciation in scale, sublime presence, spatial dislocations, and danger of falling—as in the sculptures of Serra. On the more benign side, it offers delights for outdoor philosophers and other strollers in the site pieces of Christo, where ephemeral yet strategically located nature is gently encapsulated—perhaps to show, that nature can, with sufficient wrapping, be made both impotent and sociable.

IV

A life that is consistent from its beginning to its end is hard to live, for consistency is a verdict that the uninformed make about your life when you are dead. Cartesians say we live inside our minds and make the outside world from there. Thus Descartes replaced belief in God with the undeniable truth of our existence as guarantor of the world's reality. Artists, poets, and other peculiars like this idea; it gives credence to their own presentations. But these presentations cannot (as yet) be blamed upon the brain—only on the mind—and their consistency, as best we know it, is largely stylistic. But consistency, in these speedy days, may not in fact be much of a virtue—whether in life or art.

When God left his job as arbiter of truth and verisimilitude, time and space began their cohabitation. Cubism helped out in this—as did Surrealism. The self-awareness of consciousness and its facets, and the call to introspective fidelity, became factors that replaced the older verities of scholastic truth and measured ideality. Disobedience became an aesthetic. Dada jokes and the Expressionist slinging of cheap paint at good ideas helped make the social point, for it broadened the field of high art to include ordinary stuff and unskilled talents.

Words wanted in—not only as literature, but in amalgams with paintings and graphics. Words that have pictorial ambitions have to struggle to transcend their letter-forms and so strike up new friendships with forms that are not letters. After all, the drawings on the cave-walls came first. Are there large meanings behind this incestuous ménage of recent sayings and showings? They are rife in Medieval manuscripts, and are now commonplace in both "high art" and "outsider art." The portent of this mixing is however hard to decipher—especially in these unsettled days.

We're just trying to be together, says ambitious John the interactivist to his advanced-artist friends. We will try at first to make a small medley of words images and sounds, then move to body parts and other appropriations of what is still out there. Then we'll move to a chorale of the happy harmonies into which screams of violation have been transformed into expression: Pain and death do not result in fear or pity, but rather, sitting by the telly, into entertaining fictions. After that who knows, there is always room for another symphony of a thousand.

Medieval art needed words to ensure that the images pictured were understood to be about what in fact they pictured. There was no conflict then between images and words in this art because the effort was to present divine truth, and the wise men thought, rightly, that the interplay of word and image would do more for a true vision of heaven earth and hell than each could manage separately. But there were dissident voices: In the beginning is the word, they said, and graven images are but sources of non-belief and goads to licentiousness. So, Jews forbad them. Plato didn't like them either, he considered them, as I noted, to be twice removed—copies of copies of the forms. He preferred words—but strangely, given his restless mind, he did not comment on the historical achievements in the visual art and architecture of his own time.

Christians, being more driven to spread the word, found images useful—as long, that is, as they did not stray from picturing truth. But eventually, the juices of Greek art, which all this time had been scattered around unnoticed in ancient Rome, gave the impetus and tools of style to the nativities, crucifixions, depositions, and resurrections of late Medieval times. They also reintroduced the sensualities of Paganism within the acceptable but broadening limits of subject matter.

The fascination with classical images in the Renaissance diminished the necessity for the Medieval reliance on words. Notwithstanding the demands of piety, such images took on increasingly secular contents. In the Sistine ceiling, Michelangelo's muscular Adam—languishing within the turmoil of creation—was given the touch of existence by an aroused creator. Further north, in the Venice of Titian and Tintoretto, Venus had her court, Susanna her admirers, and Danae, accepting Jove's largess, played full counterpoint to that God's intentions. There was no need for explanation. Flesh, well painted, was the image of choice and needed no surrounding chatter to justify it. There was little fuss about the balance between devotion and appreciation—the rational and the sensual—for "art" had encompassed both. This was a pact between sensuality and belief that, for a brief time in the history of the Western World, removed sin from art.

But then it changed: the Reformation put a pox on both these houses, and all diversity broke loose: landscapes were pictured without holy occupants, male and female peasants danced with each other in public. Then there arose, in contrast, a painterly preoccupation with fruits and pots, opaquely suggestive milkmaids in the light-shrouded geometry of Flemish interiors—these were images for a different, more contemplative delectation—but one that also did not require words.

The world enlarged further, and these timid yet suggestive Mannerist changes in Italy and the optical interests of the low-countries, coalesced in the Baroque of Rembrandt, Caravaggio, Velasquez, and Rubens—the greatest aggregate in any one period (pace the Renaissance) of genius in western art. Every inherited theme could be painted under any interpretation—skill and sophistication being the prime artistic virtues—and the audience, from cardinals to kings to financiers—and the growing bourgeoisie—came to realize that the thrust of imagery was both literal and metaphoric, and that their own interpretations, whether religious or secular, true or fantastic—could be accepted and even valued. The autonomy of appreciation introduced a new world for art.

V

But the openness of interpretation eventually, perhaps inevitably, leads to the vitiation of expert judgment and to the search for other vantages from which to justify ways of looking at the fragmenting, perhaps degenerate pieces of new art. One way to keep things going was to shift the ground of judgment from the artwork to the creative act. Kant offers support for this in his identification of artistic creativity (genius) with the sublime: The perception of genius, which is broader and more acute than ordinary perception, can reach beyond the parameters of rational explanation. The sublime suggests the contents of infinity through the violent extremes of nature, and the imaginative flights of artists. So the emphasis on the qualities of the aesthetic object shifts to the valorizing of artistic process—all this a prelude to the Hegelian concern with changes in art as symbols of cultural (spiritual) evolution, and to the later Freudian interest in the transcendental illness of creative making.

Modernism moves from the rejection of past styles to the valorization of artistic process. The decreasing reliance on canons of verisimilitude opens new avenues of expression but also creates new uncertainty as to what counts in making a good artwork. Such uncertainty leads to alternative strategies that often prize ugliness, non-traditional skills, and social confrontation, as parameters for making art. But these freedoms, come the transplantation of Modernism to America, cease being tools for historical or cultural criticism, and turn instead to the market place to identify those somethings that confirm the rather vague belief that anything goes—and yet identify what, in fact, will go.

Art-works mutate faster than their appreciations, and they, unabashedly now, embrace other paradigms—architecture, emblematic emptiness, communal theatre, accidental art—and so try to overwhelm the critical uncertainties that often dismember commercial success. The paradigm "fear and trembling" of existential anxiety—appropriate to those post-war years—is replaced by the "why-not-me" years of the new century. But when an artistic "something" can lead to an "anything" which can then be replaced by its equally artistic "nothing," there is reason to be cautious. But in this climate, reasons lose their ontological force. They become dismembered into petty preferences, and eventually reduce to a low if widespread muttering.

The "posts" illustrate this happenstance—"post-modernism," "post-post-modernism," "post-art." The "nons" join in—"non-representational," "non-objective," "non-art." These and their offshoots, are attempts to give "progress in art" a graspable direction while denying the pertinence of the future and the past. However, the insistence on direction continues to be a requirement for artistic ambition—whether it goes up or down, forward or back, or circles round in place. These directions are the necessary ingredients of style.

But there are other problems: The assessment of qualities in an artwork that are indeterminate gives rise to a concern with the experience of making indeterminate art. To compensate for object indeterminacy, interest moves from the artwork to the artist's life. This, actually, is a recapitulation of the romantic tradition—the steamy antics of the Pre-Raphaelites, the tasty grime of Bohemian Paris, and the grasping but sullen cold of New York lofts.

On the magic mountain, there can be found the northern sadness about the experience of art's end. This causes a quiet suffering in the mountains, which contrasts with the loud masochistic pain sometimes sought at the southern seashore. But they are both the felt signposts of art's historical failure. Settembrini dies because the end of art is real. In Venice, Aschenbach dies because he mistook life for art.

These days, concerns about artists' lives are much on the model of how we treat athletes and rock-stars—poor or good performance is justified by how temperament coincides with output and reviews—the statistics of success tell the tale. In evident contrast, an artist's behavior, in the early twentieth century days, was not a signpost of success—that linkage comes later. An artist's suffering, even now, is not a sufficient sign of redemption—although a successful artist's misbehavior might be. But in the early history of this linkage, the artist-person (the Van-Gogh paradigm) reaped no benefit—neither historically nor financially.

We must remember here, that artists of the old academies had a vocation—they accrued benefits from the excellence and utility of their products: There was always need for commemorations of major events, portraiture of important personages, and mythic titillation for exclusive gatherings. There also were assistants to help with the chores, and apprentices to paint the duller passages. Early modernists, in contrast, driven by the anomie of non-vocation, social and (often) psychological alienation—coupled with a political distaste for the residue of empire—presented the non-utility of their works as an aesthetic and, indeed, critical value. But such dark-mirror reflections—after the first flush of martyrdom—did not last. The loss of critical standards posed new problems for later art making: they revealed the need for other modes of justification.

One notion of late-modernism—that materials are ontologically equal to representations—gives birth to practices that use aesthetically innocent materials—welded metal, plastics, crumbling walls, commercial artifacts, detritus of all sorts—within the constructions of objects that are offered as art. These new subjects for artistic interest conjure up an aesthetic of inclusiveness, yet they also deny the maneuvers once required for representation. The way for art to go, in this changing climate of freedom and anomie, was towards abstraction—as far that way as artists could go without entirely relinquishing the notion of art-work. Non-representation—nominally the end-goal of abstracting—opens to the kinds of marks that have come to characterize this aesthetic—the visible beads of welding and paint splashes which drip. They exemplify commitment, and don't need refining.

The concomitant loss of academic skills and the rejection of the once blooming world of similitude had the result of farming out these concerns to the "lesser arts "—photography, illustration, film-art, and TV—and now the internet. After the heroic days, these "commercial" skills became important for the next turn. Searching the debris of the battleground between old high art and new modern art, "Pop-Art" would rescue, from fine-art leavings, useable matter for an increasingly popular (and pragmatic) aesthetic.

VI

Abstraction has its justification in the distance between the image and its origins—the further the better—and such distance is touted as best achieved through the program of a further reduction to what has become celebrated as the empty (but nevertheless valuable) end. Beckett and Mondrian are a case in point. "Emptiness," in this passage, is tantamount to "profundity"—the process of reduction and purification made necessary by the flight of practical reason to absolute spirit, thereby surpassing matter. Art at the end of art, taken one way is about essence; in another way, it is about nothing. This has also been described as an art of "lessness" thus keeping a semblance of concrete presence—little to look at but a lot to think about.

The risk to art when it continues to look for itself underneath layers that have already been well-peeled, is to become its own subject. Art as its own subject, I suggest, may be the new solipsism—but it requires an altered sense of art. Rauschenbergs "white paintings" and Cage's 4'33" are a case in point. They are about what can be done after art's end. Without this sense, the term "art" survives only as a historical reference, which no longer discriminates between present entities. But the search for "essence" and the retreat into "nothing" are both otherworldly—and by now, atavistic. The first, as centuries have told us, is too hard to find in the limited time of living—the second lurks all around us, but offers no place in which to live.

The happenings of history are often a pity, and this is one of them. "Art is about art" is collusive with the seemingly contradictory practice that "anything can be art." Both avoid the delimiting act that would distinguish art from non art: what it is in "anything" which identifies the "something" that actually becomes art. This play of categories encourages those who dote on a stylish style of indifference—something or nothing doesn't matter.

Christo's banners in Central Park do not bother much with language, but they do grace a weekend stroll. There is little piety needed here—except perhaps, of a Panglossian sort: the pretty flutters affirming that all is well with the world. Nevertheless, power shows in abundance: Who else but ambitious city leaders, and socially anxious captains of industry, would spend so much money for the project of a flutter-filled walk in the park?

There is both pain and pleasure in art—the pain is in what it demands, and the pleasure in what it returns. History is marked by different ratios. The Renaissance managed an abundance of both through its co-option of the classic interplay between concreteness and abstractness. Those artists brought the Greek gods of flesh and geometric perfection to merge with the Christian notion of transcendent being. There was plenty of room to go from Leonardo's Last Supper—to Titian's Venus Looking In Her Mirror. The quarrels between, say, Michelangelo and Raphael, or Titian and Tintoretto, were not about sensibility and skill—they all had quite enough of those. Rather, the competition was for entry into the arena of ripe beliefs that required expert picturing for their credibility.

As time went on, there were increasing numbers of such experts, each in turn fashioned by apprenticeship to the older masters, and anxious to take on the demands of princes and popes in bringing together the sacred and secular images of achievement. This codification came to be called "Mannerism," and it's ubiquity and social ambition, its ambivalence in style, mirrors something of what we face today.

The Baroque that followed was the last great style of western academic art. It rejected Mannerist frivolity and re-appropriated the "terribilita"—the grand ambition—of the best of Renaissance art. But the geographic spaces between its masters: Caravaggio in Rome, Rembrandt in Amsterdam, Rubens in Flanders, Velasquez in Spain, were further removed from each other than the time it took to travel between Venice and Florence and Rome. (There is a lovely story—perhaps true—about Rubens being sent to Spain on a diplomatic mission that foundered, but it enabled him to spend his remaining time there drawing with Velasquez. Who would not want to be a fly on that wall?)

The commonality of the Baroque, despite its stretched geography, is to be found in the novel belief that artworks can transcend their pictorial separateness and invade the living space outside—all the while remaining art. The gesture of the angel, stretched forward to include you as a participant in the painting's holy space, is of a high ambition: It at once invites you into the depicted ceremony of transcendence, and it also suggests that the parameters of art's content can be extended to include you, the observer.

Earlier, in the low countries—the Flemish developed an independent style (in keeping with their politics) that used the integration of real and fictional space, actual and imagined representations, to bridge the gap between images of persons and the figures of their belief. Van Eyck gave to Chancellor Rolin the place immediately opposite the Virgin, and while that monster's hands were dutifully folded, his expression gave little doubt about his glee in personifying the intersection of earthly and celestial power. Here, the actual meets the hypothetical in picturing both as occurring in the "same time and place."

Caravaggio's Last Supper is more circumspect. It does not demonstrate, but rather draws you into the space of the painting—not as an imperative of the representation, but to where you would be if you could bypass the illusion and touch the extended hand of the pictured Lord. The gestures and directed gaze of Christ and his disciples thread the pictorial space into the viewer's space and back again, and they raise the question, in this commingling of belief and vision, as to where, given this porosity of actual and pictorial space, one should best place oneself.

VII

After that we all went mad and some few sad, and we spent, cumulatively, near a century in denying that art is saying anything at all—anything that smacks of the old "worth-whiles." Art could not, for example, any longer be about beliefs or apotheoses, battles or immolations, but it could be about indifferent things—landscapes without place, nudes without a name, pots and bottles—and, soon, charismatic swirls and patterns without end. The coming world did not, however, want to contest these new ventures against old art—the old (as far as we wanted to know it) was dead.

Instead, we praised new things for their form (form being eternal but not historical except when, occasionally, it became radical). Pictorial frontality replaced perspectival illusion (enough already with the social disease of make-believe). Sculpture and architecture sought their aesthetic in the exposition of earthly materials: metal, stone, and glass were offered without disguise or pomp. And criticism belatedly came to find little future in salon traditions for judgments of the new art. Paradoxically, as the new art was further removed from standard paradigms, the need for a new criticism—as commentary, education, and reassurance—became greater—not only for the viewing public but for artists as well. Before, between, and after the two great wars—from, say, 1900 till 1960—novelty, expression, abstraction, progress, purity, were explanatory—if competing—catchwords for the new aesthetic.

Early Modernist polemics bear comparison with the furor of Renaissance squabbles. For both, the valued issues faced the reality of artistic dilution. Our present, despite the residual glamour of Modernism, is also a time of dilution. Art works have become too large, too indifferent to the hand-mark of high craft, to be discernible through any durable distinction from their competitors. Art's competitors are not, these days, new styles of art-making; they are ordinary objects, seducible—as are all objects now—into becoming art-works.

Artists, occupying an increasingly porous category, no longer face the intolerable problem of originality. Rather, they must measure their identities—not against the nobility of "the death of art," but against the death of vocation—the end of exceptionalism as justification for the status of "artist."

Demolishing worth-whileness in today's art is a plausible objective of those who have long chafed under the opprobrium of worthwhile art—assuming that they also believe that such destruction is better than the range of values that would, willy-nilly, keep "fine-art" going. Even at last century's end, antagonism toward established art was rife. After all, the art-academy was seen as in cahoots with a moribund social order that supported the values of class-distinctions, repressive politics and predatory economics.

Modernism soon became a social as well as artistic call-to-arms. It augured the demise of both the academy and its patrons, and it invoked the liberation of art and artists from vocation. These freedoms were allied with social democracy and its value of equality. But freedom, when it is associated with equality, leads to confusion in artistic vocation: If artists no longer exemplify the hierarchy of academic virtues: apprenticeship, diligence, talent, vocation—and yet are not angry enough to make an art that nay-says the oppressive world—what then are they to do?

Actually, there is no historical time that can identify its worthy inhabitants—whether god, king, dictator, or president—in which their images are not commemorated by patrons. But there are other times, this being one of them, when art has become so entangled with sophistic sociologies, that it is without any subject of its own, and the notion of art's special subject is not any longer useful. So our new art, with its anti-historical pretensions, has not, since Picasso, fed its audience with the latest interpretations of older styles (as in his "Las Meninas" variations). Nor has art any longer capitalized on wounded psyches (now psychiatric concerns) or encomiums to nature (which are environmental issues). And there are no bronze statues of recent presidents in Central Park. Instead, new art offers the seductions of disposable décor—analogous to super-foods. If eros is still in sight, it feeds admirers of the emaciated but still living mannequins who nourish the hidden sadisms of high fashion.

VIII

The changes in today's art are not, in themselves, harbingers of the death of art; for such a death should bring with it echoes of the awe and despair that surrounded the earlier cries of those who were busy killing God. A Dead God is by now excluded from influence in the arena of living and dying—but through a simplistic resurrection, shows up again in current politics to fortify the right against the left. This, now blame-free god, is also immune from the pleadings and recriminations that mark what Hegel calls "the slaughter bench of history"—witnessed, in our time, by silent and stupefied survivors of two (and counting) great wars.

The death of art on the other hand, signals not the end of the world, but merely the end of that art-history devoted to transcendence. Victims in this war are the multitudes of art students who were periodically assured that they could make art forever new.

The church and the academy, by the fifteenth century, were both advocates of the early professionalism—a synchronicity of belief and beauty. How else would beauty be celebrated except as a witness to belief, and how else could belief be authenticated except through its instantiation in beauty? Circular? Yes. And so is good sex—as well as Buddha's rejection of beginnings and ends. But the straight line of historicism eventually showed up, and led us here.

In our "beyond beauty and belief" days, the secular fussing about "art after-art" had its problems in holding on to some beliefs it needs—aesthetic exclusivity, for example: (Let us hope that, even if everything can be art, not just anything will be art—much less good art) or to the constantly relocating place of beauty: (It should, for heaven's sake, be inherent in the exclusive object as determined by a privileged perception). Well, yes and no.

What to do? Here's my advice: Despair to know the way the art-world works, and embrace the freedom to invent your own—for an art world, like art, is formed by invention. There is no shortage of worlds—art or any other kind. Yet we cannot live in all of them. Rejecting the worlds that include God or Art involves changing manifest belief into looser, more comfortable, but less historically grounded beliefs.

Belief is probably a genetic quiddity—to which humans are bound in the long term—the will to believe. Individual will is what we seek, but there is also the public will—which is both powerful and fearful. When belief was not yet an issue of individual will, its manifestation could be found in communal ritual and categorical demands. The belief in a solitary will that provides universal truths needs a sense of exceptionalism as regards the "willer." But after the decline of true belief—whether the source is self, king, or god, we face the petty problem of distinguishing what is true for us—and what for is true for (all the rest of) them.

IX

There is both custom and science to fill the emptiness. The rituals of custom are many and competitive—and their changes are quicksilver for the hidden reasons that combine ideology and politics. The findings of science, in contrast, are cumulative—although they are not immune to ideology and self-interest. But the findings of science can be tested—this is their strength—and the findings provide for warranted true beliefs—which are true until the warrant is itself found wanting.

Those without a restrictive calling, young artists in particular, can wander unabashed between rituals old and new, between practices pure or communal, without being tested—for what is there to test for? Yet, there are unexpected limits: failure when the Biennale ignores you, for example. Then, more severely, there is the incipient boredom—a loneliness of the long-distance runner, a too-late arrival of irony and disbelief.

Freedom for making the art you want to make after art has died has its problems. (But this is only true for those who still value problems). Purity and reduction have been the killers—although the death-throes have given us some consequential art. But little rectangles in black on a white ground (if not for their "my-end" soliloquy –and, by extension, their "end of-you-and the world" conclusion) soon came to look like home-décor for affluent radicals. What, after all this, can still be done—after the killing time that extracts from art the impact of all this history, the value of all those metaphors, and the wisdom retrieved from all that scratching? What happens then?

Well, you can stop drawing and hire a contractor to build you something eye-catching. Or, if you have residual guilt, find a way of making art that looks like art but requires computers—not handmade fussing. When these efforts prove inadequate results (perhaps because of electronic ineptitude) you should frequent post-art-and-neo-artist bars and pay attention to the drop-in critics (who do have a high turnover rate, but are nevertheless attuned to the latest version of "post"). Then, who knows, you may indeed become a factotum of the persistence of post-art presence after the end of art.

All this is painful to the historically enmeshed—to those venerables, after experiencing disasters of past wars and failed ideologies who still seek a pattern (just a glimmer of an upward path will do) through which they can oppose the decline of dedicated meaning. But the dreamy thought of such a revival need not be taken seriously—not even by the dreamers. Who could live in such an antique world? Neither you nor I for sure! Ask the youngsters. They are sanguine about worlds without end—especially those they never had to believe in and then to painfully deny. The new ones prefer those worlds that have no truck with ends—the concept of ends actually being a distasteful bourgeois tic—like a tie and jacket—a defensive response to the onset of anonymity.

There is not (if you still don't know) only a single world—nor are there too many. There are just enough of worlds to make thinking about incoherence important. This is a transformation principle that does not much matter in a single world. But a world that is one of many—even though this one may end in the lifetime of our thoughts—would eventually have to cope with the infinite varieties of beliefs that proliferating worlds create.

It comes to a matter of categories and their justification. For example: the end of art requires a prior conception of "art" before the possibility of it's ending. Art then needs a dignified way to go after its denial—a well-marked road (not an overgrown path) that leads towards a deserved post-end. But don't bet on it: Dying is cheaper than is the promise of proper entombment. The corpse of art is still to be found in the war of art-worlds—it is a residue of the battle of competing categories—art, non-art, anti-art, post-art and etc.

The "tradition of the new," Harold Rosenberg's catchy notion, absolves us of prediction, but it sidesteps the question of whether the "new" is also a factor in the history of art. Newness enmeshes us in a concept of social experience that is much like Dewey's value of "doing-undergoing." Dewey saw art-making as a model for how lives should be lived: Make. Reach out. Fail. Do it again but better. There is a populist strain here, for Dewey wants the benefits of artistic creativity to inform everyday life as well as to provide an imperative for continuation of art.

Clement Greenberg was a prime advocate of newness, but he presented his notion within the Hegelian terms of inexorability—that progress in art (thesis) can be hindered (antithesis) by reaction, but is nevertheless unstoppable in that it (art's progress) is a function (synthesis) in the de-facto ascendancy of spirit.

The newness that Harold Rosenberg espoused, unlike Greenberg's, was not based on stylistic ascendency. Rather, it encouraged artists to pursue interests that were promising, if sometimes inchoate. These changes, as in Dewey's populism, were communal not historical. They were aimed at the present. Here, the uncertainties of artistic creativity and the problems of social betterment were, at base, the same.

Greenberg's dogma of the new—which insisted on non-figuration and optical flatness as its virtues—was, in contrast, strongly historical. It required disciples for whom "flatness" and "abstraction" were inevitably marks of the new art—so he championed such artists as Stella and Noland. But "flatness" is an ideological, not a perceptual virtue. Pollock's paintings evoke Impressionist space; DeKooning's women are exhibited in Cubist—if not voyeuristic-space; Rothko presumes to present the space of the ineffable.

Yet both conceptions of the new—Rosenberg through individual freedom, and Greenberg through evolutionary Hegelianism—speak to the creativity of an art that surpasses, surprises and often disturbs through its novel presentations. In all cases, the predictable is a negative value for art. The explanatory—as a source of value for new art—is considered a negative if it grounds the aesthetic in non-aesthetic contexts—whether sociological (as in accounts of the proper role of art) or experimental (as in mind-brain hypotheses about the physical location of creativity).

X

"Newness," to my mind, is no longer a discernable guide to new art. What is new has a limited historical time and conceptual place to locate in. Something new in Brooklyn may have already been done in Rio. And in Teaneck, something else is being done that will not be recognized as new in, oh, a hundred years. But wouldn't that Jersey artist who, in desperate non-recognition, looks to science for the future of her creative life, and is told that she has a creative splice, just recently discovered, in her somewhere lobe, encouraged? Then—given this assurance—she gains the courage to push her work, corner dealers, browbeat critics, and thereby, through force of warranted belief in her physical talents, achieves aesthetic success. Good for her!

The claim that such prediction leads to good art is as proper in its falsity as is Van Meegeren's success in duping even the finest sensibilities of his time. "Of course it's a Vermeer, I have spent a lifetime of looking, and I know one when I see one." Then the chemical analysis says it is not a Vermeer. What is lost? If the chemistry had found otherwise, an industry of critics and dealers would have used the many virtues in the painting to affirm that it is indeed a masterwork. What follows? Van Meegeren, you remember, saved himself by admitting that the paintings he sold as Vermeers were, in fact, fakes that he had painted himself—and so he escaped the deadly charge that he was trying to sell masterpieces from the collection of the Third Reich.

We know that aesthetic judgments (such as beauty, skill, and portent) can be confounded by empirical judgments of provenance and authenticity. But are we, who on the cheap have bought a Van Meegeren Vermeer, doomed to minimize our appreciation of our buy, because of the (now more evident) qualities of (so far) true Vermeers?

Authentication is indeed an esoteric enterprise, buffeted by narratives of who sold what, and by whom it was deemed to be or not be. Van Meegeren fakes, better painted than critical opinion then had it, are now much in demand. Van Meegeren the fake-forger, plummeted in value at the height of European Modernism. But his individual fate went against the values of the time. A fake old master, these days, can be seen as an anti-institutional piece, a revolutionary gesture directed against the decadent chrysalis of authenticity in the history of art. A "fake" can become an "alternate mode of discourse," challenging such held values as "identity" and "authenticity."

Alma-Tadema, the delicately dissolute Victorian artist, poses a different but parallel problem—namely, how, in the face of extreme social changes, to assign aesthetic value to an ouvre that celebrates the tastes of a historically decadent tradition? How do we countenance naked nymphs frolicking in Roman baths when both rich Victorians and poor Bohemians have a reputation for only occasional bathing? The nymphs are said to bathe a lot—it helps their future.

Both Alma-Tadema and Van Meegeren qualify for using postmodern ploys. They employ secret beliefs for their own aesthetics: Alma ignored social ills in making an exclusivist art that fed the tastes of the perpetrators of these ills. Meegeren fed fakes to those who prefer images of a clean and glorious past (what could be less controversial than a Vermeer) to the reality of a dirty brutal present.

The critic Arthur Danto, writing about a recent invitational show, used the phrase "art of lessness" to describe its general tone. In what followed he was more circumspect than, say, I would have been—but then, he was undoubtedly thinking about next year's show where "less-ness" might reach a sufficient level of insufficiency (the end of "less-ness") that would require a more fulsome rhetoric—a denial of the intentional fallacy, a repudiation of the pathetic fallacy—all with a mind to encourage the just budding but already sturdy shoots of a new "more-ness."

A word of caution: Do not, in the next few years, look for moreness in museum annuals—much less in halls of the most exclusive galleries. Look, instead, for Keep-Out signs that designate entry into places where artists heap their works in mounds of smelly, sometimes dangerous, Piles-of-Art. Look also for moreness art in the carvings, weavings, animal bones and bits of holy flesh that can be found in the bazaars of third-world countries. Look especially in the small midwestern towns, the bayous of the south, and ice-huts on a northern lake, places where art-history-as-we-know-it has no currency. In those places, more-ness is a way of celebrating the occasional fecundities and excesses of a simple life.

More-ness is in the disposable images that our dissidents hang on the outsides of their houses, paste on their trucks and kitchen stoves, and wind around their bathroom toilets. When the houses they own are all covered, beyond the possibility of living-in, there is always Aunt Effie's inheritance with which to buy another crumbling shack down by the river that needs a coat of arting.

More-ness can also be understood through the perspective of a universal (yet historically sensitive) critic, who will enter the spaces of the serious old—those still working but no longer hoping exiles from the world they once thought they owned. And then this adjudicator will pull out the deserving few and bring them to the enthusiastic notice of the next art-world—if not here then elsewhere.

But late intercession that brings worthiness to the notice of the world has always posed problems. Worthiness is like an ill-tended mushroom patch when it is finally brought inside—it needs nourishment: earth, fertilizer, and water—and it needs critics, those who will claim to be the first to promote this patch as the originary source of the essence of mushroom. Many mushrooms smell unbearably. Saints and the like usually do not smell good either, and yet they are as good as mushrooms at encouraging us to brave the smells that emanate from our own journey.

XI

A pity, this. It hurts like a toothache, although not enough to consider pulling. But it does suggest a cinematic scenario: Alert, alert! Some invading rascal art-terrorists have penetrated our precious ideological library: I can hear the thugly cadences: Boomba-nobelieve-a. Pull the shabby-shit off the shelves, they say, and burn it—but not all—the leather-bound ones might be worth saving for the downtown market. Cut the paintings from their frames with a dull knife—but store the good ones (as above). When the academic crowds begin to mill and ridicule our undeveloped tastes, knock them down, sit on them, and pluck out each and every hair. Then into the night we go, laughing all the way. There may indeed be art after the end of art; but in-between, there will be some old fashioned destruction.

The waiting game for post-art art is suited for those who are indifferent to outcome—a way of neither winning nor losing—that will give the waiting a last minute purchase on the way things actually go. But there is a spoiler here too: If art is life twice removed from reality, then life is art through all its performances of reality. Life ends before it completes the imperatives of its style; art ends after its style has been around too long. There seems little way to bring the two together: Art lacks life's durational density (in life there is always someone—if only one's self—who cares). In contrast, life lacks art's self-containment (an art-work, when it is done, is finished, but not ended –as long as someone wants it). Art and life do both end—but for different reasons. Life is never complete—according to descriptions of the after-life given by the sages of after-death. Art, in contrast, never ends as long as it remains art—according to the sages, mostly dead, who attest to art's intrinsic importance.

But what happens when we no longer understand the issues in this struggle? Some folks, especially in recent times, have tried to make life into art. A few of them may well have succeeded. I would be less than honest if I did not admit that I am jealous: all those parties—food by Escoffier, the finest companions with limbs and attitudes in disarray—perhaps not as fine as last week's, but they will do—and someone to drive you home.

But they all, and I too, will go a-moldering in the grave—or float as ashes strewn upon cold Mississippi waters. Best, then, to demand of art that it be more like life—that it give up its exclusiveness. But this is not easy: Art, when ended—destroyed, forgotten—does not end. Rather, it loses its uniqueness and joins the realm, the residue, of entities like us—it becomes the object that it is.

This brings us to the notion of post-art art: things and events that still desire the honorific "art" even as they face the imperative to discard the term when what it designates cannot be distinguished from anything else. They must then hope for a future where the distinction can again be made.

3

Dying after Eighty

I

There are things to be said about dying at any time in life. But there may be sayings specific to after eighty that would not demand as much attention within the broader frame of birth through death. I am not yet eighty, but close. When you read this, I will be—if I am—well over eighty. It is a propitious time to focus on ends rather than spans, to look for a clearing just up ahead instead of glancing at vistas passing by. Vistas, after all, are full of themselves while a clearing is an emptying out—a better metaphor for ending.

We think of death and dying when such thoughts are not overcrowded by visions of sex, or derailed by feelings of joy or fear—which do not count as thoughts so much as grasping for purchase on the life we now have. Unlike musings after sex, thoughts about death are about nothing in particular; and there is no post-coital lassitude to let us slip down slowly into the pool of mutual perspiration; there is only dry thinking about the absence of something.

But "absence" does not entirely cut it—for the absence of "something" (if we don't quibble) is "nothing". To say, then, "there is nothing" (after death) affirms an existent, namely, nothing, which, logically speaking, is a something that is nothing. Heidegger made much of this, even putting nothing into action by pairing it with its very own verb resulting, famously, in "the nothing nothings." It remains unclear (to me) as to whether nothing has a choice in the matter—or whether "to nothing" is what nothing necessarily does (in order to be nothing).

But there must be a nothing beyond all swordsmanship: A nothing-plain that can be a prime metaphor for the state of after-dying. It goes beyond "no memory" and "no consciousness." It is the metaphor that scratches at non-existence, and it offers the denial that "nothing" can be a value of a variable. It is the iron-gate clanged shut at the end of our existence, shutting out life and language from admittance to the nullity on the other side. Deadly-dull this ending, so it is not surprising that both populists and esoterics reach for more—something, anything—to circumvent the blankness of the separation. Even "blankness," as it is an attribute, does not do the job of un-describing the "nothing" which, when totally bereft of attributes, should be beyond the capacity of thought and language.

I retreat now to the broadest realm I can codify that remains within existence, one that includes "nothing" when it is conceived as having a "nature." Within this realm, the nature of nothing reaches for the experience of an existent that has no characteristics except for our awareness of it (its negativity). We then, the not-yet dead, continue to supply such a nothing with terrestrial juice. This has precedent: Philosophers, painters, composers—even some theologians—have offered characterizations that strive to give the living a peek across the gate.

But there are also contrary moves. The church these days, as I have read, is forsaking Limbo, a place which, historically and theologically, is reserved for the innocent and premature—folks who were born too soon or died too young to be baptized—quite unintentionally to be sure—but who are nevertheless assigned for all eternity to a place, it is said, of a suffusing gray, a continuity of sameness in which are dissolved all end-life anxieties about the absence of bliss or the threat of torment. While the climate in Limbo may be dull and constant, there seem no restrictions on the climate of the mind. Those actions must indeed be lively: ancient philosophers telling newborns about the varieties of existence, and those newborns, prematurely dead, bearing witness to the experience of a blamelessly lived life.

When we consider these images, however, we must wonder about what counts as being fully innocent or historically premature? How does it matter that Plato was born before Christ—it was not historical location, but his obdurate rationalism, his unwillingness to leap from the Forms to God that is at issue. Or ask why children, those diverted to limbo, have a space in which to die before they are absolved of original sin but are not yet old enough to commit even a fledgling fault. Why does not giving them the chance to do the dirty, doom them to spend eternity among ancient philosophers—whose dirty doing occurred before it became a sin?

But for all that, it does seem that Limbo, however expedient its origin, has lately become a political liability—too accommodating to special interests: all these children encouraged to be born just to die too soon. For a church now under siege because of tensions between the rigidity of its formal categories and the obscurities of its informal practices, the notion that there is a separate place for souls not beholden to heaven or hell—but with nothing to aspire to either way—can be an embarrassment. Nevertheless, if the docents do away with Limbo, the problem of the spiritually un-and dis-possessed remains. Where does one put all those premature sages and transient infants? Perhaps in heaven with its vast demesnes, there is an outlying place—an exurb if you will—that can be developed for just this purpose, a place that is a bit shoddy and weedy, but yet quite suitable for souls whose inadvertent lacks prohibit the hope for heavenly bliss. Can you imagine, on a back porch overlooking the unkempt lawn, Socrates having all of eternity to talk to a gaggle of kids?

As a counterpoint to the stasis of Limbo, there is the accretionary state of Purgatory—which, officially, is not (yet) under siege. I understand this latter state in more Hegelian terms—through the evolution of spirit—in this case the passage from guilt to redemption. The guilt involved—as contrasted with what can be seriously done within the agony of the world—is minor. It is called a venial sin, a slip of the lip in adolescence, a nibble on a cracker before communion, a casual cruelty in a drunken party, an indifferent response to a cry for help. But all committed when we died before we made confession. Here, in Purgatory, all these timid would-be miscreants find themselves—not without hope, as in Limbo, but with a long way to go. The evolution through stages of hope is instantiated by the passing of a time that has been secretly assigned to each inhabitant. Kind of a jail sentence it is—"pen-indef" as they called it in the pits of Brooklyn. But given that there is all of eternity in which to expiate, and Purgatory's evolutionary march never stops nor becomes sidetracked, it surely leads the non-irrevocably unredeemed towards the distant goal of Heaven. Hope is the catchword here. Purgatory, unlike Limbo, remains in (some version of) consecutive time. Penitential souls in Purgatory—and they are by fiat, studiously and unreservedly penitent—when they have trudged their upward path through all millennia, Heaven finally is: Where? Why, there! Just go around the bend and follow the glory road to its end! Then, as you step over the line, time both metaphysical and material ceases forever; there is no now and then, no before or after—just unremitting bliss.

Don't worry pilgrim; you'll get there; there is no downward path in Purgatory, no backtracking, not even a permitted second thought about alternatives. But consider: There is no free will in Purgatory, not even a mere trace of volition sequestered in the most hidden being of its resident penitents. The compulsory ritual of cleansing and showing can at first be disconcerting to the newly-arrived in Purgatory, whose discipline must transform "what did I do that was so bad?" into a seamless "mea culpa." In Hell there may be nowhere else to go, but yet—as a residual notion, perhaps, of a still more ancient mode of judgment—there is freedom to regret: to invent, between yowls, fantasies of what might have been, and to protest, between moans, the injustice of it all.

There is time in Limbo, but unlike in Purgatory it does not move; it is of the kind to be extrapolated from the present awareness of forever. Limboists, like old Floridians, greet, upon waking, the same day every day—and rejoice in the security of recurrence. The contradiction of time's non-movement in Limbo matches the contradiction of its role as a punishment of the guiltless. However, in a further contrast with Purgatory, there is full freedom in Limbo to contemplate alternatives—not personal in this case, for there are no Hellish fires to keep you focused on yourself—but metaphysical, in the older sense that the dialectic of Plato's ascendancy of reason here holds sway. There is free will in Limbo, although its exercise resides only in the capacity for an endless prolixity of concepts.

The powers that devised this place, threatened perhaps by the excessive liberality they allowed their first creations, saw to it that in Limbo there is no "should" that can be pursued. Calmed by the grayness, the unruly horses of the appetites have been cut loose to forage in the lowlands; and the soul thus freed of its smelly companions for all eternity, exercises full rights to contemplate about what there is available in the reaches of pure thought on that small island situated between the continents of dark and light.

One notable difference between Purgatory and Limbo is that the former requires a baptism that is later sullied, while the latter is linked to a time that is prior to the splashing of holy water. However, notwithstanding their different modes, these are both states that intrude themselves into the transition between life and death: Limbo, given its wealth of classic worthies co-inhabiting with innocents, does not need a doctrinal interpretations of post-life reality.

In contrast, Purgatory is populated by penitent survivors of "Severe Judgment"—not that they've gotten off scot-free, but that through accepting a regimen of copious, persistent and continuing penance, they have become part of the heavenly program of indefinitely prolonged, yet unquenchable hope.

Limbo escapes the horrors of hell by holding firm to Socratic rationality, thereby maintaining the pre-Christian equanimity of warranted belief—wherever it takes us. Purgatory, in contrast, is forever reaching past the demonstrable through a process of faith in a movement that necessarily leads to nowhere else but Heaven. The air in Purgatory does get thinner with the passing of each millennium, and when breathing altogether stops, the world will end—and all those now fully molded into righteousness will have reached their promised land.

Heaven is different; it is a realm in which nothing moves—anyway, not from here to there. Heaven is universally understood as the completion of being—beyond desire and time, within an unbounded place that yet is everywhere immediate. What remains for doing in heaven is the privilege of those fortunate souls—instantiations as they are of cosmically chosen being—to enjoy nothing less than heavenly bliss. But there is a problem: Does not the combination of immediacy and infinity that characterizes heavenly bliss, leave its souls only the undemocratic recourse to bliss—to partake of everything good and true for all eternity? Well, yes—as far as I can tell from here. Heaven is the conjunction, without otherness, of the present and the eternal. There is no room for space as location, for time as change—or for dialogue (such as is actively practiced in Limbo) about issues that once, in earlier venues, were presented as imponderables. God, as the ancient story goes, once permitted free will in Paradise. But that freedom to depart from the rule of even self-evident truths, gave Eve the courage to offer the Serpent's apple to Adam, and so unleashed Satan's disfiguring insurrection—which both then and now requires a goodly portion of the heavenly host to keep in check.

Were I asked to choose, I would prefer Limbo. Of course, I am not eligible either historically or sacramentally: I was born in Brooklyn in the twentieth century, was baptized without my permission, and went through the rituals of Communion and Confirmation to please my mother. Given all that, I have, I confess, tried a bit of preliminary exculpation—on Sundays putting on the hopeful smiling face. I have tried I have, but I always had to turn my face away. So Purgatory, however much it is touted as a road of advancement to the better offices of eternity, I will forsake in favor of the Limbic coffee house of lesser virtues that welcomes those, however wrongly born, who have come to celebrate an indifference towards the blandishments of both Heaven and Hell.

Consider now some secular supports for my conjectures: In his discussions of will and idea, Schopenhauer argues that once one has renounced the will, experience continues to be of living but no longer of desiring—an achieved disinterest in changing. It is a living,—as the painter Ad Reinhardt said of art—that is about doing the same old thing. This notion of constancy—don't change for goodness' sake—is a fitting extrapolation of Schopenhauer's thought, for it evokes a constant state, perhaps like Limbo, where the pressures of ambition are exchanged for the steady-state of serenity. Ambition is the timely affirmation of desire; serenity is its timeless denial. Will-less achievement is independent of sacramental or historical goals. The denial of will can be practiced anywhere, but the flights of memory that recollect will's wantings can be discussed into eternity only in the coffee-shops of Limbo, in that impoverished place, precariously situated between the antithetical realms of Heaven and Hell—those behemoths where the will, in full divine or diabolical manifestation, contends against itself in the battle between Good and Evil.

The description of Limbo I offer is based on an awareness that is will-less in that its content changes through recollection rather than desire. This approximates the awareness that Schopenhauer seeks in the journey from will to idea. Limboists, in this regard, have it easy because, as they are dead, they need not strive for relief from willed action. They have all the latitude, however, to imagine what the action and the striving might be like. Schopenhauer's freedom-seeking soul strives for that achievement in a traditional way: abnegation, self-discipline, denial of desire, the obdurate passivity that confronts temptation. Yet, these difficult choices on earth are simply modes of discourse in Limbo—where one can consider everything yet remain instrumentally aloof.

Schopenhauer's life-way of assaulting will does roughen the path to its overcoming. If rejection of the will can be so well accomplished that no residue of desire remains, then why do we, having wrung out all that wiggly stuff, still have to die—when all the material perils of willful living have already been paid for and overcome? Consciousness is the last temptation of the will. It is the state that retains awareness of self as still conjoined with the material will of the world. Is will, then, through the perversity of its remaining after having been overcome, the last living consciousness of dying?

II

I began this essay with a discussion about nothing. The object was to counter the conceptual if not physical void which some understand as death. I have suggested alternatives, and support my case with inventions, theological and mythical, which confirm that, for some ways of thinking, there are indeed celebrated alternatives that extend physical demise into realms of continued being. The question, of course, is not whether any of these are materially possible, but how one or another supports the valuable notions about life we entertain before we die.

It is an ancient truism that a belief in after-life makes more easy the transition from self to death. I don't know, but here I want to discuss a realm, found in various philosophical speculations, which is much like the theological constructions of Purgatory and Limbo—the flimsy bridges between life and after-life. This is the realm of "sublimity" which, like these others, is systematically incomplete, and so well positioned between the contingency of life and the finality of death.

Sublimity is more a nineteenth century designator, but I offer it here as a way-station along the traverse, traditionally of high but fearful aspirations, towards nothingness. It is a concept that opposes death with narcissism and so offers a peek across the abyss, a virtual dying—yet with the chance of scurrying back to the land of living. Sublimity is where the incompleteness of life, the sense of its fragility and finitude, the indifference of natural death, can be experienced (and conquered) as an idea if not as an actuality.

Kant speculates that the sublime is reason turning back upon itself when, because of unbearable fullness or unfathomable emptiness, the world goes beyond our capacity to know it. He suggests that this turning—mind's ability to think its own incapacity—is a cause for reason's celebration: the mind continues to make sense of what overwhelms the senses. Kant also assigns this capacity to the imagistic power, the infatuation with (being) "nature's voice" that artists have—those reckless gifted ones who can use an overwhelming of ordinary sense as a conduit for aesthetic content.

Hegel, in contrast, regards the sublime as an absence of determinateness which he associates with historically early cultures, something that, systematically, he delegates to primitive notions of reality. Hegel's sublime is an early way-station, a temple for a not-yet-immanent

God. Yet it fits well with Purgatory, for it is on the early road where thought rids itself of sensory contamination and mythic illusion, and eventually proceeds to the plateau of the pure idea—knowledge of the absolute through the office of the contemplating self.

For Christians, this supervenience can be understood as a purifying mechanism for sinners in Purgatory. On a secular level, It is also a much- remarked description of world-process by political Hegelians—the inevitability of an all-world resolution.

Schopenhauer follows Kant in separating the sublime into dynamic and mathematical parts, but is more willing to use poetic metaphor in distinguishing between the various modes. An early grade of the (dynamic) sublime is "a very lonely region of boundless horizons, under a perfectly cloudless sky . . . the profoundest silence." Here is offered the vastness of the empty desert as a place for those who would set aside the need for acting—a place not unknown to early saints. But Schopenhauer's modes of the dynamic sublime increase in violence and totality, until the natural forces that pose a threat to human life—those previously experienced in only distant awe—become immediate, deadly, and inescapable. Sherlock Holmes and Professor Moriarty, each stuffed to their weskits with righteous will, struggled mortally at Reichenbach Falls until they fell, still fighting, to their deaths. The natural sublimity that is the falls engulfed them and their heated wills with scarcely an extra ripple—it is, after all, all the same.

The sublime in all such manifestations is necessarily incomplete, for it disappears just when its promise becomes actual—when we are swept away in the cataclysm which we can no longer represent to our dispassionate selves because we have come too close and so must die. The capacity, then, to perceive what is beyond measure, requires a split between action and perception. The risk to life must be vicarious, a perception of threat but at the safe distance that imagination brings to an enveloping and destroying immediacy. Schopenhauer treats another version of the sublime—the mathematical—in perceptual terms as well: "never by an empty space, but only by one that is directly perceivable in all its dimensions through delimitation."

In this version of the sublime, there is no threat to our being except in the immensity of the star-filled night whose spectacle brings us to contemplate time and distance that has, in fact, no earthly measure.

I take sublimity to be the very metaphor of partiality and incompleteness. If we fully experience its proximate impact, we die; if we contemplate its incomprehensibility, we abandon the world of sense. for Kant, however, there is an peculiar amalgam of sense and reason when he offers the sublime as an embodiment of genius—the rara avis that personifies what otherwise cannot be thought. It seems here that sublimity reaches a truly modern point in that it teaches sensibility what is meaningful, and therefore, what the ego must encompass to bridge the gap between the profound and the trivial. Schopenhauer, also anticipating modernity, allies genius more with madness—as an often fatal impasse that can be socially illuminating, but which destructively reveals the transparency (or collusion) in the "sane" world between will and idea.

Keats offers another version—the "egotistical sublime"—as a way towards immortality by incorporating the world into the self so that "it and I" together "are" reality. It is a way of ingesting the outside so as to overcome the anxiety of separateness. The egotistical sublime reaches out for completeness, yet its existence is threatened by the particulars of criticism, and by the fluctuating arrogance and despair of self-love.

The last time I remember the word seriously used in art was in the title of Barnett Newman's mid-twentieth century "zip" painting titled "Vir Heroicus Sublimis."

III

Our very lives, considered on the distaff side as art, have something of the sublime about them, for they too are indeterminate—ongoing performance pieces that seek to incorporate our world into ourselves. But the elaborations that the future brings with it prevents this, as do the shifting memories of our past, the sense of never knowing ourselves completely. But neither can we so know ourselves through our reflections in the mirror of our present, for to know that way, we would have to discount the biased images in our loved ones' eyes and the errant unbidden dreams which demand that we transform ourselves. To attain the knowledge of what we "really" are, we search for a way of retelling ourselves by probing for our central place. Such probing, if it is to be will-free, must be an action that is not so much historical as sporadic—a flitting between feeding stations, a choosing for no willful reason between what should be held fast and what let go.

Schopenhauer makes a distinction between the states of nihil privatum and nihil negativum, the first a consequence of removal, a taking away until everything is gone, the second, a conceptual feat that underwrites a knowing beyond experience. The first (privatum) is the story of our empirical lives—in which bits and pieces leave us, via the extracting agency of time, as we begin to age—and it remains in force until the last piece of living leaves. The second (negativum) is not in or for experience; rather, it applies without regard to our flourishing or withering, and it remains in force even after the last pieces leave. Nihil negativum, like the true mathematical sublime, is a conceit of the mind that congratulates itself on the capacity to think itself, and thus to give rational credence to its empirical antinomies. Indeed, this so-liberated mind should even know that which is both everything and nothing.

Nihil privatum is the content of the fear of dying; nihil negativum offers an opening for an afterlife—if only of self-narrative. Schopenhauer contrasts death, not with life, but with reproduction, (as Freud did in his pairing of "eros and thanatos") and in this opposition he has death take on the homely identities of orgasm and excretion: "generation is only reproduction passing over to a new individual . . . just as death is only excretion at the second power"

On the level of nature—his "second power"—death devolves into nature's shit. To avoid becoming merely shit has been, throughout the ages, a concern of the living.

"Oh death, oh death, where is thy sting?" sings the tenor. It is a fair question, and has provoked many of the answers that try to do away with death's dominion. The philosophically inclined, especially those whose thoughts about dying do not reduce to dogma, would be pleased if death were indeed boundless and undetermined but could still be thought after one's having died—even if such thinking is forever captured in a Limbo of infinite retelling. But, given the alternative specter of no thought at all—that awful threat of "just being nothing"—this opening seems most welcome. For is it not the very disappearance of thought that makes death such a conundrum and so fires up conjectures about how to retain a wee bit, however constrained, of thought in and after death? If thinking can somehow remain after all else is done, and even if there are only the shards of the completed life to have thoughts about, then thinking after dying is supported, if not enabled, by the inexhaustibility of memory. Memory, in this scenario, whether it be individual or collective, consecutive or cyclical, remains a challenge to dying. The "persistence of memory" is a way (perhaps the only way) to counter the nothing that, however finessed, lurks at the end of living. But, as Sartre puts it, "nothing" is the little worm coiled at the center of things that acts to preclude any connection between actions and their consequences. Why then, if dying signals the end of living, does it also preclude the possibility of memory—of continuing to narrate one's life in a way that discounts the nothing in which one is dead?

Benign Buddha offers you reincarnation, according to your just desserts, into another being like yourself, who will have yet another chance at climbing past the rung of your best achievements. This is punishment and redemption removed from the individual will and transferred to a cosmic beneficence where the solitary time-bound soul unites with its others, past and future, and eventually outlasts the treadmill of—even cyclical—time. This is like the state, much esteemed by Schopenhauer, where oppositions vanish. We are off the wheel, both alive and dead, enjoying the mediation between mind and soul, between the contingent and eternal, between the intuitions of time whether configured as a line or as a circle.

Nietzsche, poisoned perhaps by Wagner's darker side, takes the transcendental circle into the forbidding cycle of the "Eternal Return": If, say, a million monkeys painting (more or less) for a million years are able to produce a Rembrandt, why cannot the cosmic processes repeat, through all eternity, the stages we individually are all passing through? So we will live forever, says Friedrich, and it comes about by reliving our lives exactly as we now live them, although (and this is the heaviest darkness) we will not know that we have been there before—thinking every time that this is the first (and only) time around.

Derrida, more recently, as he considered the fact of dying, refused the binary opposition of life and death (as he does in his other attacks on the "excluded middle") and he offers, instead, the notion of a "trace"—something not fixed as memory or influence, nor even as persistence, but yet the not quite nothing, the something that can extend being, his being and other such beings, into the empirical future. In Jewish lore heaven is sometimes conceived as one's power of benign influence on the continuation of progeny, and hell as a lack of influence, creating an anonymity whose individual fate is simply to be forgotten. Derrida distrusts his own widely acknowledged influence, and instead wants, in death, to be only a trace, a quicksilver impression on what will come. Modest, certainly, but also a way of never dying.

I am not happy that the tail ends of the Divine Story are limited to a dialogical two or four—an either-or of life's resolution. If Heaven and Hell are so theologically wanting as to require the symmetrical buttressing of Limbo and Purgatory, then the whole story is vulnerable to endless apologetics—a contentious yet evenly divided legislature that relishes the safety of its impasse between good and evil.

So I say: Unbalance things. Get rid of tacky Purgatory and make Limbo the third member of a newer tri-logical, and thus indeterminately evolving, eternal state. (Hegel might appreciate the action here.) Limbo, in this new array, would function as the locus of remembering where those of us are who submit to dying but never to quite becoming dead. Like Scheherazade, we endure as long as we keep telling stories. Through this telling, we engage in an indefinite (perhaps infinite) task of remembering—which is tantamount to being in the third state that mediates, more strongly than do the dual pairs, between the transience of life and the finality of death—between the kinky hopeless of Hell and the self-serving righteousness of Heaven.

As I have said and sung, if I had my ruthers about the place in which to end, I would pick Limbo. It is compatible with Schopenhauer's state of quiescence where will is not suppressed, or re-directed, but only put aside—as in settling down an unruly drunk, a sometime friend, whose presence is to be tolerated and a bed assured. But this needs some finessing. It is in the earthly experience of the sublime that the human will falters through its own incapacity. In the dynamic sublime, the ferocity of nature's impact renders the will powerless to pursue its agenda. In the mathematical sublime, the abstractness of its projection leaves will no object to pursue. Comparing the realm of Limbo with these versions of the sublime evokes the conditions of passage between the states of life and death. Ending up in Limbo is circumstantial—not a matter of volition. Achieving will-less-ness, in contrast, is through an extreme act of willing that, if successful, comes to deny itself: the will that denies volition. One cannot be held to account for being in Limbo, for it is a strangely non-normative manifestation of theology in history. And one cannot be blamed for lacking what is required to achieve complete mastery over the will while alive—for it is impossible—perhaps a cosmic contradiction.

IV

Libraries contain forgotten books. Most libraries are made for such books—the musty and arcane ones that slip from memory unless periodically assigned as readings for graduate courses. Libraries, while always interested in attendance, are indifferent to the attention that their charges, the books, all seem to want. Books that occupy the distant out-of-fashion stacks, are not sanguine about the world's indifference. But libraries, as opposed to the books they contain, are very specific in their ambitions. Libraries, like museums, want to go on forever.

Books, in contrast, are more like people who grow out of fashion as they get older; and it is particularly this obsolescence—not so much in body but painfully so in taste and language—that has them crave recognition as past contributors to the intellectual enterprise, to be candidates for the immortality of ongoing mention. But I overdo this gloss upon bookish ambition. What books really want is the simple pleasure of being read—again and over again—for there is no rubbing of the genitals that can compare with a book's titillation by a readers gaze.

On certain nights, especially in late summer and before the advent of the fall rush of students, an optimal reader can enter into the ideal library and listen to the sounds of books reading themselves. Books are exemplars for humans of what we crave—to avoid the dying while yet living. But most books, as they grow older—especially if they are not included in some literary list—or are obdurately difficult—are less often read by readers seeking the more easily obtainable parts of wisdom. But hey, old reader, don't despair! Any attention you can muster, any mention or quotation you can bruit about, is better for your charges than is their simple moldering in the stacks. So let us imagine that these books, our proxies, dusty, unread through those many decades, will take their identities in hand, and in the silence of the night begin to read themselves (listen to the sounds of their silence). They are separated in their place of reading, not by content or history, but by degree of neglect—by the intensity of their need to continue themselves—if only by insinuating their pages into the time of someone's, anyone's, listening.

I remember a place in Mexico City, Piazza Garibaldi it was called, in which Mariachi bands would audition for hire in festivals of various sorts. What impressed me—in addition to the soft summer night and the weaving celebrants of pulche streaming in and out of the bars—

was the meticulous sense of space the groups were able to establish between themselves, so that their individual musics could be heard without overlay from the other bands. It was an immaculate distribution of performed sound within limited space (a rare occurrence anywhere music is played), and it also showed a finely tuned tradition of knowing each band's needs. All the musicians were dressed to the nines, with sequined jackets, pants hugging the thighs and flaring below the knees, and the wonderful sombreros that look too heavy for a mortal head to bear, but give authenticity to the scope of their music. The music was not much about the commercial use of its performances, but about what had been learned and practiced between generations. To acquiesce to this auction of their talents, the musicians must have been quite needy—but they seemed indifferent to the denigration of playing for hire in weddings and cocktail parties; they were like nobles from an older more subtle culture who found themselves entrapped by a nation of aggressor people that value only practical delights.

The books that read themselves have similar problems of spacing—how to separate voices intoning the quiddities of the ages, or the later modernist perspectives, without running out of room. Fortunately, libraries have copious stacks and can usually assign the more aggressive of self-readers by appeal to the statistics of listener circulation. But serious books, however disheartening their immediate appeal, also try to remain competitive. In some large institutions, a long period of being-out-of-print leads to a secluded placement that, in fact, is acoustically favorable for unfashionable declamation. Neglected books that still have the will to read themselves tend, like angry malnourished people, to continue sounding off, beyond the busy day into the empty night. Have you not heard, night-owl, the insistent chatter coming from the far reaches of the stacks?

But face it; who listens to the reading of forgotten books? Traditions of ancestral respect, as with other attempts to right a skewed world, are being quickly cast into the oubliettes of electronic practices where books, their excerpts, synopses, gists, and influences interchange to form new entities that do not require identity or longevity. It is not simply a matter of a growing estrangement between books and their texts, where authenticity gives way to expedience; it is a denial that that there is, in any important sense, an originary book served by its faithful text—that measure of the unitary meaning of what someone has written. Books which obduratedly hold on to the traditions of their making, their tri-partite identity of writer-book-reader, and subscribe to the ideality that holds this identity together—the value of continuity, and the need of the members for ontological sharing—are threatened by the void in which all that remains of books are notations.

Our bodies are books. They will molder—as books do. What we should not relinquish, according to my thesis, is our texts. Texts are to books as the soul is to the body. Yes there are differences, but these are mostly of an instrumental sort: A text can have many books, but a body—so it is said—can only have one soul. Books are never that faithful; they are modified by circumstances of editing, abridging, modernizing—even by denying that the original ever was a discrete text—only an accumulation of changes to earlier changes. A body resists the nothingness of death through the continuity of its soul in the episodes of its living. A book resists the nothingness of disregard by the perseverance of its compliant text; the body endures through the accretion of the novel texts that are its memories—aggregates of its soul.

Yet, these must both be read—book and text, body and soul. Every so often, they jointly refer to a something—which is a scraping of the inner side of the shell whose outside may well be nothing. So we write and paint and procreate and win or lose our battles great and small, in the hope that they will be read and seen and treated well in and for posterity. But we also know such hopes are illusions—warranted ones, but illusions nonetheless. They are offered as gifts from the dead to the living; they are meant to assuage the guilt of those who have come to understand why the dead are better than we thought. Hegel lives, yes—but if not read he dies as shabbily as we. Why, then, do we still continue to propitiate the gods of our fathers—even as we succumb, even when dying, to the seductions of new gods? Was the old man better than I thought? When I read him—and we should all listen—you will see that I am just like him—better than I thought.

I would like, for all eternity, to be a book that reads itself. My life has not been grandiose or even modestly sublime—but it has had the sequencing of unique moments as, I suppose, has every other life. Grasping a life is splitting it so fine that no one recollection will exhaust all that has happened. So I do not fear, when singing starts, that I will ever finish myself.

V

Artworks die as well as we. I am troubled by this parallel because I consider myself as both art and life. So I offer the conceit of people reading themselves—the way for us to remain alive is in what we continue to say about ourselves as art. People who are prone to dying should want to make a noise that identifies them as not quite dead. But if I commit myself to this enterprise, is there not the danger that however much I argue for my infinitude, I may very well, one ordinary morning, read myself right into the summing-up that will end me? I have only this defense: I find that I cannot, even if I would, arrive at my self-summation. Each day I configure my life of memories in the way that seem most true; but another day I modify that way into one that seems more true. It sometimes seems that paranoia enters even into Lucian's Arcady. Can it be that others are secretly inserting a summing-up into my ongoing story—those smarter assholes who remember what I have forgotten, or know (because some other asshole told them) what I never knew? Yet, I have a small philosophical advantage over such barren souls: Paraphrases of life as art or art as life take each other as subjects. But as with warring siblings, none will ever accept what each says about the other. So I orate on, nourished by a never-ending array of steamy dishes of description, cogent and incoherent theories of meaning—and so I am not (much) concerned with the mortal threat of a reductive certainty. My dishes, (no memories are without their tastes), are fashioned to fit the appetites of changing times, exotic guests, and warming seasons. There is no scold left in me who would limit the amount that others should eat of what I offer.

Lucian, you are a bore unto yourself. You want to read yourself forever, buttressed by the argument that there is always something to say beyond what you have already said. That largesse, you expect, will fill each day of the new millennium with a splendid variety of stories. But where, may I ask, in all of this, at at the sum of times, is the real Lucian?

Look who's here with this disgraceful question! My half-brother of essentialism! It must be the Wladislaw recently returned from the bureau of obscurantist objectivity! You have a rule book for defining the likes of me? Who let you in to spit your vitriol into my home-made-stew? Out with you! Our stew may be unfinished in body, but it is in form immaculate. All you worthies, come—now that he is gone—and eat with me.

There are indeed books that for sentimental or economic reasons, are revered as objects: a well-preserved rare edition offered at auction; an out-of-print curiosity found in a flea market; a musty leather-bound collection of Shakespeare's tragedies passed down reverently through successive generations but never read by any. But we party-goers know the difference between book and text, and we find it obligatory, if the party is to continue, to separate the two. Were people simply texts that supervene on their bodies, dying would be trivial—a mere mortification of the body that frees its text to indulge elsewhere in the collusion, interpenetration, fragmentation and regeneration that characterizes the community of creative spirits.

Perhaps the soul in this regard is like the text of a book—tested by unpredictable currents of opinion into modifying itself in the hope of pleasing the gods of literary value. True, texts are more intrinsic to books than are souls to persons; we can more readily consider people who have lost their souls than to imagine books that have no texts. But then, people, in this comparison, seem to be more important as individual selves than are books. Death, accordingly, is more troublesome to people than is, to books, their being out-of-print. Books die when they are forgotten—when there is no text left to celebrate their source. The soul, however, has no such out; it cannot deny, after the fact, the body that has caused it such discomfort.

One strategy to overcome this interdependence between soul and body is to rid yourself of that connection: Enlarge on the modern practice of separating text from book by denying that there is but one soul per body, or, for that matter, one body per soul. Insist, to the contrary, that you yourself are not simply the sum of your memories—for, as we have argued, there is no such finite sum. The soul, so disencumbered, can more readily be read selectively without letting in riff-raff memories. But this may not work. We all, after all, have creeps in our past—as we are all creeps in others' pasts. It may be, after years of telling, that the memories you had wanted to exclude will have taken on the same patina as those others who are also trying to survive their oblivion. So why not propose instead that the riff-raff of your dreams join with the ingredients of your waking appetites—then you can become a Mulligan Stew of Lucian and his others, undiluted by a tidy separation of gross from fine ingredients: Bones and fat come together to surround the snooty meat; tendons, without so much as a "do you mind" penetrate demure sweetbreads; gristle commingles with prime filets; over-age potatoes insist on rejuvenation with young and aromatic herbs. For dessert, Twinkies may be washed down with good cognac.

But it is time, after all this gastronomic flexing, to return to dying, which is, after all, the theme of my tale. Death, as I argue, should be mitigated by enlisting the principle of infinite recall into the telling of life's escapades. This is a good way of not-dying after death, and it rests upon the view that life is inexhaustible, at least in its telling, which after all is the infinite aspect we most want to contrast with finite living. Narrative strength is a rare gift however, so it may be of benefit to practice storytelling before one actually comes to dying—so that a certain familiarity with eternity is achieved.

VI

When I was ten years old, I fell in love with a girl who lived next door; her name was Joyce. She had a way of standing that threw one hip higher than the other and she pointed her feet at right angles to each other, the forward one being beneath the higher hip, the sideways one, which bore more of her weight, beneath the lower. It was the first time I noticed the promise in a girl's hips and its relation to the disposition of her feet. The adjoining houses in which we lived were two-story Brooklyn brick, and they both had stoops in front, four steps high, each of which led to two doors, one to the lower apartment and the other to an upper, usually rental, apartment. Joyce lived in the lower apartment, and in the mornings, before she began the walk to school, she would stand on the top step of her stoop and asymmetrically align her body so as to achieve the proper diagonal between her hips. She did this before my wide fixed eyes although she never looked at me, even though she knew—how could she not—that I would be there each and every morning. The diagonal did not change in slope nor in the time of its achievement; but once complete, Joyce would bask in it for a moment before she skipped down the steps and walked away. Sometimes, at that point, she would look at me and say "oh, hi."

We never walked to school together, although we were in the same class. Sometimes, in bad weather, her father drove her, other times groups of her friends would come to meet her, and they would all surge down the street and across the avenue that led to the Public School. I lived next door to her, also in the lower apartment, which belonged to my aunt and uncle who owned the building. I lived there with my mother because my father had left again and we had no money to have a place for ourselves. I guess Joyce's father knew about all that—there were no secrets in those parts of Brooklyn. Also, she was Jewish and I was not, which was lethal to young infatuations in that time of Brooklyn.

Once Joyce was absent for some days at school and a teacher asked the class if anyone knew why she wasn't there. I said something, probably nasty and untrue, which I can't remember now—but perhaps after a thousand years of telling, it will come back. Another student, the spokesman for the class, a future corporate chief, turned in his seat and snarled invectives at the vile and sneaky nature of my statement. He was right, but I only wanted to hurt Joyce for showing me her stance and then ignoring me all the rest of the time. The teacher then said something in return which expanded upon my comments—perhaps she too was taken aback by Joyce's protruding hip. A few days later, Joyce's father came up to me after school and asked me what the teacher had said about his daughter. He knew, he said, what I had said, but that didn't matter to him—I being what I am—but he wanted to get at the teacher.

In our last elementary school grade, Joyce and I were placed in an English class where we read Shakespeare. The teacher (he was tall and skinny with a moustache which partially masked constantly moving lips) assigned sections of various plays to students who would then be asked to perform them when the regular readings lost their way. I found myself cast as Othello to Joyce's Desdemona. Why? Perhaps our teacher knew we lived close by each other; perhaps he noticed my constant attention to her slightest twitch; perhaps he enjoyed the discomfort given us by his assignment of roles.

Joyce and I rehearsed our roles in her father's living room, declaiming the bard through, over, under, and around the family photographs and nickie-nacks that crowded the space. Joyce orated to her possessions; I spoke to her private parts. I, at least, was faithful to the Moor's lust and love, if not to the substance of his sayings—although I hoped she knew that I too would have grasped the (un)circumcised dog by the throat. But I was not, in real time, any danger to the large boy she was then favoring. Joyce didn't much try to understand Shakespeare's script although she seemed to like the sound of her voice as it bounced off the family heirlooms. I relied on the lines that could be imparted in groans and bellows, and so intoned Othello as close as I could get to the bard's sense as my lusts allowed. In the hotter parts, I dreamt I would come to prick her squeamish flesh with my bared bodkin until she squirmed asymmetrically from the top to the side of my sweaty un-formed frame. I grasped the text in one hand, and I fished for reasons in the lines to touch her with the other; but the inches separating us were unbreachable—she never looked at me even when I was supposed to kill her. I don't remember much about our class recital, except that I was numb and vocally diminished. I had memorized my lines; she, perhaps to avoid all misunderstanding, read her lines from the script—so she didn't have to look at anyone.

The first year in high school, Joyce, who would not even acknowledge my unrequited pain by going to another school, became the girlfriend of Louie the Italian star quarterback on our outclassed football team. The gossip was that they went to wild parties. But high school had many avenues, and I no longer saw much of her for I had become involved in the higher pursuits of literature and handball. The generalized perfume of sexual attraction throughout my classes distracted me from my lust for Joyce's crooked hip. I even remember wondering at some point if it—the diagonal—was not, in fact, an affliction. But one day, on my aunt's front stoop—yes, my mother and I were still living off my aunt's largesse—Joyce's father proudly announced that his daughter was about to be married to a son of a family friend, a doctor-lawyer-financier whose prospects were impeccable. Joyce came out the door, smiling at all the envious neighbors who wanted the same or better for their own children. She did not especially smile at me—but it was okay, that time had past. She looked matronly, dressed in anticipation of the life she would soon lead.

And lo, her weight was distributed evenly on both feet. We were barely seventeen, and yet, there she was, transformed before my squinting eyes—straight in stance and complete in life. She looked thirty—an age for parents—what with her starched new clothes and sturdy stance. No, the diagonal I admired was not an affliction, only a strategy, and so I wished her well—despite her indifference to what we could have had, even if for a moment, before she had to become symmetrical. I walked slowly down the side alley to my aunt's backyard. I was going to college; she wasn't—although she was smart enough. I pursued my fantasies of superior purpose by dwelling on images of the primping that would embellish the impregnated closure of her life. My mother would soon be dead.

VII

Joyce, you fat suburban bag, I would fuck you even now. What do you look like now? Plump as a frog I'll bet. Are you instead now dead—without ever having had the thought to read yourself to me? We could have intoned the Bard's black and white of it into the most distant wanderings of time until we got it right. I would have put on blackface like Olivier if it got you hot. And I promise you, I would not have touched you for a hundred years—after that, of course, you would have to wrap one leg around my neck and the other around my waist unless, of course, it seemed more fun to go symmetrical. But who would care by then? Not I. I would not remember whether your diagonal had once descended from the left or from the right, or which one of us is Jewish; it would not have any bearing on your matter at my hand.

Perhaps, despite my snobby disbelief, Joyce did find her way to read her life. It was probably at least in part my doing: Perhaps she was infected by the little creatures in my spray of spittle when I intoned "Un baccio ancora." Perhaps she sensed in some damp viscous corner of my enthusiasm that I knew she was made for better things than Larchmont or Long Island. But she did reject me—that syrupy creature. Considering her later life (the one I did not wish on her) of tacky comforts and hovering boredom, she would need some secrets to merit an ending through selected reading. But Lucian, what do you know about her life? You were free to flail your arms and spout high-school naughtiness in a Polish accent because you had no prospects, not even small expectations of how your life could be. She did; she knew that all the good things her father described would come to pass, if she followed the rituals locally prescribed for creatures of her kind—maidens of her tribe. She was pretty, precociously diagonal, with a high forehead and wide-set eyes—and an upturned nose to boot. I could only appreciate her breasts and backside indirectly, because I had no standard then to measure them straight on. During some dark oblique and moisty moments, I did imagine how they would look in the light of a bed-side lamp or in morning sun shining through the window. Whoo! The images become clearer as they move into my geriatric twilight. Joyce was good at getting into other people's dreams, and she had expectations that everyone would open up a space for her. What a father she had! I have no memory of her mother.

How does the Joyce that keeps coming back into the memories of my old age affect the way I want to extend my living. She is my age, and it may be that she too had recoiled from the standard ceremonies of dying-time—the confectionary rites that sweeten the way for those who sit in folding chairs while watching people gasp and rasp in hospital beds, and who suppose their presence has helped the dead to die well. During all these hidden years, she may have been a closet poet, and is now fulfilling her secret obligation to let it all come out—so that I, yes I, can see that mostly because of me, she just won't die.

Joyce, I remember your clouded eyes and skittery legs. Despite that memory you are welcome to join me in my readings. I think you did not really want to find your self through living; it was waiting around that more suited you, waiting for the next scenario someone would assign you, a scenario that, as with the others, you neither did nor did not want to be in. You always did (didn't you?) what was wanted by your father and, I suppose, your boyfriends and your husbands. But when I covered you with protestations of Moorish love, you waited me out, feeding back your lines and not caring, so it seemed, when the session would end. Why didn't you just tell me to go jump? So now, let me ask you: When did it occur to you that you were not willing to die? I imagine it was the time when you began to look for memories that are about yourself. I am (look for me) in those memories—skinny, poor, gentile, opaque for all of that, hovering around the edges of the games of after-school. You only feigned indifference—isn't it so? There was something about my pronouncements in English class—my abstract pomposity and Slavic gesticulation that caught your attention—wasn't it so? I was on the way to the life you didn't dare pursue. As I remember, you had skills in talking the after-school talk I didn't have—but I hoped then that it wouldn't be important later on. You never looked at me when I stood and talked my precocious Polish-talk in class. But I was sly. I would sneak successive peeks at your dead-pan face, there, in the corner of the classroom, and then there, in the center of the schoolyard, cheek to jowl with your scowling quarterback. Perhaps I misunderstood; perhaps you were thinking that I was more serious about myself than anyone ought to be. How could someone stand this droning bore, even for a day? You should have tried. Others did; but by that time I was flying wild and you were knee and elbow deep in propriety. But I never quite left, you know. I had decided, although I didn't know it then, that I would become a worm chewing through the categories of my life and yours, making holes that show how they both connect.

In truth, however, I don't remember thinking of you past the age of, oh, fifteen or so. Do I remember you now? The slanted hip and upturned nose remain forever; the rest is less clear. But, Joyce, you are a perfect icon of unrequited love, the kind I really can use now that I have passed eighty.

VIII

Why then, I ask, after a half millennium of not a word, and never a glimpse of pink, would she show up to live her eternity in the same library as I—in the adjoining stall, even. Joyce, I certainly did not expect to hear you intoning yourself, in your chirpy-nasal Brooklyn voice no less, when I moved into the space that somehow, most mysteriously, happens to be next to yours. You must have died before I did. Or perhaps we are still somewhat living, but must face the choice of place where we will spend, you know, the after-living. Noise can be a problem. Not that I could reduce you to orgasmic screams. Remember, I am on the other side of the wall—but I would if I could—if the rules allowed—elicit the most howling yowls heard this side of life. There are practical concerns, however: Soundproofing between cubicles, so they told me as I entered, has not yet been included in the budget. Such official inadequacies, as is usual, encourage its victims to find other ways of coping: Grunt if you must, but don't make loud sounds. The protocol of a cosmic largess, as it is slated to last through another eternity, must naturally have glitches in its development. This particular glitch—the lack of soundproofing—causes readers, ostensibly engaged in private recounting, to hear the voices of other readers relieving themselves in much the same way. And my nearest neighbor, can you believe it, is Joyce!

Begone, distractful spirit! I have sung enough in choruses. I no longer want the shrill of women's voices to divert me from the subject it has taken all these years to find—namely, me. This point is not yet clear; I don't too much dislike where I am—assuming, of course, that I don't get distracted again. Why then, would I want to listen to the harpy who so muddled my adolescence? Who wants to view (certainly not any longer taste or smell) the adumbrate of wrinkles liver-spots and sags that undoubtedly now adorn the vessel of that voice next door.

Anyway, according to the rules, we cannot leave our cubicles to sneak a peak; and I do not have the courage to shout across the wall. So there is nothing but to speculate about the origin of those transgressive cadences: Can that raspy cackle I hear really be the voice of Joyce? I remember that she always started talking on a high note and then let the words that follow disintegrate into mumbles; she also dentalized her final "t's" and sprayed her beginning "p's." Yes, yes; that's the way it is! It's Joyce all right!

The plan and procedure for eternal readings must have been started in medieval times, when father-superiors had the status to adjudicate between the needs of lay candidates. By their nature, monks are sensitive to the psychological frissons that might erupt between adjoining readers, so to keep things peaceful, a number of rules were developed: 1) No simultaneous reading –whether in unison or in harmony—is permitted between adjoining voices. 2) Ogling, fondling, or the mingling of fluids—is expressly forbidden. 3) It is understood that reading one's life, by post-Pagan definition, is a solitary act; therefore, duets or trios, being by their very nature, erotically tainted, are seldom, if ever, permitted. 4) Heavy breathing, muttering, squealing, howling, or any other noise that would be corrosive to the clarity and rhythmic continuity of the solo recitations is usually not allowed.

Such rules are understandable. This state of quasi-death, to remain politically acceptable unto eternity, requires a purist cast: Books are the essence and paradigm of the act. However long one reads, if one reads well, nothing else than reading happens; all that can be done to stoke the content of the readings has been done. Continued doings—were they still possible and still fun—would generate post-existential chaos: Just imagine the scenario of readers who find that the subjects of their readings are the very readers who, as it turns out, are also reading about them in the adjoining cubicle. Well! A living orgy in the after-life—a transgressive denial of both mortality and morality would be the result! All incompletely attenuated (read: inadequately indoctrinated) readers would then demand (as should be expected in a welfare state) to get back to steamy living. But the cost of rebellion is severe. These backsliders will find, whether because of orgasmic persistence or conceptual insufficiency, that they, in fact, are really dead—and the whole mythic enterprise of eternal reading, once acclaimed as a victory over the old tradition of life-death bifurcation, will fail—as the conservatives in heaven have always hoped.

Nevertheless, there is a group of radical readers, veritable terrorists as many see them, who would recklessly strive to erase any distinction between living and dying. Such attempts are disastrous for what I am proposing. Eternal quasi-life is not easily attained, and a poorly thought out proposal to modify it could, in fact, risk a return to the old system where we all become dead without appeal. Fortunately, the sages who decide between the really dead and the reading dead are indifferent to radical rants. They speak for an institution that, while not immune to pressure, has the historical perspective that gives them protection from the rabble-chants periodically emanating from below. In the course of adjudicating between candidates, these sages are quite sensitive to the residue of earthly desires. For example, they often help deserving novices in solitary reading locate the conceptual whereabouts of their obsessions without having to violate the space between them and their neighboring readers.

I never expected to be among those who chose—or were chosen (I don't yet know how that goes) to read a life of dying instead of being merely dead. Ancient Greeks, who had no truck with mummies and pyramids, and instead looked to the eternal power of rationality, might have been the first to discover this alternative: Why did you not continue talking in the quasi-death of exile, Socrates, instead of just becoming dead? The arguments you gave for not doing so are not very philosophical; they are mostly about your pride—about how demeaning it would be in exile. In the years that followed the abasement of Greece by Rome, and Rome's abasement by the Northern hordes, the dedicated after-lifers got so strong a hold on the collective imagination that, with their wondrous works of art and most subtle theological disputations, they gave us the choice of Hell or Heaven.

As to our present state: The failed historicism of Europe, the re-emergent pietism in America, the dogmatic time-indifference of the Middle East, and the wanton destruction in Africa—none of these has room for a notion of self-revelatory dying. However, what with the recent death of God and the post-modern disbelief in progress, there is again reason to look for a narrative solution—an art-way—that extends beyond what happens in a short and brutish life.

The authorities in charge of the reading-art have not yet found a foolproof way to keep communal sound from impinging on solitary navel-narrating. We all know the practical difficulties, but at base, this is a theological matter: It can be argued that color and form—as in the heyday of abstraction—are not considered factors in representation, but valuable in themselves. At other times—mostly the older times—

such factors are tied to images of passion and devotion, landscapes fecund or barren, subjects exalted or despised. Such images, it was believed, can better determine the ways we should see our lives. Even sounds, the ancients say—referring to the great masses and cantatas—must be safeguarded by their sacred words, and only then are they immune—as much as any art can be—to the pollution of desire and memory. Plato, for metaphysical reasons, thought picturing a pernicious distortion of truth. He also considered certain musical modes—those hoppy-dancy ones—to also be conducive to irrational conduct, and he excluded both from the ideal state. The more recent sages, those who first conjured up the idea of dying as reading, still do not want participants to commingle, but fortunately they seem bureaucratically inept at keeping reading in its designated place. The word, it is true, has a history of penetrating unlikely spaces: "In the beginning was the word" they say, and the monasteries have long resounded with sung and spoken admiration of that original captive word.

If I were sure that that sound next door, that high-pitched nasal caterwauling was truly a Joycean emanation, I would defy the prohibitions on taking a peek—even if it would mean my dying dead for it. Not that nostalgia drives me to this extreme—simply an irresistible fantasy. I am curious unto death about the way we two would now look side by side, without Othello's intercession, or her fathers imminent return, or the dangling threat of her quarterback's uncircumcised pecker. If she too was chosen for inclusion among the reading almost-deads, then I hope she would have discarded her vacant-beatific mode and let us know—we who are still determined to peek into her cracks—how something, anything, really feels to her. It's OK, Joyce; I do not come at this late time to fuck you. You are a fat old wrinkled still more crooked toothless warty saggy hairy hag by now, while I—why I am tall and robust, a bit gray, a little stiff, but still muscular underneath the modest layer of paunchy fat, more so than you would remember if you had ever thought to look. I recently lost a tooth, but all the rest is there, ready for the foraging.

Would you believe that I was nineteen before I knew enough to imagine how it would be to chomp on you? But by then you were already a matron, with your twittery voice made harsh by screaming at your many kids and berating that bloated pretender you once were so happy to marry. He's fucking his secretary isn't he, and laying out a pretty penny to keep her from telling. But anyway, you yourself wouldn't know how to spend that money in true sybaritic style, so maybe it's better that she have it—after all, she's looking to improve herself.

In truth, I'm a bad choice for this self-reading thing—because I'd rather look. Maybe I could find a worm-hole, of the kind that galaxies are said to favor when they need quick transfer between times, a hole that would let me look into the cubicle next to mine, and discern, however dimly, whether it is really Joyce who is reading there. She would, I'm sure, would no longer have those fine boned feet and ankles (which drove me crazy—I wanted to tickle them). They've been submerged under well-aged fat and bulbous bunions. But no matter, Joyce. I, myself, am long and wrinkled, with accumulated muscle overlaid by saggy skin. However many curls and squats I perform each day to reclaim young dreams, I cannot rid myself of gimpy legs.

When I first heard the low drone, Joyce, of your expounding in the adjoining cubicle, I did recognize it—even though your voice back then on East Fifth Street was more staccato. You see? You can't hide! I immediately retreated to the childhood memories of waiting for my manhood. Then I gathered up the tools provided by those memories—broadsword, lance, mace and chain—and I smashed through the wall, yes I did, that has so long separated us.

You look better than I had expected, Joyce. You show some fine lines beneath that caftan: gluteous curves and mammary swellings that although they are larger and hang lower than in Brooklyn, should be more succulent by far. And you must admit, if you would care to look this way, that I, a sometime seeker after bigger lats and pecs, also look better than those fat priapic hairy nakeds you have grown accustomed to.

Joyce, you never knew me and I didn't know you—for knowing didn't start that early in pre-conceptual Brooklyn. But you did give me, even then, measures for lusting, loving and hating, that prepared me for the oncoming world. While I didn't know you then, now I know you well and not at all. But after all the calumnies I spattered across our memories, yours and mine, I turn to you for help in managing my fear of death. This is a good return now for what I wanted then.

Can you imagine, though, if we had managed to get it on early on—naked and playing in the backyard of wet and sooty Brooklyn—

and had retained those memories of how we used to leaven our organs with each other's spittle, why, we could be doing it even now; albeit in slow and ancient cadence upon a period couch in a rent-stabilized cubicle where only oratory is officially allowed.

Imagine further, though, that through another hole in the wall (I made more than one) an itinerant filmmaker (a one-time student of mine) is setting up. He sees that our clandestine dance, highlighted by rattling bones within folds of stretched-out flesh, could be immortalized as his first pure documentary—a performance of sex among the almost dead. This filmmaker is young of course, still complacent about his own dying—a journeyman who has avoided post-mannerism, and is now going beyond the neo-cynicism that followed the failure of the new globalism. His peeking, therefore, is free of any discernable ideological overlay. He simply, he says, wants to capture—and show on prime-time—how far extend the ways, even unto death, of the sexual urge.

We all know that practices change a lot between our first fast gropes of puberty and the almost imperceptible reactions of old age. But this is nothing (as I trust our filmmaker knows) when compared to the ancient varieties of love-making that give the lie to the notion of progress in history: Transgressive putti uncovering uncomplaining goddesses for the delectation of the gods, make way for the return to earth where hairy heroes are engaged, part-time, in rural rape. In towns large enough to sport a castle, noblemen exercise their rights of coerced seduction as a tax on bumpkins who marry pretty girls; and in later larger cities, bohemian souls who, having little access to washed and wealthy ladies, celebrate the needs of their inner-selves by alternating modes of pleasure with equally deprived and smelly partners. There are always, of course, the crotchety rich who, throughout history, parade their nubile catch for the envy of their best buddies—who then must catch a trophy-worthy vessel of their own for the next showing. Down below, despite all of this, there are the legions of un-enchanted poor who try to get it up (what else to do?) when they come home in an alcoholic haze from the neighborhood saloon—the first stop, each and every evening, when the last of work is finally over.

But how could we, Joyce, even now—given our separate mullings over the sometime pleasures of fleshly coupling, hide the assaults, in both deed and language, of monotony. Monotony is also an aesthetic failing—an incessant grinding without the promised end—which, if not banished—could undermine the layered program now being devised by the liberals in celestial governance. The literary contributions of the not-quite dead are expected by the celestial bohemians to be novel—indeed, a bit racy. But its speakers—who are not yet celestial, but who represent the quasi-dead—must be beyond reproach.

When I was little, I thought that tasting flesh was mostly in the body; it took years before I understood that it is also in the mind, and even in the soul. (tri-partite schemes, I have come to learn, always explain things best). But it now seems that some who have been chosen as self-readers will want to taste their memories immediately—in whichever place they may occur. How then, given the austere rules we are subject to, do we cope with the desires we find still shining—true, in many different colors—that illuminate our various parts?

Not to worry—we are joined with all those others who have been selected to put death back into living time by recounting the programmatically incomplete infinity of themselves. At an earlier time, the ancient festering wounds between the body's mind and the mind's soul would have been staunched by the deadly beat of ritual. But no longer.

The proposal that we, Joyce and I, are party to, (Isn't it true, Joyce?) is that we heal this bifurcation between flesh and spirit through a new cosmic plan that re-coheres the universe through the stories of those of its inhabitants, like us, who have stories to tell. This proposal is nothing less than a plan to wed the future with the past, and therefore reinforce the present through the demonstration of a concept necessary for understanding eternity—to deny the inevitability and arrogance of temporal process. For how better can we know what happened some or another time, than to hear the past recounted in all its variations by those who have lived it—and who, by virtue of critical recognition, can tell us, the still living, the way it was at that time before we were alive.

Let us then, Joyce, speak our memories, and share them all—early and late, trivial and profound, salacious and spiritual—with our audience. What one remembers today, anyway, is fallible before tomorrow's more authentic version, which in turn gives way to a resurrected early version. If time were finally to stop, then we could know, by looking at the last version that made the cut, how it really was. But time will not stop—and so it seems, on face, absurd to long for the truth about the way it was. Tomorrow's memories won't behave, and they always manage to put the matter differently.

IX

> The day that I left my home for the rolling sea
> I said—mother dear oh pray to thy gods for me
> And then, 'e're we sailed I went a fond leave to take
> Of Nina who wept as if her poor heart would break
> Nina if I should die and o'er ocean's foam
> Softly a white dove on a fair wind should come
> Open thy lattice dearest for it will be
> My faithful soul loving come back to thee
> —La Paloma

I must go down to the sea again: "guarda il mare quanta bella." How nice it must have been when Luciano sang his farewell and sailed off in search of pirate gold never again to return to his faithful Nina. Why didn't he come back? Oh, shipwreck, storms, a knife between the ribs, a Peruvian princess—or perhaps a water-carrier with a shapely back and to-die-for thighs who offered him acceptance into her tribe. But maybe it was a good job in Venice—as an overseer of loading pilfered artifacts onto foreign vessels.

Nina pined, but not overlong, and then she married the local apothecary, newly widowed with three young children, who offered her laughter, good provisions for their meals, and only occasional demands on her body. Nina learned to cook, tell funny stories, and to wash as befits a wife of status. So when the dove returned with news of Luciano's demise, Nina took a broom to it. Heartless yes, but consider before you judge: They could have made a go of it back there and then in Naples had Luciano the clarity of small purpose to open a bait-and-tackle shop for the American tourists. And Nina would have encouraged him even while knowing that local success would turn him from a flame into a husband (which, after all, is what she mostly wanted). But they did neither. Nina stayed mum as befit her familial leanings. (One might think she really wanted him to leave). And our Luciano (looking, I suspect, for a way out of the husband thing) took the wider world as a more fit terrain for his mother-given swagger and ambition. But he had too few brains, and his brawn meant little before the expertise of mercenaries and the guile of merchants. So he died early, not thinking so much of Nina but of what he could have gotten had he done this instead of that. Nina did the minimum of grieving (they were not wedded after all) then cut off all conversation about that past ghost, and proceeded to marry well and put on weight.

Nina talked a lot, and most everything she said was what she had heard someone say the day before. She loved the comfort of not saying anything out of place, nothing that might slant the four-square life she had built with her apothecary after Luciano left. But as what she had to say had already been said by the many like her, her dear friends—advocates of why the future should be like the present, and the present as much as possible like the past—her efforts at originality were ignored by the sniffing city-speakers who come by occasionally to convey to all back home how it really is. Luciano had a problem with talking—he preferred to sing. He sang songs familiar to the people he was with—but sometimes, when it was safe, he sang songs from far away that made people cry—although not many understood the words. When Luciano did speak, it was mostly about repairing nets and washing smelly underwear in cold salt water. Rarely did he acknowledge with a complete sentence the inner thighs of those who wanted to be appreciated, and who hoped to build even the smallest appreciation into a life of many children and a place with a yard in which to drink wine on summer days and let the dog go loose. Luciano did not much think about such things, but he had no words to tell himself why—so when he became irritated by demands he just left. Eventually he died—because of war or greed or a storm at sea—but he said nothing anyone remembers about all that—or about anything else.

I once wanted a life at sea, girlfriends that one can sail away from in the morning, songs sung in foreign tongues before the mast on calm nights, strange ports with cobblestone streets and doorways from which would waft the most enticing smells and plaintive cries. When was it that my admiration for such kitsch turned to disbelief? I really did admire Luciano and his easy ways with Nina, but I found I could not be that way; so I transformed admiration into envy and envy into disbelief—then into disdain. Nina, I would not like you as you became, and after the first hour of drinking, I could no longer talk with Luciano. Why then, do I even bring up such chimera, spawn of my childhood needs and their trivial dreams? A fair question—but we cannot only talk the lives we wanted to have as we proceed to die. I need to show how the transition from Luciano to Lucian shows how tellers of stories might be chosen. It is not the breadth and grandeur that is at issue: Luciano has more breadth, and especially in storms, more grandeur than most. It is the function of choosing, uninteresting to him, that I am after—the sense that the living life is itself a story—one which finds value in finding what is worthy for the act of telling.

X

> Sei unser Schwester nicht bose
> Du trauriger blasse Mann
> —Heine

Charlotte came into my life much later, somewhere towards the end of high school. She was not like Joyce; she was very nice, and liked me for reasons I still don't understand. Charlotte was a little turtle-like, bent in on herself. She presented her back and crossed arms to the world—defense before attack—and yet, when she raised her head and smiled, I knew I would be safe in her shell with her. She was also somewhat pigeon-toed—which gave her every step a purpose, a way to a place that was seriously waiting. Years later, I told my daughter about the merits of turning her toes in when she walked—in the manner of Fenimore's Indians, who could walk swiftly yet silently through the brush. I liked the way Charlotte walked, and we went out once or twice. Went out? Hah! We went where my scrupulously saved five dollars would take us for a movie and some food. I stopped dating her, not because of the expense, but because I had just discovered Greenwich Village, and (would you believe it?) preferred the company of the pre- and post bohemians: psychotics, messianists, and messed up girls, to sweet Charlotte's arms (not that I had ever really felt them). One night I brought her home—it must have been our second date—and after we said nice time and see you soon (it was her parents' apartment after all) I grabbed her and bent her back to kiss her—just like Errol does in the movies—and she shoved me away, showing her distaste for my imagery while leaving some liberating room for my education.

Well! I didn't accept the rebuff. I was then on a mission to escape the bourgeoisie—no one anyway was after me—and here I am being chided for the mildest of countercultural affronts—which, according to all I then knew, was a hip way to get (get!) a girl. So I crossed the river to Manhattan and didn't see Charlotte again until years later when I was strolling on Broadway with a sleazy friend, and she passed us with her date. When she saw me, she turned and smiled the same smile of understanding and forgiveness that I had run from in the first place. Charlotte, let me ask: Are you a member of the after-life club? You should be because you're so nice, much nicer than that Joyce who

I'm sure got her appointment through connections. If you are a member, let me know; I really want to hear about your life, Charlotte—as a way, perhaps, of redeeming some of mine. I want to hear what you said to others when you smiled at them, and how you sound when you make love.

4
Place

I

What place, Place, do you have in art?
Do random visits create clutter in your spaces?
In my house, tidy sweepers safeguard clarity
And promote friendship between the lookers
    and the runners in place.
When die Reine, die Feine, die Eine, comes knocking, I let her in
Knowing that she knows I am as one with her
    despite our many names.
Truth, Goodness, Beauty, need no further subordination
They are engorged—enough already—with their parochial instances;
    and cannot be further reduced to just one.
But their progeny: the purely factual, wholly universal,
    and indisputably tasteful, although spoiled,
    can be made friends.
They need a nice cold shower in the all-together
Which would merge their separate quivers into one big shaking.
Otherwise, the long contention between their inherited forms
Begins to smell of dirty socks and ancient armpits.

Red-spot-here-now, you are not invited to my place,

For you are prone, with your cowboy hat and downtown spurs,
To cutting my continuum into pieces.
You do not care, alas, that each true piece of reference
When bereft of out-of-date compliants,
Becomes more high-strung and nasty than the next.
Why don't you then, failed reference,
Abandon the church of the context-free,
Avoid the true assertions of the good and beautiful,
And join the flow of beer, brats, and bragadoccio
That cools us on a summer's day?
This is the last space in which I can hide from you,
Nit-pickers for the knowable.
And now I have to let the sweepers go,
In order to let alle Reine, Feine—and Meine—stay.

II

Poems are easier to write than the other stuff because poems, like butterflies, flit blamelessly to the outsides of the page just in case they must protect themselves from the demands of a prosy notion that is longer and wider than the places set aside for song and sentiment. There are fewer places now that are suitable for the old narrow ballads, the ones which, beyond their rhyming, used to tell only what is important for us to know.

When did poetry relinquish its calling for the telling of higher truths? Perhaps when truths became democratic and lost their categories—when most any truth like "the cat is on the mat" could qualify for all levels of profundity. Sad time.

A poem is easier to end than prose, for the descant rhetoric of historical intruders and the knocking at the door of imported common-sense, signal the poet that it, the poem, had best be brought to an end—you could well have ended it sooner. Long poems, after Dante and Milton, are difficult.

But prose has its own problems. It can be deadly dull because it usually is too long—and even when short and to the point, its reading is tainted by the drowsy anxiety of something missed. Most things, these days, move faster than their readings, and so, as paragraphs grind inexorably on, what they, the things themselves might say, can easily be missed. But however the readings come at you—in script or on the screen– few now have the fortitude to slog through others' memory games—especially when the authors say that what they purport to show-and-tell, in the there-and-then, is really about us all, dear friends, in the here-and-now—which, as we know, happened a while ago.

Revolutionaries don't provoke—as Tamirov said to Gary C. when Spain was burning. But authors—after the bombing is over—begin to peep out at us, however firmly the Fascists stuff them back inside their sacks. Painters who paint self-portraits fare better than do auto-biographers. The latter carp about the pain of art mostly because they are afraid of flatulence. They have eaten the tasty grease of promiscuous evenings, and are later faced, when they wake—together with their consorts or alone—it doesn't matter then—with the farts of morning. Painters are less concerned with smells—for one, they stand more than they sit, and can thus spread their gas around the ample studio space; and sometimes, because of reasonable fame and fortune, they are led to burrow under covers with foreign connoisseurs of outlandish odors.

Painters are trained to paint themselves and significant others in all the ways the winds allow. One must note, however, that it is a mark of exceptional talent (like Velasquez) for a painter to paint an ugly king as ugly—and get away with it. Van Gogh painted his ugly self, but the painting lets you know that he-himself did not match its beauty. Rembrandt looks sadly out from behind his magic glazes at bourgeois frolics—even while Saskia encourages him, with his bulbous nose and all, to find the older beauty in her naked plainness. Cezanne modeled himself after that mountain in which geometry clarifies the form but lets no sentiments intrude. Picasso veered between insatiable and analytic as his women and career dictated.

From that high point of ambivalence, art descended to become more easily fashionable, and so more profitable—a loss to art if not artists. Despite this loss (if such it is—I think it is) painters—although they seldom paint themselves these days—continue to treat themselves more kindly than do writers. Why this is so (and those boozy parties tell me that it is) is that words tend to make one small, dry, and prone to chronic guilt, usually centered about the gonads; and so writers direct their words upward to where the sensations they cause can be enjoyed without fear of shrinkage. Their syncophants agree, however, that elevated writing is preferable to the deep diving of paint which reaches bottom through the uncouth smell of naked boys and girls.

The Sardonapalus of Delacroix reclines in moody musing while his retainers kill his concubines—which he had so often made public use of, and which his thugs could not but have desired, had they not been dulled by a life-time of obedience. Just think: Those brutes, rather than killing, could have fled together with the girls—despite the tyrant's empty roars (after all, his enemy was at the gate). Then they—however little more they were than lesser beasts—and the girls not more than much-used beasties—with freedom they all could have crept, grunting and giggling, past the carnage on the road, onto a long life of fucking, foraging, and planting in the wilderness.

For painters, the tension between the highs of depiction and the lows of expression—the swoop from narcissism to anxiety—encourages the use of cheap wine to mask the smelly end of a sweaty day that despite the leaping and the diving has not gone too well. The art of film employs lots of people, and so the smell is more communal, but perhaps because of the commonplace of sweaty scents, the aesthetic possibilities of orchestrating body-odors into art are ignored.

Film is particularly good at portraying the social disconnect between odor and, for example, lusty love. But can you imagine what Marilyn or Clark or Ingrid or Humphrey smelled like at the end of an all-day shoot?

There once was an attempt, called the "Feelies" as I remember, to electronically introduce distaff bodily sensations into the central visual meat of movies—but it got nowhere last I heard. "Smellies" would probably do no better.

Paintings still have something left to call their own—perhaps only memories of the ancient power that has been discounted by self-conscious moderns. The aesthetic pilgrimage that would revive this power begins with looking, and continues into listening, tasting, smelling, and then, reflecting. This is the message of Plato's Symposium. So I began to put my writings into my paintings. Yes, I painted my writings onto the canvas—sometimes I typed them out and glued them on—other times, with a gesture to the good old days, I did them free-hand. The other sensations I'm still thinking about.

III

The "what" of us is concrete; it can be looked at and listened to, probed in public daylight, felt nightly under privatecovers, and then confronted snarling in the morning mirror. This "what," when washed and combed, becomes the self we present to those who for a reason pay attention—probably in the hope that if they accept this our presentation, they will get from us what they want for theirs.

The "who," in this dualistic scheme, is the antipode of the "what." It is the stuff of extravagance, illusion, loneliness, and—now almost forgotten—the sickness of the soul. We here assume geriatric privilege, and unload our "who," without pity, onto those who still come to eat and drink at our now unfashionable table. They, the stumblebums, one-time artists' models, and dear-old-friends, are now outnumbered by errant gossips and mal-formed critics—the usual suspects. But because they all come to eat our food and drink our wine, we are free to slop them over with our "who"—as with the hot-sauce of barbeque—so that they can taste the acrid distinctions we make between the "who" and "what."

Why, anyway, should those creeps believe me when I show them what they are and who I am? It is a difference, they might say, that is important primarily in the exercise of taste. As I am taste-free, they don't believe that there is a difference between, say, my who and their what. Sometimes I don't either—although, in my dotage, I care more about believing who it is I was, than what they, if they are not careful, soon will be becoming.

Belief is everywhere—all souls have a few beliefs through which they put the world to bed for another night. But in its more singular, philosophical versions—as in "warranted belief"—belief becomes more (Anselm) or less (Parmenides) civilized than knowledge in that it escapes the arrogance of the true belief that knowing needs. Belief, in its best manifestations, includes uncertainty within our efforts to seek hidden and peripheral memories that, if we were to push them into a clearing, would be seen as true or false.

Consider the difficulties in linking what with where—which linking was once considered a foolproof way to distinguish what's from who's. A "what" needs a "where" (to be somewhere) more than does a "who." "Who's" never need be sure as to where they are. It doesn't really matter to a bona-fide "who" that there are all these "where's"—inhabited by professors and investment advisors—that are required by "whats" for any knowledge of the way-to-go.

"Who's" have alas become unfashionable because they contribute more to obscure poetry journals than to the real-estate interests of a "what" in search of a "where." So it is surprising that the few "who's" who are left are still brave enough to step into the waning light and proclaim that the controversy between them and the "what's" continues to makes a difference. There, e.g., still are "who's" who believe, despite all physiologic evidence, that they are (essentially!) independent of their "what's." And then there are "what's" (now in the majority) who believe that a "what" is to a "who" as "brain" is to "mind"—the latter term in both cases, being an atavistic disjunct of only historical interest.

The ancient battle between the inside and the outside has been won many times by one side or the other—only to come back into contention in the guise of new and different interests. Believing that my "who" is embedded, embodied in, yet supervenient on my "what" is only a way-station on Hegel's grand dialectic train-ride aimed at bringing who and what together in a final synthesis. This completed synthesis, one that transcends the two-ness of body and mind, will not occur, scholars note, until the reversal of the big-bang—that (finally) timeless moment, past the end of Armageddon, when development ceases being a method for spirit. But for now, the play is between our present antagonists: brain and mind, feeling and form, history as progress or as random change, time as inexorably linear or as prolix in its patterns.

Some say that believing in "what" is not a belief but an empirical matter of fact, and that believing in "who" is not even a belief, but an instance of wooly fabrication. How dull.

If it should happen, then, that you come to my party, you are free to believe in "who's" and "what's" in whatever configuration you like—and you are encouraged to drink wine beyond the limits of dualistic propriety in any of these modes. Indeed you are free, as the night goes on, to reject any one or other mode (do not reject them all—or you and I, without a mode to our name, no longer are) and then you can walk away, if you still are upright, with no further obligations.

Introspection is a venerable method of searching for the "who" in us. Its signs are familiar in literary circles: furrowed brows and undirected frowns, a quivering at the corners of the mouth, and excessive sweat during academic and communal gatherings. However, these signs are not always reliable, for they can also be imputed to gastric upset or ingrown toenails.

Historically, introspection is but one of many names given to acts of plumbing the depths of self. Others are: confession, ecstasy, talking in tongues, babbling up the underlying-hidden because of drugs or torture. All such pulled-up contents are justified (in their special frameworks) as being otherwise inaccessible to surface scrutiny. Looking for one's "who," then, is as reliable as are the interpretations of its signs—although there are indeed differences between signs from the Inquisition and those of Freud's couch.

In the absence of duress, successful clients, having earlier solidified their "what," will approach their "who" in the latest health-spa style. They will want their "who" to be depilated, cut-up for bait, denied tenure, or otherwise neutralized—and then thrown back to splash with the other antinomies that occasionally emerge, still-quivering, from the unexpectedly deep depths of Golden Pond.

But in every age, there are divers for whom going deep is not merely a point-of-view—it is a response to a needed, however poorly imagined, reality. The effort that will dredge-up demons, despite the danger of their non-existence, is preferable, they say, to paddling toward shore with friendly minnows and other surface-riders. Those who go obsessively down below the warning signs on the rope (deeper than the limits of clear thinking) are just those who will tolerate the darkness and fetid damp that signifies the latest location of "who"— even when, because of proximity to the unspeakable, that location can easily transform into a variant performance of the Liebestodt.

Deep diving in the psychic waters provides access to the excess of nitrogen that counters the oxygenated clime of surface truths. The inhalations of air when our heads are above water is at one with the rational middle, while the deeper mixes, because of their narcotic content, are deemed antithetical to rationality by sober surface critics. (Imagine offering, at 400 feet down, your limited air to deprived fishes, and then tout it as an example of the proper way to run a country).

This feud—between surface sippers and deeply infused inhalers-is a version of the ongoing historical quarrel about the way to achieve a self—to distinguish between the "what I am" and the "who am I." Such acrimony can be traced to the schism between the tribes of Cain and Abel; it shows up in the tension between Plato's love of the beloved and the austere needs of his Republic; and it still figures in the latest attempts at mapping poetry onto brain-waves.

"Who" and "what" are the contenders in this conflict of identities. "Where and "when" are the determinants of the terrain and the strategy of battle. We ask: Where? Why, there—the place beyond the bushes—although the getting-there has become harder in these passing years. But this is so because "what's" have so proliferated as to challenge the success of their own where-discerning technologies—it's a matter of overgrazing. "Whats," in principal, are eternal optimists—waiting only to be discovered and codified. They are the constituents, as we say, of the objective world. So too, is the "when" of a "what"—for a "what" needs a "when" just to be somewhere. But a "when" is not immediate—it is a "some-time" which does not contain the fiction of a "now." Our cognizance of a "what" is a factor of its material claim to our attention during some highlighted "when." Not attending to a "what" does not make it disappear, however. Our neglect of passing "what's" may lead to their decline, but it is not a sign of non-existence—simply a matter of the "when" and "where" of a "what" not having a "who" to recommend them.

It is different with the existence of a "who." There is no "who" who is external to our interest—for if there were, it would on closer inspection, turn out to be a "what."

"Who," unlike "what," has more "where's" than can be located, or "when's" that can be arrested. The "where's" of "who" do not satisfy a determinate location. They only map the changing places where a "who" may alight in order to affirm, within a particular sojourn, who it actually is. But no "who" can be fully captured by a "where"—even though where we may be tells us something about who we are.

The rock in the desert has more resting places for a "who" than does a what-infested corporate boardroom. (I recognize my prejudices.) A bordello may reveal more fecundities of definition for your errant "who" than does the daily affirmation of what you are by, say, your butler. (I recognize your prejudice.)

The "when" of "who" is quicksilver. When did it happen that I spurned my sweetheart for the Jezebel across the river? It began while I was being born and it is still happening—as I write just here and now, and whenever I buy plums in the supermarket to give as sweets to another who. We then, you and I, are caught in this ménage-a-quatre of "who, what, where, and when." All participants in this performance vie for dominance—for a leading role in the action. That such acrimony likely will not end before the death of language, should show that there is no hope (except in the realm of Forms) for a coming together of thinkings about the encompassing real within a single reading.

IV

How is it, despite all these categorical anomalies, that there are openings which encourage ontologically naïve daredevils to move between the worlds of sense and sensibility—between their "what" and their "who?" Nostalgia is the remedy for their bruises, indeed a folk remedy, an age-old salve for painful bifurcations. Nostalgia also breeds memory—of a sea that once parted and thereby opened a path to the opposing shore—which blessed path allowed the worthy to come across to their salvation—only to be disappointed yet again.

Imagine a world in some undivided past in which the good-folk celebrate the union of discrete identities. That world and this one are not incompatible—but traveling between the two, across a non-parting sea is indeed precarious. Be careful of the battering of the ancient waves! Look ahead, instead, and ask which players in this contest between mind and brain have already won the game? The winners are the ones (check it out) who embrace the plea of no contest.

The relation between mind and brain is indeed a hard problem. Either way you play the game, you lose: Maintaining the separation evokes an untenable distinction between thought and reality—between descriptions and the world. But denying that distinction puts our cherished needs of infatuation and imagination into the unfeeling hopper of stimulus and response.

Despite mailings from the ministries of "who" and "what," I remain divided. I once believed that art helps us find our special place by offering historical contenders for the meaning of life. But as I look back from the vantage of the morose present, all this arting is mostly pain-in-the-ass memories of allegiance to causes that (had I looked more carefully) showed themselves as spittle on the chins of aging advocates for the latest way. When one is young and wanting, watching spittle form on bearded chins can be worth emulating. It is better than wandering the Brooklyn streets from dry twilight into dull night without finding an opening, not a glimmer, for the "who" of such a deserving one as I—who should certainly have been anointed by multiple loves, and shown, step by step and drop by drop, how to get into the better world.

But there were no harbingers of redemption in those poor streets. My chance to climb the ladder leading to the institute of redemption came through the free city university—where I was shown how to compare my opaque darks, however much I loved them, with others' wiser brights. I soon became a locust in an early art-world swarm, buzzing fitfully by day in Brooklyn, but come evening, joining the other locusts that would dare to cross the river and invade the seedy bars that separated the bohemian village in Manhattan's downtown from its ethnic—Italian and Chinese—neighbors.

Two beers in Cedar-Street-Bar is what all night you need to buy; and for that you gain access to the latest expositions of painterly strategies, affirmed by all the other artist-boozers as art's final freedom, which, when assiduously adhered to, will resolve the old (and old-world) traumas of stylistic change. The final separation between art and history! For two beers! What a bargain! Also included were ad-hoc demonstrations in gesture, arrogance, and the aura of talent—all that and those girls with radical hairy legs and long dank hair. We danced under the penumbra of art and life together—within the protection of the style of styles—that will last (as someone, I forget who, said) a thousand years.

These days, I don't much think about other days. But I paint a lot. My paintings are now often written on, and sometimes on them good-things are glued; and then, when all has dried and settled, they are again painted on to see if the brushy natives, having been forced to hide in the tall grass, can reclaim their homeland by matching ancient craft with the distaff strengths of intruding words and pictures. These intruders, although also ancient in their origins, have regained the courage to come across transgressive borders. Sometimes, like uninvited immigrants, they behave like colonizers—and so present challenges to painterly complacency. As to whether this dance in climates of sun and shadow, wet and dry, raw and cooked, past and future, can bring together the painted with the written and the photographed—not to say the smelled and tasted—is an academic question.

The trick, I think, is to keep them, the natives and intruders, both separate and together, living austerely for themselves and yet promiscuously engaged with each other. I attempt this by laving them with loose memory yet insisting on strict method. It is easy enough to scribble words on paintings or paint over photographs, or paste exotic images to juice up wanting passages—all to the sound of hoof-beat in the snow. But the additions to my paintings are not remedial, although they do share a communal shelter when the weather turns or boredom threatens. Memory is a good resource for determining the parameters of promiscuity. The extensions of the canvas, when they include a palette of memory, become more fluid—more concerned with permeability and diffusion than with the rigidity of borders. But to guard against transient seepage, I daily draw-up estimates that map the further limits of cohabitation as well as warnings against excessive dissonance—estimates, which I admit, may well be too restrictive for other artists. But we are in the here and now—my cast of characters and I. We enjoy our strolls—ogling and preening as we go around what used to be the village square.

V

It is good to enjoy art—but you know, of course you know, that artworks, whatever their inherited ambitions, have become less important than when they were more important. These days, the best are in thrall to visionary architecture or radical theatre; the other, more timid works, can no longer find contentious images with which to please the pope or shock the bourgeoisie. These-days' artworks are also obscenely abundant (everyone I know knows an artist who makes works of art) and so the porosity between notions of work and non-work increases and the distinction between them is lost in the mist of an older times. Non-works—those weekday foibles that sometimes dress up on weekend holidays as art—are now more in demand than are works that seek exclusive and stubborn status throughout the week.

Non-work works are usually made by those we know and love; the free gestures of giving and taking that bind the ties. But if our friendship sours, its tokens can be disposed of without guilt—just throw them in that dumpster where other objects, still waiting to be art, also can be found. However, anything that insists on always being art is disturbingly ambitious for these days; we have no cogent critique of "always," and no way of paying due respect.

Pretensions to immortality are some of the more fanciful stories artworks tell in order to be noticed. The term 'Artwork,' for a long while, has had a sacred ring to it: Artworks, like "Good-works" and "The Devil's work" are important to the distinctions cherished by believers—distinctions between what is deeply meant and what simply happens—between a rational and an accidental world. Early works, those that have survived and are now indubitably art, maintain their importance for us while they celebrate the historical accomplishments of power and glory. But recent artworks, those that, in this democratizing surge, admit to being some-time-part-time art, lose their celebratory role shortly after the moment of their viewing.

Refractory old-line artworks, however, those that insist on immortality, must counter the ephemorality of single viewings. We're in it for the long haul, they say, leavened by constant contemplation, and we must make our case within the category of full-time works that are slated for immortality. This is the received history of art—the evolving pact between masterworks always insecure in their ascendancy and prescient aspirants for that niche in history which will assure them—and their chosen predecessors and sometime successors—a continuing line in the system of "begats" that regulate art-works within the history of art.

All art-works are objects of some kind (for those of us who have placed the mind firmly within the brain) but only some such objects have been anointed by history's quarrelsome judges as incidentally objects and consequentially art. All such anointments, however, can be reversed when a something, deemed to be art, is no longer art on the occasion that object and work no longer overlap. The tension between such determinations is adjudicated by the conflicting demands of epistemology and fashion. Sometimes this tension, so prized by late-night devotees of aesthetic value, dissipates in the morning light of a later day.

Heroic images, once undeniably art, often lose their historical claim and become pigeon-glazed effigies in some central park. Patriotic anthems attesting to great state victories are sung to general indifference at ball games. Parades commemorating saints and heroes float down the avenues of large cities on kegs of beer. Concerts sound-off until they have played their music out—a short time, really—and then the subscription holders will wend their ways through the fugue of honking taxis, while the cheaper seats, still beating time, wait for the allegro of the oncoming subway-train.

In film-land, there are movies about undeserved executions where sullen stars are interrupted in extremis by flashbacks of their previous lives as hardy hunks well tended by lissome ingénues. In other movies, the characters talk so fast and smile so broadly that the storyline never gets beyond the content of the pleasant present. Then, for the latest private tastes, there are age-old roles played in multiple ménages, which are caught on tape and shown on weekends for the delectation of old and trusted friends.

The joining of all this slipperiness to a concept of place remains difficult. Place-concepts, as I have described them, are not sturdy. To those who consider all artworks to have a place (however "place" is modified by the niceties of "editions," or "performances") the reality of "no-place" works, in contrast, poses a serious threat to art-ontology.

I remember a student in a sculpture class who, when asked to show his work, pointed giggling to some near-by woods. "It's in thar," he said. We, the faculty, dutifully walked among the trees and rocks and bushes and, in effect, found many works. We didn't ask him which was his for fear he might start giggling again.

There are works that elide their objects in other ways, works that need to be disassembled and reassembled. In one Anselm Kiefer sculpture, shards of glass are scattered around its base. When the piece is moved, the glass is swept up, later to be re-scattered in some approximately similar order, in another location. In constructions by Eva Hesse, strings of latex tubing coil around each other eventually to be pulled apart and re-entwined in a new installation. A recent work by Richard Serra comprises massive sections of steel (torqued elipses) plunked ponderously down onto the reinforced floor of a masochistic museum—which, it now seems, has long been waiting to be despoiled by this latest enormity. When passion fades, the hope remains that another place will bid for the aging balabuster and so prompt a further move—perhaps out onto a cove where its rusting and the rust of old abaandoned ships can form a neighborhood.

There are works that, so they say, cannot do without a place of their own. Such works resist a move; they hole up in the studio or gallery until they are promised that some new place is really more venerable, and so befits the change from a youth of shock and awe to the place lit (although more dimly now) by the regard of retired tycoons. But as public attention shortens and art proliferates, maintaining place grows more difficult. Serra's museum pieces in New York weigh more, I am sure, than any artwork this side of the Sphinx. Conceived in Manhattan, cast in Germany, shipped across the wide Atlantic, craned aboard waiting trucks, and then re-craned—while traffic stops and people gape—onto the level where, once the installation is deemed safe, the curators and significant others can gather, drink, and softly cheer their triumphant entry into a new art-history.

The sphinx, eight stories tall, has stayed in its place for millennia—it is a matter of religious mystery and national pride. Also, it is in the desert, populated more by sand and camels than by art-lovers. The Sphinx's present place is in books rather than on real estate. A photograph and some commentary will do—no need to go and see for yourself. In a few thousand years, if someone is still around, the Sphinx, as with the glories of Ozymandius, will be as one with the desert sands, sustained only by its myth—but it remains somewhere in the confluence of sand, images, and words.

The "David" in Florence was dragged through the streets amidst cheers that he had become so large after his biblical victory (not to mention the triumph of the Renaissance). But Michelangelo's sizing was small potatoes, handled efficiently by a horse-drawn cart. He (David) got safely to his place, where he still stands, and where he shows his splendid proportions to the many viewers who prefer him to the Sphinx because, in addition to all the other art around, and his great cock and balls, the local food is better.

Some nay-sayers consider all distinctions between works and non-works to be elitist—in the way that impinges on the enjoyment of advanced living. Among the complainers are anti-art artists and dyspeptic social critics who are always ready to spot collusion between art, advertising, and high finance—a malevolent brew, they insist, which queers the real aesthetic deal.

But art-works, as things-in-the-world, move around to find their best niches as avidly as people do. The historical imperative scatters its pieces over the landscape, and each piece, like a seedling, takes root within the soil in which it finds itself, and then mirrors both the nutrients and privations of that soil. Art has a populist way, these days, of taking public root in poor communities. The impetus is both celebratory and critical. The celebration is in walking through the colors and windings that a neighbor's child has made; and the criticism is about the dullness that plans for neighborhood improvement offer as a way of experiencing the mediate world for that child.

Serra and Christo challenge the power-builders with whom, quixotically, they are kin, through their intrusions into permissive public spaces. Architecture-manqué they are, presenting themselves as the latest instructions—more pure and to the point than buildings or cloistered artworks—about how to live and love within the extravagances of a great city. They have forsaken frames and pedestals—and for that we should thank them. But in doing this, they require, more than other art, that we collectively pay attention.

VI

There are many outsiders who live in places where the forms of things around them need no aesthetic instructions. True, the "Lightning Fields" and the "Spiral Jetty" are out there—but they are lessons more for visitors about how to view—rather than live in—the surrounding country. But the cliffs of Capitol Reef, and the glaciers that preen just off the road between Banff and Jasper have been there before the rise of acquisitive appreciation.

True, there is competition even within the natural landscape: Schopenhauer's "Will, " is located in nature and in the psyche, and its appetite pits erosion against upheaval in occasions that surpass—and continue past—the conflicts of our willful living. This will in nature is indifferent to the ideologies of its human counterpart, and it shows no appetite for stylistic reformulation.

In the main, the arid cliffs resist human intrusion– the lessons needed to survive in that waterless cold and heat are too hard for most of us to learn. Not a pity. When I sit on the cliffs at sunset, the crimson and pale ochre of the waning day revert in the late light to fading umbers and worn violets. The coming of night is restrained from abruptness by the glow the sun leaves on the higher rocks even as it sets beneath the lower hills. Yet, even in the desert, it seems a barren conceit to denigrate the power (and accomplishments) of the encroaching empire of glass and steel.

Kierkegaard asks of "speculative philosophers" that they include their own condition in their attacks on faith and belief. My condition is of rescuing my now-old self within a purple-painted house with an open view of the Mississippi River. The river sometimes floods, but when it just flows by, I sit on the porch and watch the barges pass, drink cheap chardonnay, and write what you are reading. When the weather cools, I go to a shack that my love turned into a studio, and I make art-works that you are less likely to see than you are to read this. I have little reason to assault an empire that, because of strategy rather than benevolence, leaves such as me alone. There are benefits to this mutual neglect. I am indubitably myself (no one around to doubt me) dependent only on an academic pension that I have some reason to believe will last me through my span. Being free, the zealots say, is an acquired value. I say it's a good way to scratch your ass and do what ever else you can still think of doing.

The red-rock canyons in Utah are a good place to find one's freedom. The rocks don't care—for they no longer have a soul. They are too old to chastise the trees and bushes about the infernal goings-on in the ravines—millennia of scraping and sighing, of sprouting and withering, to no particular purpose. So you should know, that in such an indifferent place you won't be getting any praise for being free. They are all free out there. The chipmunks and the rattlesnakes are free; and yet they sometime seem jealous of my freedom, which they suppose to be less regimented—more broadly circumscribed at least—than theirs. So they bite if they must, or eat my grain before it's safely stored. I began guarding my freedom with a shotgun, but over the years, I never managed to shoot at any creeping, running, or flying thing—I swear. My resident snake knows where I walk and I know where he hunts his mice. We both keep our distance; I kick some brush to give warning; he no longer rattles at me but wiggles slowly across the path so that I can admire him.

Did you ever see a storm race across the roofs of ghetto tenements? It skims the surface as if it doesn't want to get involved in the deeper social problems. The buildings picked by ghetto storms are mostly three stories old, but the top story has long crumbled into the rubble that takes the place of once well-tended gardens. There are many hidden places in all this sadness from which to see the darkling clouds and lightning streaks as they give notice to their arrival with barabooms of thunder. Crumple and rubble, when washed by wind and rain, will glow for our attention to their beauties.

But strong storms, especially in the mid-west, are more insistent than the niceties of enjoyment; they overdo their stay, and we the living are grateful when they finally move past our space. Not that we don't like storms, you see, but because storms, like the rest of us, are nervous; and once they've preened and strutted, need to notice the lateness of time—so they give us a last boom-ba, and move on to share themselves with others.

Storms, unlike divas, are not affronted by audience hostility. A stormic notion of place and time is not ours—although, if one were to ask a storm to stay longer, or leave earlier, it would wonder whether we want to control its cosmic role or make it into art. But we already have too much art that wants to stay forever. If you please then, storm, just go away when you are over—and thanks for showing us what the spaces of your place are like.

Storms on the inside are much like their outside cousins; they attain their clearest form when they are over. "So, how do you feel now that you've vomited and had breakfast? Let's take a walk; the sun is coming out." But inside storms, beneath their sometime need for expurgation, have a differently calibrated intensity than those which occur outside. Their assigned place is within hailing distance of the gateway to the heavens: it is a small and modest but potent nook located somewhere between the pineal gland and the gonadic hang.

Such storms are more circumspect than the ones outside; tief wie das Meer they may be, but what we see are only surface ripples. Inside feelings are never fully expressed (the sound of fear, lust, hatred, despair –shush, what of the neighbors?) If such storms should surface, they are quickly dumped into institutions. But there are other internal storms that elude cures, and generate more than most can show they feel. Annotating such extravagant disturbances is primarily a task for culture-heroes—those who can dive deep down, brave the bends, and bring the weird-fish wiggling and biting back upside, and make them into art.

The red-rocks do not want translation into art; like outside storms, they have no regard for our feelings. Proposing an ontic unity between the duration of cliffs and the flow of our living brings together subjects that have only the whisper of a common place. Some of us do indeed talk familiarly, even conspiratorially, with rocks—but our feelings stay with us when we come down from the cliff and drive home. Because rocks have no feelings they don't miss us, and they will endure for eons if left alone. In their desert sanctuary, rocks protect themselves from aesthetics. Wild rocks, unlike our wild feelings, need no art, and so are not subject to the transient batterings of criticism and good taste.

One can deplore this incommensurability between us and rocks; but whether our human quivers of inadequacy show in the thighs or lips or tender-foot toes, we must have courage. All these red and green encrusted sentinels shall, someday terrible some-day, succumb to human avarice. They will catch the eye of a vile developer and soon be gone. Developers do not talk to rocks; they make them into landscape ornaments or crush them into gravel—either way rocks will lose their separate selves.

I think about the places we almost bought—places that could bring the extant rocks and our own quivers into an irrational but satisfying union. Perhaps it would be better, the sandman says, if you just visit the cliffs from time to time. Better? Maybe si maybe no. There is an old-fashioned metaphysics lurking in my aging bones—a wish to protect primeval nature before it is too-late corrupted by inhuman uses. If we had bought that decaying cabin beneath the cliffs, (you can't see it anymore) we could have said back then: "These rocks are real and we will be rocks among them." But we didn't know that rock-talk would soon be the fashion.

Where I am now is where no one much wants to live. Oh, it's a beautiful place, down by the banks of the Mississippi with sandstone bluffs on either side. Rafts little changed from Jim and Huck compete with barges along the river; catfish and deer are staples enjoyed by the old and inbred families. But there are no jobs to bring in more folks, and few poets are left of the kind that would probe the hot and sweaty river-rat infested perennially flooding land and push their toes deep into the muck along the shore. So here, a Polish-boy from Brooklyn takes his geriatric stand—typing what you now read, painting and pasting on un-stretched canvas, and awaiting the next ten year flood which, they say, will only submerge half the house.

There is no direct way to describe the trip that brought me here; my attempts at consecutive memory are waylaid by fictions of how I came to be—and be here in this place. So I write and you read, and we both face the mix of memory and embellishment that took sixty-odd years of highways and back roads to gel into a pudding of one old Lucian. Well, however it happened, it happened, and I now sit and watch the Mississippi flow by—a river quite as indifferent in its passage as is the stolidity of the desert rocks. The river flows past the troubles of the old-folks stretched beyond their time, and sometimes drowns the young locals, three times divorced, with children they never learned to love. All rivers –as I am told—are like that. But on a winey summer's night, we all—loners, losers, slackers, strivers, meth-heads, and me too—gain absolution from this our own big river—which mostly shows a forgiving face, and gets angry only when the winter melts are more intense than usual. But the river has a lot to teach us. Its practical wisdom can be learned by those who fish, farm, hunt, or just sit and watch the flow come late afternoon.

VII

Place is both a location and a state of mind. Place as location is unsettled by the competing metaphysics of eternal place—those states of mind—from which one views what is true as such, and the particular places of the where's and when's of one's life . Both such places do not comfort a mind that wants the world to not be the same as the day before. They are also of scant comfort to those who want the Good to remain the same.

Mind, when considered in its purity, does not show us something in a place; rather, it shows us that there is nothing in experience which can construct a something that denies the inevitability of change. Those minds which are appalled by the notion of a something become nothing will want an after-place, one that conquers time and encloses change—even when that requires making a nothing beyond existence into a something which we can value as the source of our becoming us.

There are some, Magians mostly, who do not want anything to come from something, or end in nothing. For them, existence stretches infinitely in both these ways as it mounts a challenge to the nothing that others, mostly Christians, say lurks on either side of beginnings and ends.

Those who have Faustian souls say we begin at birth, but do not end in death—as we are a mirror of the world that begins at its own inception and will only end at its end—which is not so much an ending as a resolution of all that has happened. Faustian souls, although not existing before they became themselves, do end after they have become everything they are.

For those of us who would rather have no commerce with soul (a goodly number now) birth and death is all there is. Speculation to the contrary is just so much poetry. So much for poetry.

Although some may reject theological solutions to the question of ends, there remain the difficulties that have to do with the relationship of mind to body—a recapitulation in modern dress of the "who, what, where, when" fugue that has provided continuity for both art and philosophy. Mind that has no place, and a place that is empty of mind, are unsettling notions. Past attempts to resolve this have successively championed one or the other as the only feasible view of reality: Either we create the world through our perceptions, or accept an unperceived world that we don't live in. Will God exist after all intelligible life in the universe has ended—or does He (continue to) exist in a context which is no longer teleological? What after that, then, might He have in mind?

Post-Magians believe that we do not, anymore than do tadpoles, create the world through our perceptions. The world is antecedent to the unexamined solipsism of tadpoles—and it also precedes the fretful solipsism of our own existence. Whether it will continue beyond us, is a matter of extrapolation from the evidence that it was there before we came.

There are those, however—often caricatured as the wooly ones—who affirm the value of "there- thinking" wherever the thinker may contingently be. "There," they say, is neutral between some and nowhere—a good place to hang out. But anywhere (whether "some" or "no") can move us from ecstatic certainty to analytic affirmation. The object, then, is to find the "where" of a "there." The materialist view—a low level of abstraction—locates "wheres" within neurons in the brain. This, dualists counter, is of only elliptical help in such inquiry, for it does little more than illuminate a consequence of brain-surgery—a "there" we can no longer think of when our brain have been altered.

Ideas which propose a brain-free (brainless?) existence for "who's" wherever are their distaff "where's"—typically follow the early morning pee, or come to rosy bloom abetted by the wine of late-afternoon, or perhaps finds their evidence in the sweaty dreams of midnight. The more extreme thesis that offers "who's" who have no "where's" the belief that they (who's) do not need them (where's) deserves respect for its attempt at a new spirituality. This thesis, of course, is open to criticism, and is particularly vulnerable to the rejoinder that "where-less who's," while they may exist in a place ancillary to our rational world, do not share the same modalities, and so cannot offer us evidence that upholds their existence.

A counter-argument to those that would separate "who's" from "where's" offers the hypothesis of common co-existence in time and place, the (widely held) belief that for an event to be characterized as an occurrence, it must be within a physical framework at a certain time in a particular place. Thoughts in the mind and actions in the brain, on this account, are experienced as simultaneous—and through formal if not temporal prioritization, become causally connected.

But the rejoinder argues that terms such as "events" and "occurrences" are static and abstract.

In every time and in all places, there is a programmatic uncertainty about the nature of times and places—even to the point that the locutions "every" and "all" presume a totality that is beyond specification.

One solution, of a religious kind, is to suppose that all variability and uncertainty come together in a brain—not yours or mine—but in an ideal brain that contains all the possible variations in existence past and future. This thesis, among its other virtues, provides defense against anxieties about the threat of nothing—the fear that when the brain stops, the mind ends. It is a comforting faith to believe that one's individual demise is not a chance occurrence, but a proper part of cosmic necessity—a necessity given its law by a (necessary) deity. Our small ripple when we die rejoins the larger waves off shore.

The thesis of an ideal brain can also be found in a secular context. Such a brain locates itself in the expansion of our computational efforts to encompass and encode the material processes of mental function. Its program is to give us a this-worldly version of the transcendent mind: If we could get it down pat, if we could put all the variables, past and future, that are implicit in experience, into one grand self-correcting scheme—we could then grasp what knowing and what knowing that we know, and what knowing we know that we know … finally comes to.

The places of Place do not, these days, compete in the academic lists where the prize is peer acknowledgement of one's true belief about what there is. This reticence is a recent one, its modesty a defense against the forces that categorically champion place as concrete location.

The few adherents of the opposing view—that mind is not reducible to location, are a grab-bag of myopic Hegelians, retired relativists, some artists and nostalgic flower-children, and those skeptics whose interests are directed to undermining reductive theories.

Such skeptics typically don't believe that translations can be definitive or that explanatory theories are cumulative. They believe, instead, that theories are only richer or more meager—depending on what they say that we can use or marvel at. At stake, here, is not the notion that mind is located in the brain. It is, rather, the present poverty of the theory's explanatory and, indeed, predictive function that is at issue. Adherents to the theory of "place-as-mind," are heartened in their beliefs, when they peer across the fence and see how poorly the advocates of "place-as-brain" fare when they try to map the "soft" problems of ethics, aesthetics, consciousness, and the hard ones of strife and warfare, onto a neuronal matrix. Not quite yet but soon, they cry: We'll have an organic handle on all those differences, and will soon be able to offer explanations (as well as panaceas) for every problematic place that has been hindered in finding its empirical location by atavisms of mind-speak—the poetry that refuses to stay in its place.

But mind, the mind-ists say, is not a location. Rather, it has places which it shares (physically but indeterminately) with the brain—but it can also be located (metaphorically) in places that are not the brain. The task of mind-defenders is to fend off the locationists and reductionists whose victory would be the (illusionary) finding that we can locate all this flotsam of thinking, willing, feeling, creating, wanting, despairing, rejecting—time past and time future—within the brain-scans of our bemused compatriots in the medical schools.

The study of physics, as I timidly understand it, has gone beyond location in its search for reality. Quarks, in experimental situations, appear in time-spans that occur only in our recordings. The accelerators that produce ever-smaller, more basic variants are increasingly subject to observational parsimony. How miniscule can these variants be before one can say only that they are fictionally observed—although perhaps not (actually) fictional—for they exist as they are—even when not observed. Now there are strings—a celestial conceit if ever there was one—which are said (finally) to underlie the whole of material nature. Although strings can be figured and reconfigured in theory—as being the most inclusive and explanatory ur-phenomena we have yet to meet, they, by their very formulation, are not subject, being multi-dimensional, to perceptual verification in plain old space and time. They cannot, alas, be so strummed as to (finally) sound the music of the spheres.

The notion of consciousness is analogously difficult. Consciousness, too, is a phenomenon in and of the world—but it is not reducible to the empiricism of place in time—even when it is explained via a tangle of firing neurons. Someday we may sort out each and every tangle—who knows? The "ideal" lurks behind every scientific theory. But for now, the philosophically ambitious mind has become a victim of the medically innocent brain. Brain is now the new pineal gland—the doorway through which we will—very soon—bring together mind and body. Descartes' hope for a seamless transition between the ineffable and the matter-of-fact foundered, among other things, on bad physiology. But there is no doubt (do you still have some?) that everything the mind conceives has correlation with actions in the brain. Where else? Well, also between the toes and out the runny nose—or maybe under a field of ancient thistles at the end of winter—or even in the courts that decide on what should transpire between the where and when of lovers.

"Where else"—that arrogant question—implies that someday we can cap it all: We will finally find the ultimate physical particle and, at the same time, we will stuff mind and its misbehaving surrogate, consciousness, so completely into the brain that there will be no distinction left to pester us.

But some things, you know, are always left outside—those peripheral irritants that test the boundaries of every explanation. Think about the defunct certainties that girded the attempts to reduce language to sense-data and then, through construction, into objects: "Erlebs" join "Qualia" in the salon of benighted visions of transparent reference. This overflow of certainty, these failures, I accept as travails of the soul. But here I give the term 'soul' a special usage—as a name for programmatic uncertainty about what is left over from all attempts to squeeze mind into brain. Soul, in this usage, need not retain a religious sense—although it may. I offer it primarily as a way of marking the distance between what bedevils our present aspirations to become complete in our theories, and the conundrums that in time diffuse our every success. Can we still be optimistic Hegelians without accepting Hegel's final stage for the achievement of spirit? Theories explain only what they say they are about. Everything that does not fit is irrelevant, unknowable, in need of the practice of dancing, the correspondence of scriven images with the moving world, music heard out the windows, and writing poetry about all that.

VIII

Speaking of the soul can indeed be poetry, but that does not exclude it as a way of truth-telling. Soul need not be an ecumenical scold; it is in good company when it is offered as collusion with the mind that has no better offer for a merger during this political impasse with the brain. But the soul is also a conceit of ecumenical promise. Let us give this a poetic transference: Soul is firmly in the brain, to the same extent that the mind is there as well.

A secret pact seems to be afoot! Soul and brain together, in serious negotiation with the mind, could mitigate the uncertainties that afflict each separately. Mind, in this pact, does not have to choose exclusive alliance with either soul or brain. We may agree that mind is a phenomenon of brain, but this only is to say that the fully explained brain will take some time to account for all that mind is about. The disparity between times, the residue that bubbles up between succeeding explanations, is what I term the soul.

Appetites, ambitions, loves and hates, are indeed rooted in both mind and body—good and evil is there, ugliness and beauty too—as are ideals, pledges of allegiance, blasphemies and travesties of justice—as well as the ordinary mindful acts of living lives. There is also contained, through a categorical ascent, but with doctrinal disguises, all that is in the soul as well. If we want to be stubbornly empirical and insist that all this containing is only in the brain, we should locate our arguments outside of the consciousness from which we argue.

My objections to mind and brain identity need not be taken as an affirmation of mind-body duality, much less as a soul-mind-body trinity. I question, instead, the notion that there is ever an achievable completeness of explanation, specifically, the notion that explanation, when systematically pursued, and given good will and ample time, will merge with the subject of explanation, namely, itself. If mind and brain indeed would merge, the explanations that define both, and the circumstances of their union, will, to my mind, have to face the charge of question-begging—of ignoring what and who the merger needs to remain outside itself for its success.

Ruben's painting of "The union of earth and Water." is a masterful depiction of an ideal communion which, despite the drama of lustful storms cohabiting with needy droughts—and the allure of its principals—is not about to happen.

Carnap famously distinguished between two forms of judgment: one made within the system of inquiry (the workings of scientific method), the other, about the system of inquiry (the philosophical justification of scientific method). Someone in his group asked: What, then, is the form of the judgment you have just made? It is neither within the workings of the system nor about its justification. So it must only be about validating this sense of theory through a further judgment, one which holds that this first pairing of distinctions is not the fundamental basis for the system of inquiry. The impasse thus created, between the logical impossibility of finding an innocent object-language ground for the proliferation of meta-languages in explanation, threatened to break Carnap's theory. All such justifications require their own justification—and the loop thus formed does not supply a starting point for the wanted construction that, for the theory to succeed, should be based upon pre-linguistic certainty. Given this, the hope for a veridical correspondence between language and the world, upon which empirical claims can unequivocally be based, becomes an illusion. Such theorizing then breaks into an array of claims—each justified more by separate pragmatic needs than by unity in their modes of explanation.

One variant of correspondence theories occurs in aesthetic writings by Monroe Beardsley, although here the correspondence occurs not between the world and its descriptions, but between art and prosaic efforts to explain it. Beardsley attempts to account for literary meaning through a consecutive and cumulative series of paraphrases. each shedding more light upon the latent meaning of the art-work. The question here is: Can the sense (or meaning) of, say, a poem, be exhausted through an array of literal explications which, with time and diligence, gets ever closer to the actual sense of that poem? In this aesthetic, the critic usurps the role of the poet in presenting us with more precise versions of poetic meaning. The explication becomes the source of meaning; the poet the provider of latent content.

We could agree that art-works of all varieties come to a richer understanding through their interpretations. But then we should also say that interpretations change and meanings dissolve as taste and history stir the pot. There is no "meaning" (contra Beardsley) that an art-work finally "has," however tall the stack of its paraphrases.

Explanation requires a supervenience (not a theory of analysis, but a process of accumulation) which supports explanation by gathering past memories, present descriptions, family attitudes, forebodings about the future—as well as the day to day accounts of pain and pleasure—all of which identify, not meaning, but an arena of shifting interests which contains those things that we, from time to time, notice enough to want to explain—to give meaning to.

This sounds slippery, I admit. How does one do explaining without clearly circumscribing the landscape of concern? How do we delimit the aggregate of possibilities from all we can surmise and dream to what it is we are explaining?

Art and its practitioners have had no problem with limits—exclusion is often more valued than inclusion; it signals a change in style and a deepening of historical imperatives. Change in art is a signal that extant efforts are exhausted—not devalued—only done with. Philosophy, however, has a different take on historical succession. Systematicity, here, is greedy: what we include in explanation refers back to the errors in all that we have discarded. Philosophy, given Hegel's prodding, has had hopes for a theory of everything; but, as in physics, the hopes are at this point more metaphysical than they are demonstrations of how the world is.

Art wants a world; philosophy wants the world. But philosophy also has a habit of avoiding the part of the world that is not susceptible to accepted modes of explanation. Art, in contrast, is irreverent, wanting and yet dreading the incommensurable that becomes actual, and—as monsters often do—offers itself seasonally for a new mode of appreciation. Neither art nor philosophy should be vocations. Arting, in its practice, has no way to win or lose; philosophy depends too much on its seduction by irrelevant sources of argument.

There is, of course, the ancient quarrel between art and philosophy, between appearance and reality, truth and feeling, the world as it is and as it is perceived. This is a quarrel that will not be resolved. Nor should we, on pain of boredom, want it to be. Accepting the inevitability of this quarrel is an insight reflecting the ancient wisdom that not all things can be brought together, that human existence is not a whole—rather, it is stitched, and unraveled, as on an n-dimensional tapestry, through its contrary descriptions.

Each array (theory, system, style) is limited in its time while continuing, even after its run, to clamor for attention. After the praises of achievement become dim and sporadic, the created whole, and the credibility of its array, begins to crumble. Art needs new subjects; science new insights, and philosophy needs a new mission that can recast its old insights.

IX

Artworks have no place, no more than they have a physical description that circumscribes the particulars of their artness. The marble carvings and the welded beams, with their privileged sites, are no more in a particular place than are the printed versions of successful poems.

Think of the Elgin Marbles, named after an Englishman, first scrutinized by ancient Greeks, in passing by Turkish invaders, later, as pillage, affording neo-classic raptures to Victorian Englishmen, and recently, in facsimile, adorning university stairwells—reminders for undergraduates of the relevance of higher education. Where then, among all these is the place of the Elgin Marbles—that place in which their meaning can be ascertained, their qualities best enjoyed, and their influence on the future of art and life most clearly assessed? Evidently, there is no such place. Instead, there is a narrative, itself incomplete, of places and responses, and the more we read, the more this narrative rewrites itself—as do the greater histories of which it presumably is part.

Physicality does not confer identity to art. I wonder, in passing, whether anything or anyone achieves identity through a material place: Maybe in the country—but even there among the corn stalks, the old familiars die, the young permit the weeds to grow, their offspring uproot the weeds and sell the place to speculators. So too with the relics in Grandma's attic, sold upon her death to the wily antique-dealer, and now cohabiting with Kwakiutl carvings in a pent-house condominium.

There are places where art can hide and avoid bringing its makers into early prominence, despite being given hopes by the older to the younger that, by playing hard but within the style of a thousand years, they could be among the acknowledged living and remembered dead—like us.

Old art is a vampire that demands a string of progeny, with ancient perpetrators biting young and willing necks—so as to ensure that the originary line is closed to outsiders, yet alive in familial derivation.

But young art, unless it dumbly succumbs to the toys and joys of ancients, has no mandate to be kind to those old scribblers of the ineffable. They, unspeakable elders, limp divers into the core of moist young things, fractured planners for the once large reach—still dreaming of their place in the all-inclusive theory of everything—they deserve no rescue.

Titian's nudes never smell; Rembrandt's sometimes do. But, ah, the musk of the girls of Rubens and Courbet. After Cezanne's bathers, though, nobody wanted to know whether the local girls smell or not, because they all have lost their ardor.

They have (how did it happen?) become abstract—except for some old-age Picassos, where he winds his dark-green brush up the cleft in the backside of a surprised cubist nude. Abstraction is bad for smell and indifferent to taste—although it is wonderful for sound. I am for the reintroduction of smell into painting—so as to confront its role of just hanging placid on a wall.

Smell is a good authenticator of place, because you cannot indifferently pass a place when it smells a smell you can't but recognize. Brothels once perfumed their places as beacons for my stumble-bum forbears; and the latest salons of fashion now insist we cannot know the difference between scent and stink unless we come inside, have a glass or two, and be shown the price of fashionable smell. Most places are connected, like most lovers, with their smells, and the interpretations of artworks should include the smells of places they have passed through. Van Gogh, Gauguin, and friends did not smell the same in the café Momus as they do hanging in the latest hallowed halls.

The place of art changes with its smells; even the most enduring of our loves smell different as the years go by. Does a Titian Venus attain a sharper edge of funk after we have looked our fill at Dekooning's women?

Wagner and Kandinsky wanted, in their ways, to bring the senses together within an aesthetic place and time. Wagner strove to establish his works as the foundation for the (historically inevitable) synthesis of all art forms: the Gesamtkunstwerk. Kandinsky was less political and wanted only to affirm, through his own work, its offering of the common elements found in the all the arts—namely, art as a source for the trans-sensual unity of spirit.

John Cage permitted random sound to join with whatever noises his compositions make—an experience we can also have while listening to Bach by an open window. It depends, as Cage accepts—and Bach—who knows?—on what we listen for. Kant famously did not like the sound of music because he found it intrusive—they say the daily hymns required of prisoners in the jail just down the street clinched it for him.

The sound of paintings and the look of music needs a more empathic study—one that should bypass the many tedious attempts to uphold the sanctity of realms. But then there is the sense of taste. which needs to distinguish itself, all the more these days, from taste to value—"good-taste" is not the same as "tasting good."

Taste is intimately involved with smell. If the receptors in either smell or taste are compromised, the other does not function well. We can smell at great distances: the acrid smell of forest fires, or the upbeat smell, when crossing Brooklyn Bridge, of the coffee-roasting plant, or the fetid stench from garbage dumps on the south side. Taste does not have this distance—you put your mouth to it, and wipe your chin or smack your lips when the tasting ends. But both taste and smell have first claim on place in memory, and both marinate our older years with wafts of once upon that time. We then shake our heads and stand erect, although less straight than once ago, and we fasten onto nearby sights and sounds as protective barriers against what we remember smelling and tasting back in that some time ago.

Actually, memories of how things smell and taste is a young pursuit, fitted to the feral forests of prey and love. Remembering is more for older folk, pork-bellied by maturity, who cannot any longer run down a deer, nor have the derring-do to rip and slurp what others have left at the entrance to the cave. Rather, clearing a space between the bones, they concentrate on slow-low-cooking, even as they slap at the also-hungry flies. Some young folks do that too, but they are quicker at coming to the end of it. Not having memories of ancient gluttonies, they are gone before morning to find some of their own.

"Good Taste," in these late days, is not much about tasting; it leaves its intimate companionship with saliva and looks for a more distant partner. Taste now abdicates its youthful role as enabler of prurience, gluttony, and other life-preserving functions, to assume a role as referee of aesthetic and cultural value. So construed, it takes on a putatively normative mode, the referee between high and low taste, which, in our social scheme of preferences, addresses the important choices—those by which we acquire a valuable artwork, or ancient items of décor, or an admired companion—and so enjoy the acclaim of privilege and success.

Choosing while knowing that your choice does not fit with the tastes of others, can sometime affirm your sensibility as one which exhibits superior—even novel—taste (for serious consideration in the salons of the future). But it can also be likened (accompanied by a wash of giggles) to baring the plebian backside of your tenement past—where memories of musty smells still survive. Why on earth, then, should you risk evoking these memories and their qualities- for the titillation of pure-bred high-steppers?

Well, no, I don't want to. It may once have been that, but it is now because these memories, and their evocations, are all I have left to offer to slow the demise of my "who." They also provide a measure of what I was and where I still want to go. You, my lovelies, can fill in the spaces between.

There were chances to go to the place where I could have been more were I not me. I now think of those places whenever I sit on the pot, and I remember my young infatuation with the ideals of lust and ambition. When I get off (the pot, that is) I think about how—and occasionally why—it ends up where it does? But ending is only an idea of sufficient closure—as dying is nothing but the indifferent way-station to nullity.

Where dying actually takes place is mostly of sentimental concern; where ending occurs is impersonal and historical. Ending is a function of how what one has done continues to be exist for those whose birth is not yet in sight. And so ending is more feared than dying by those of us who suspect they didn't do their best to be something more than what can be seen in the residue of their death.

X

Lucian, what a scold you have become! Yes, I agree—a perk of aging. But you, young folks out there, I say to you that mortality vies with consciousness as a way to discern the value of life. That we must die is a reason for our periodic need to hurry the best construction of our end. Otherwise, we give up to silence all we have done and want to do (and yet by god can still do!) as penance for all those frippety times-wasted that scolds say lead to merely dying.

Affirmation, albeit with due celebration of the end of effort—that is the usual response to dying; There are the familial visits: (My, how good you look—Does the pain bother you?). Affirmation can also be (an ancient custom) the sharp and fat-smeared knife given to old sled-dogs, so that their licking, in the unfeeling arctic cold, will enlist their own blood for a tasty way to slip into the dark.

It is comforting to think that dying is not fungible—it parochially goes one way. In contrast, ending, as here considered, recurs whenever someone in another place fishes deep and reels you up from your solitude in the archives of the lower depths, that is, if you have done enough to be counted with the other deep-water fish that also offer fine fillets.

Have no illusions; you are not being brought to a later surface to live some more. Your role (as an end) is only to be subject to a consideration of what you have done. (Your dead friends contribute to this consideration—but bear in mind that they have end-related ambitions too).

Is ending, then, with all its post-life calumnies and only occasional after-life faint-praise, preferable to simply dying? I think so, yes. But why? Because we yea-sayers believe that the coruscating judgment of who you are as an end—as laid out by judges however corrupt or prescient—is preferable to the pain of having just one death, without reference to your end, and so, just dying.

Death has no place—it does occur in places someone knows, but then it vanishes into the context of not being anywhere that is a somewhere. The old trilogy of heaven, hell, and purgatory no longer does the trick of placing anything you might be interested in into a "where." Avoid death, I suggest to you, if you can. Ending, on the other hand, is stronger; it has a different reason for attracting folks like you and me—a reason that demands recall as a paradigm for continuing to get attention. When you do not, as the poet advised, go quiet into that dark night, your roars (complaints, demands, entreaties) will be less about dying than pragmatics for your end-game.

Listen and look, the street-person says: It is what I have—the only thing—but it is more, at end, than is your dying. For I am none other than old Joe Gould—and in this bag, somewhere in there, is my "Oral History of the World." It is, as you know, not finished. How could it be? But as no one else is reading it—perhaps because they cannot find it—it has not yet settled into its ending place. But there is, yes, one such place—a secret one, which, although obscure, does not allow dead Seagull-Joe to end.

The chance to do a shuffle that substitutes ending for dying in the play of life is worth paying attention to, especially for you young folks who are barely alive as yet. Ending, for the reassurance of still-ambitious liver-uppers, occurs in many places—and each end is expected to accrue in value between generations.

But some ending-places also do well in fallow times—despite the fixations of collectors, art and life change in their attractiveness. Selling too early is always a mistake: you can't buy the better place of a more prescient ender at a price you can afford.

Then, without a good place to end, you anyway will die. The aftermath of dying, in-itself, does not have a place. But even the absence of a no-place in which to not-be might be preferable, after all, to opting for the fuss—as designated by factotums of such things—that continuing to end in actual places will be like. Maybe just dying, is better—don't you think?

5

Before Beginning and After Ending

I

The universe begins with a "big-bang," and ends with a "slow-burn." So go recent theories about the beginning and ending of everything. Whether these are true or not, or whether they get truer (with finessing) as we go along, seem to me questions of impenetrable duration and profundity; truth and falsity may not extend that far. My interest here is only in some implications of such theories: What is the state of affairs before beginnings and after endings? Does the obvious answer "nothing" have any meat left in it? Are there other answers, and if not, are these distaff "nothings," facing each other across millennia, the same?

To ask what it was like before anything began, requires a lot of conceptual discarding. To begin before the beginning, one must put on hold such notions as "time, space, and causality"—for they are specific to our own circumstances, and lie within the parameters of "after it began" and "before it ends." What we replace them with is much harder—"how it began" is more mysterious than "how it ends"—the first more easily centered in theology, the second more empirical.

The terms "world, universe, and cosmos" have multiple, often overlapping meanings in ordinary usage: The world is where we are and what we can know about it. "World" is also profitably used as a limiting term—the world of politics, or fashion, or our inner world. Its external reference stops at the outer limits of our intended locale, or at the internal limits of the crawl space into our intimacies. The term also serves, more neutrally, as a contextual demarcator of what we want to talk about: "Let us consider the world of . . ."

"Universe" has a larger referent—as large, mostly, as we can make it. The universe is not ours, as contrasted with "our world." It does, however, contain our world and—if we believe in such things—other worlds as well. "Universe" includes all that is knowable, but follows along the edges of its own expansion into the unknown and thus raises the question, akin to the "where" before it all began, namely, the "what" into which it is expanding. There can be many worlds, but there should only be one universe.

"Cosmos" is an all-purpose term—ranging over "world" and "universe" and the subject of the academic study—cosmology—that, purportedly, is of everything. It is also a slippery catch-all: "Cosmic" replaces "cool" (or "hot") in popular circles, and serves as a pendant around the erudition of an overblown sage. Use it cautiously.

The past of our world can be represented, excavated, causally configured, idealized, appealed to, or denigrated when unruly events dictate, or even (at our peril) ignored. The past is something of a plaything for our present—although we are still too young a world to understand the directions that our past and present will take it in the future. The past's insistence on its presence in our present mirrors the incessant slippage of our present into the past—as well as our fear that, in the process, we have forgotten something that needs remembering. Would that there were some way to keep our present in the present— to keep it free from obsession with the past and from anxiety about the future. Animals enjoy this—but we have no way to do this—even though there are morning chants and stretching exercises devoted to its realization.

The further back we go in time in our search for what "really" happened, the harder it is to keep the narrative orderly. We have now (some of us) delegated the Olympian Gods (my, aren't they an interesting bunch) and Buddha, Brahma, Mohammed, and the Judeo-Christian Jehovah with his triune offspring, to imaginative constructions of the way it must have been for it to be the way it has become. These constructions evoke a reality for which there once was no better explanation. Whether the eternal—or, now, occasional—gods still have appetites and perform ablutions, whether they (still) lord it over us whenever they get our attention, and whether we will really feel the flames of hell as an eternal sitting on a red-hot stove (the sensations in heaven are harder to describe) are questions we no longer care to answer, except within the competition of poetic conceits or the cynicism of tawdry politics.

II

What happens (let us use the timeless present) before the beginning to make it begin? This question, as best I know, remains a conundrum within "big-bang" theories. There is little problem with the milli-seconds after the event—for causality starts just then and is expressed in both space and time. Nor are there problems with the rate of expansion that takes us from a first "b" into the constantly expanding universe of our present state of affairs. The conundrum lies, rather, in the nature of "pre-bang" inertia (or pre-existential indifference). "Why?" Leibniz states, is not an illegitimate question to direct at nothing. So why, then, would "change" come to "germinate" within the nothing that precedes (but contains the "seeds" of) post-bang process. How does "something" occur within "nothing" to produce something else?

This is a language of metaphors which may incidentally be poetical but which shows the difficulties of finding words for the concepts at issue. "Process," "time," "change" and the like, are all terms that describe the reality we experience. The "scare quotes" lift them out of ordinary usage into a more exotic—if more befuddled—context; but they help us wonder. Another way, however, would be to find terms for a reality about which these empirically bounded terms describe only a part: not the part that begins after the big-bang, but the part before.

The conundrum of ends has different, if related, difficulties. True, nothing we know—that we call beginnings—has ever ended; we see beginnings and endings as simply transformations from or into something else. There is no creation out of nothing in our experience (although there can be in our imagination) nor is there any extinction into nothing—we cannot free ourselves of the residue of the something that keeps us—within the world of being—"us."

But there are other considerations that show the asymmetry between the extremes of "pre-being" and "post-being." We know that we will end, although we did not know, back then before our birth, that we are about to begin. There was, for us, no anxiety about our birth—although there undoubtedly was discomfort. There is, however, anxiety about our death, whatever the discomforts. We are anxious about the end of consciousness because we will not (then) know that we have ended. We (now) know that after our ending, we will have no further claim to our being than have the galaxies that are swallowed by ever-ravening black-holes. But such galaxies will continue to have an existence, however diminished—although we surely have conceptual difficulties in correlating their compression with our non-being.

If it so happen that our sun burns itself out, resigning itself and its particular galaxy to the quietistic seductions of entropy and the absolute zero of stasis—then no one of our kind will remain as a witness to a changeless burnt-out world. This situation, however, retains existence although it is located just this side of nothing. Therefore, the end of our world is not a denial of time—merely a caesura in its flow.

Such a motionless time—even in the juice of its contradiction—does not mirror the timelessness before anything at all began, because the fate of future time is understood by us to be a consequence of causal change—and it thus remains an (empirical) prediction, as well as a (universal) memory. Then too, our solar system—our world, is not co-equal with the universe, so that while our own residue may be doomed to stasis, other suns, other worlds, may well provide conditions for life and change.

Against this, the thought that "everything ends"—even if only concerned with our meager patch of the heavens, leaves us buried in romantic retrospection, or sullen indifference, or eschatological gladness that the end will finally come. This end depends on our end.

This transition into the nothing after ending is not as devoid of notice as is the nothing before the beginning—in the way that our death is not as devoid of anticipation as was our time before our birth. We, the living, are still here, thinking about this second nothing—and our poets and physicists continue to raise the possibility that, elsewhere in the universe, there are observers to watch our slide—and perhaps to effect the rescue of something that we are—even after we end.

III

How it is before the universe began is best approached as a linguistic question—about the contextual use of "before" and "after." How the universe ends is, however, not only a linguistic question (although it is that too) but also an empirical question because we can theorize about it here and now. Unlike the matter of "beginnings," about which we have no antecedent knowledge, "ends" is suffused with our history and our science, all of which we can use to ruminate about the conditions on the way to just before our end. These conjectures about "after ending," which rest on the slide of time into stasis—that state of "frozen duration"—are more conceptually friendly than are conjectures—on the distaff side—about how non-being is transformed into (our) being. With endings, we have no need for the transformation of nothing into something—with beginnings we do.

If we take a benign view about all this and poetically identify our own death with the universal end, we can think of both as "proper parts" of cosmic process. This is a soothing alternative to extra-worldly intimations of heaven and hell; it also proclaims our independence of the something that remains after we are nothing. Yet, our belief in the rightness of separating our selves from the base materials of our remains may only be a ratio-centric poultice which covers our fear of the attenuation of something (that is not quite nothing) into the just nothing after death.

"Rightness," here, deserves a last aria, in which our reflective life, despite its brevity, is sung as contributing to the cosmic process. Free-will ends with death, and death is, alas, a given. But our living (as opposed to "mere" life) is, if anything, the exercise of a considered volition. This is species-centric, to be sure, but humans have historically voiced concern that the cosmic creaking of the expanding universe does not encourage disruption (or re-direction) by an exercise of free will.

III

What to do? Well, we cannot do without language, but we can rid ourselves of some baggage. I offer a few considerations that may suggest a way out of this impasse: Let us imagine the state of affairs before time to be an unbounded lottery in which infinite combinations or "arrays" of components (on the model of "numbers") configurate into the conditions that lead, or do not lead, to the transformation of possible worlds into potential worlds—to an array being a candidate for actuality through some version of a "big-bang." How many such combinations are there? Can there be more than one big-bang? Hard to tell: Before the fact, possible worlds are as infinite as are numbers. So becoming an actual world is not a necessary outcome of "pre-being"—although, evidently, it is a possible outcome. But even if becoming were somehow inherent in the nature of pre-being, there is no necessity that any successful array would result in our own world. If we (taking ourselves as evidence) consider our becoming as a necessary characteristic of "pre-being," we can also consider our being as a luck of the draw. Other possible worlds are also candidates for such becoming—although, to be sure, such worlds may be inaccessible to ours.

I use "number" as the metaphoric name of the components of the arrays that generate becoming because numbers are good metaphors for the constituents that link being with non-being. Although numbers do not occur in non-being, they suggest distinctions that make it easier for us to consider the grounds of any such occurrence (and there must be some such) that results in (at least) our being.

Numbers are prior—conceptually if not historically—to graven images in the Western tradition of cosmic wonder: Number is for the explanation of reality; images are the facsimiles of actuality. While numbers "in-themselves" are infinite, as used here they become finite constituents of each array they enter into. Otherwise, there would be no arrays—no possibility of "winners"—only strings of infinite extension—which would not permit the candidacies of any specific arrays to compete for the prize of potentiality for being. If there were no limit to the constituents of arrays, there would be no finite difference between, and no limit to, their strings. They would then all fail in presenting themselves as the "winning match" that provides the onset of "becoming"—this first disruption in non-being that continues on through possible into potential into actual being, and hence into a world.

No array in pre-being is dependent upon (our posterior calculations of) probabilities for its chances of success as a potential candidate for an actual "big-bang." In the no-where of pre-being, all candidates float free (untouched by temporal or normative agency) in a universe that is composed of nothing but infinite alternations of numerical arrays.

So how does it happen that something (the choice of a particular array) does happen? One is tempted to posit yet another level of abstraction, as with Plato's "region beyond the heavens" in which universes lose and take on value through the inscrutable actions of a "Demi-urge." But we here cannot know the nature of such determinations in any non-theological sense of knowing—no more than we can know whether there is pre-being, whether it is composed of arrays that engender universes such as ours, or whether there are universes with priorities other than ours. We cannot know, but we can conjecture based on what we do know.

How the transition between pre-temporal uniformity and temporal differentiation occurs is a critical issue. First, we must question our dependence on "limits"—as with the beginnings and endings of life, the rise and fall of empires, geologic creation and calamity in nature. Against all this we posit the realm of the unlimited: symbol systems such as number and language, and musings about the scope of eternity and infinity. But the former are our life-and-death concerns, while the latter, of course, are our defenses—the weapons of our exoteric language. Our efforts to reconcile these contrasts lead to such puzzles as "nothingness" taken as a "state," and such bemusements (to which I contribute here) as pre-and post-being—that is to say, the "state of affairs" that subsists before anything begins, and the one (surely not the same one) that subsists after everything ends.

We can imagine the achievement of one combination of numbers, out of all possible arrays, that in fact generates the conditions for the being of our own universe: time, space, causality, and development. There are other combinations, we can also imagine, that generate the conditions for other possible worlds—which may have much or little similarity to ours. A question here: Is not the exit from non-being into being compromised by the possibility that we are its only issue? Why such cosmic histrionics just for us? We then (shaking off the admonitions of inerrantists) more humbly ask: How many promising arrays (potential worlds) are there in pre-being?

One way of answering: The distinction between "possible" and "potential" raises the issue as to whether "non-being" (unrequited nothing), devolves into "pre-being," (differentiated nothings) and so permits the distinction between "possible-world arrays," and "potential-world arrays." All arrays in non-being, let us say, are candidates for being. The demarcation wanted here, then, is between "possible" and "potential"—"possible" being a logical description applying to all arrays; "potential" being an insertion into non-being of the competitive seed of being. Pre-being contains as many arrays as there are possible combinations of variables—there is an infinity of those—although there are only finite variables within each possible array. In this way of measuring, there is closure for the time-anticipating transition between possible to potential to actual worlds (from non-being to pre-being to being).

What, then, is the "competitive seed of being?" It is to be found in the mind-blowing move from the possible to the potential. We could hold that in pre-being only some few potential worlds can occur out of all possibles. Then we could winnow this further by holding that only one actual world (ours, perhaps) issues from all potentials. This direction of thought, however, requires appeal to a choice-making agent (or agency)—the inscrutable action of, at least, a Demi-Urge; or the aggressive preferences of the Christian God. In any case, we need a mover here (not necessarily "prime," but one conversant with the characteristics of non-being) to adjudicate the transition between possible to actual.

But it may also be that distinctions between arrays are due to patterns of their "rubbings" against each other. Nothing needed here of "creation." What comes to pass is the consequence, as in a lottery, of which numbers make it through the hole between possibility and potentiality—and, on another day, between potentiality and actuality. What then is needed is an opening adequate to the passage of numbers, and a vessel or "receptacle" that admits just the number (of numbers) that makes a world.

We can also theorize that there are cases beyond ours of this transition between potentiality and actuality. The notion of proliferating worlds independent of ours does not require that there will be interaction among them. Let us suppose, then, that alternative worlds are indeed independent of each other at inception—in the scenario that gives each world its own big bang for reification and expansion. Assuming that time is the enabling factor for being, we can imagine alternative worlds that, as time goes on (why are there many worlds but only one time?) may indeed come to intersect with ours, when constituents overlap (or mirror, or otherwise are compatible with ours) in such properties as, say, geologic similarity and symbolic capacity.

IV

Still, this leaves us with the same problem that faces the advocates for our uniqueness. How does the bare concept of "possibles" generate a freighted concept of "actuals?" How does our world, and perhaps worlds other than ours, become actual? The term "possible world" is often used as a modal strategy for prediction—to codify the variables of knowing and not-knowing so as to determine the epistemic paths to worlds, actual or fictional, that are parallel to to ours—whether these locate in spatio-temporal contexts that are not ours; or whether they are merely aesthetic constructs of of the cognitive difficulties we encounter when our four-square view of reality fails us.

Here, I restrict the term "possible worlds" to arrays in pre-being that are candidates for potential and, hence, actual being. There are no possible worlds in "being"—only actual ones; as there are no actual worlds in "pre-being"—only possible ones.

The actual world we know has certain features: It changes, becomes more complex (in our way of viewing) progresses and becomes more ordered (in our way of hoping) expands the borders that define it (in our way of measuring).

In the previous section, I suggest that change is a factor of interactions between actual worlds whose components overlap. "Development" (at least for us) indicates compatibility (a mutual interest) between properties of possible worlds, while "disarray" is a corrosive redundancy (antagonism) between intruding properties of other worlds. "Progress" can be seen as an expansion of the fields these worlds inhabit, with the further possibility of a unity of fields—which (some say) is the source of "good" in our—and optimistically—other worlds. "Regress," in contrast, is an incompatibility between the interplay of multi-world properties which reveals the debilitating possibility of randomness or premature closure. Here, determinate change is supplanted with chaos or constriction—the source (others say) of everything that is bad in our world.

We typically embrace the good as manifest, and blame the bad on the vagaries of our own efforts. We might instead, following my scenario, direct praise or blame onto the intersection between our world and the worlds accessible to ours. Choosing between these is much like our present efforts to predict our future—but with the difference that prediction is forever anxious about what has been left out, while accepting a possible world into our actual one, might be based on something like a diplomatic agreement—how much of mine and how much of yours can we share—and how much of the residue will we both be willing to ignore?

V

Moving away from politics into cosmology: The play between "dispositions" (to act) and "actions"—the transition, across the "big-bang" between potential and actual—may offer clues as to what prompts the great cosmological prologue to our first conundrum: "How is it that something comes out of nothing?" This is a more optimistic question than is Leibniz's "Why is there something rather than nothing?" "Why?" wants a reason; "how" wants a description; "why are there" is theological, "how is it" is evidential. In the human psyche, dispositions precede and do not always entail actions—but sometimes they do. As our world is a consequence of the "big-bang," it is (at least inferentially) feasible that it (our world) replicates the forces—dispositions and actions—that generated the primordial moment.

We usually relegate dispositions and actions to the human psyche. But I suggest that these terms are also apt metaphors with which to describe both sides of the "big-bang." To consider "pre-being" as a uniform nothingness from which (unaccountably) erupt the seeds of our universe, seems less satisfactory than going the other way. I use the term "array" to describe the minimal differential that distinguishes non-being from nullity, and so effects the progression from possible to potential to actual. In doing this we work from the differentia of our (actual) world and regressively exclude them. The arrays that define possible worlds are the minimal differences that we must maintain in order to separate something from nothing. There should, then, be "something" in pre-being—if indeed the supposition is at all cogent.

Reversing the direction of conjecture—from being to pre-being—it becomes easier to describe the conditions which an array in a potential world should satisfy for it to become the action that results in our existence. These conditions are like the conditions that govern our actual world—but the developmental force of "like" remains a mystery. Relieved of empirical responsibility, we can suppose that such a "likeness" occurs in germ in some "disposition" that differentiates between the arrays, and further suppose that some pattern of likeness engenders a first action, the "big-bang" that produces an actual world.

This, of course, argues from known conditions to their unknown ancestors. The array that corresponds to the creation of the actual world is unknowable until after the fact—but its consequence is that we have the capacity to marvel at our own being and the fecundity and variety (if we see it that way) of the world we live in, and then we can suppose that our capacity is like that of its antecedent conditions.

The arrays in pre-being do not result in action except when they do—and we are the example we know. The terms I use to describe human action and desire only metaphorically apply to the conditions for the "big-bang." But they do suggest that there is an analogy between our psychological dispositions and the characteristics that distinguish between the infinite arrays of "pre-being"—so that, when some array is "disposed" to elude the conventions that govern non-being, it "recognizes" its difference, its precocity, and crosses over into being to create the novel dimensions of a world, our world—and we are the result.

There are, however, conjectures that would counter the story here being told. The "big-bang" hypothesis, after all, is a fanciful tale, supported by indirect evidence, beautiful mathematics, and bolstered by such considerations as the subject-predicate structure of language, Hegelian notions of "progress" and "dialectic," and the theory of evolution. There also is Christian eschatology—the story of creation, death, and transfiguration.

But there are other stories that take little notice of the preoccupation with beginnings and ends. Plato, famously, diminishes "becoming" through the (ontic) dependence of its subjects on the unchanging reality of his "eternal forms". Aristotle views actuality as the achievement of potential—a perfecting of the promise inherent in all types and species. In neither case, though, is there concern with beginnings or ends. The eternal forms, by definition, are eternal, and so are indifferent to notions of becoming and ending. Aristotle, although he is more amenable to sequence than is Plato, also requires all actions (and even dispositions) to cumulatively match the perfection of its kind. Even Heraclitus, of the ever-changing river, does not deal with questions of origin and destination; it is enough that the river changes, imparting an admonitory note to both our identity and mortality. But its hypothetical origin in the northern trickles, and its end in the delta of the southlands are for him of no philosophical importance. Compared with these ancients, the Christian preoccupation with beginnings and ends—the "original sin" that starts it all, and the "state of grace" that ends it—shows more anxiety about the perils of achievability than do its classical antecedents.

VI

The question of "what it will be like after the world ends," carries the taint of philosophic futility. It would be tidy if we could just reverse the procedure that got us here—if we could turn our linear worlds of action into a circle, and adopt a version of Nietzsche's "eternal return."—that there is neither end nor beginning—only recapitulation.

But this now makes little sense. The "big-bang" may have begun the universe, but the death of our sun will not end it. There are other galaxies around—they are there, even if beyond negotiable distances. So our descendants may then (a long time from now) migrate to other sites, perhaps in other solar systems, before the "big-burnout" occurs. But I wonder. Technology, once the engine of expansion, could suffer incremental defeats as the world cools without our permission.

With space-travel become more than a dream, the ones at the end of our world could enjoy the historical asymmetry that they, as contrasted with all the middle-voyagers, are actually there—watching the hurricane come ashore. We and they both know that no one was there when the gas expanded at our beginnings—but this only reinforces the asymmetry, and draws out its implications: that these last ones will face the question—which we have, through the ages, been putting off—the question of whether this is all there is.

Some say that in fifty billion years or so, our sun will be done, a charred cinder in a cold region of space; and our precious planet become a speck blown by winds that nothing notices—"noticers" of our kind, by that time, being long gone. The special configuration of our "big-bang" has indeed given us a good ride, but we do not want to tell the tale about when it ends—or about the special relationship between beginnings and ends—just to appease the god of symmetry. We will-be-enders must face the task of accounting for the world before everything is gone—even as we try (a harder task) to account for the non-being from which everything came. That tiniest moment we trace back to beginnings is at farthest remove from the radio-active decay that, we suppose, will mark the end of our world. But this end, however long, is not the same as the end of time. It is only the end of time as parochially measured. One difficulty with my earlier story is the posit of finite components in the arrays of pre-being. These, I argue, are necessary for anything at all to happen. Now, extending my story to endings, I face the reverse problem: Endings are in time (not our time, but the still finite time of the big-bang). Is there, however, a way with ends that will have their exhaustion augur the end of time, and so replicate, through the cessation of becoming, the non-event of pre-being?

Here the knowing subject of "ends" faces a different circumstance from the knower of "beginnings." "What was it like before the world began?" is an optimistic, even poetic, question. We were not there, but we, after all, are here. We enjoy the gift of consciousness; and we can therefore spin our tales about how we, and all the rest, came to be. We are here, we say, somewhere between the big-bang and the big-burn-out: The former begins time, and the latter stretches it into indifference. We are in that tiny span between the two in which we can explain time through number, and, because number is powerful, we create variants of time to fit what else needs explaining. But we cannot, if we accept the notion of "beginnings and ends," deny the thesis of the big-bang and still accept time—for its denial challenges number—which may be a basic ingredient of our consciousness. The big-bang thesis rests on the irreversible progression, delineated for us by number, from just- before to ever- after. The universe, however infinitesimal before its start, scatters its first components—like lobster-fry released from the hatchery—into the expanding universe of the ever-after. The exit from the blow-hole of pre-being is a one-way affair.

The universe need not have begun at all. But now that it is here, there seems no way to push it back into non-being—so we must let it take its course; (what else is there to do)? But if the numbers that demarcate time stretch out too long and too far (whatever "too" means) they may end—even if logic speaks against it. The situation of a world of entropy and inertia, within a universe that flees away from us as from a wake, is perhaps where time as number ends. Then, what remains can be called "post-being" if only because it has neither time nor reason for change. But perhaps pre-being was also like that—until it wasn't. Then, time and change occurred, and eventually, we began.

VII

Circles are comforting. There is the geometer's circle which, properly done, goes unendingly round and round without a break. This circle is an icon of being for mystics—as it supplies no entrance or exit. It cannot be lived in, only contemplated as a propaedeutic to a seamless life.

Then there is the calligrapher's circle, whose refusal to submit entirely to geometry creates a schema of fits and starts, dark pressures and whispery brush-strokes, which, unlike the abstract circle of geometry, must be read as sequence, or beauty. This circle is for romantics—circle-makers (of which the Japanese are best) who relinquish claim to the absolute for immersion in the uneven processes of time and history. They live their circle while the geometers conceive their circle. The affinity between the two, however, is evidenced in that both reject the notion of beginnings and ends. The pure circle is a salutary lesson for the tired ones who want to get off the aggressive line, while the calligrapher's circle is an admonition to the revelers who believe that everything changes for better but not worse.

For the linear champions of the big-bang however, no circle satisfies—there being no ambition in circles. The problem, as I have indicated, in not with ends but with beginnings—for beginnings breed the (non-circular) expectations of ends. So I take a last look.

There is a flaw (taken structurally), or a blemish (taken aesthetically) in non-being. This circumstance is the reason (and agency) for the transition from non-being into being.

The flaw in non-being is structural in that it condones a replication of numbers within arrays—redundancy in an otherwise infinite sequence, which permits numbers to form arrays in which they "recognize" each other—and, so encouraged, "create" a bang. This upsets the neutral equanimity that is the oceanic character of non-being. The enactment of difference through the joining of numbers into (potentially) successful arrays begins a "pre-temporal" action that eventuates in the structure of being and time.

The blemish on the face of non-being is aesthetic in that it shows itself as an asymmetry, which challenges the self-sufficiency of unexceptional completeness. The notion of blemish follows upon the notion of flaw in that it suggests that flaw enables numbers to seek their counterparts—inverse replications that fulfill but do not erase each other—as in: back to front, bottom to top, in and out, first and second, now and then, and so forth—each an asymmetric, potentially active relationship. All replicas, however aesthetically grotesque or seductive, are composed of counterparts and so affirm the flaw in the pre-time of pre-being. The particulars of an array, and their mode of joining determine the kind of universe that can be formed. We post-bang denizens sometimes take "our kind" as an ontological preference through which we describe our world as "the world."

Flaws and blemishes on the face of being are a consequence of their origins in the bowels of a latently imperfect non-being. But what is the origin of the imperfections in non-being? There are two choices: One can invoke yet another metaphysical agency—or just leave it alone.

The first choice threatens a conceptual regress: The "unmoved mover" sits nervously on the throne—as did the Titans when confronted by the Olympian Gods, and what tamper-proof Jehovah faced with his redefinition into three. The second choice—to leave it alone—admits to our conceptual exhaustion when we see we must, but must refuse, to admit an "unconditioned"—even when it seems the only way to explain both the incompleteness and non-origins of non-being. I recommend neither choice, for I am more happy than not with imperfections at both the beginning and end of explanation. But imperfections never cease to irritate, and this is a price one pays for rejecting the circle.

6

Art and Brain

I

Art, typically and traditionally, has been seen as a specialized product of talent—a vague if suggestive notion, yet with strong historical credentials, that only recently has seemed fuzzy enough to need pursuing into the brain. There is little disagreement that artworks originate in the minds of individuals who (mostly) are highly sensitive to the histories of past accomplishments and the demands of present tastes, and are also skilled in articulating the formal structures that bring the two happily together. There is also little disagreement that such sensitivities, as with other kinds, are locatable in the brain. Where else?

But there is a parallel tradition of explanation which has had a normative—if not behavioral—role in determining its subject: Great art is of more lasting consequence than even great misdeeds; it remains with us as a document of cultural change; it gives credence to the idea of social progress—and it's value is authenticated by the hallowed inquiry into the nature of the activity that creates great art.

One problem, here, is that "great," in this context, is more cogently applied to the past than to the present, and is always suspect when applied to the future. Art-audiences do relish surprises when looking at new art. Yet, critical support for present artistic innovations, however media-exuberant the art or its accolades may be, is not reliable as a predictor for future greatness. Artists feel this as well—in their fluctuating need to balance the verities of tradition with the promises of novelty.

Another problem is the territorial tension between aesthetic and ethical judgments. Although both fall under the rubric of "normative" judgments; the aesthetic version, however strategically made, has an aura of permanence that ethical judgments lack. A learned consensus that a work is a "masterpiece" entails its being done by a master—if the attribution holds up—while the attribution of "good character" to a person is usually the impetus for covert anticipation of a fall, because of hidden foibles, from grace.

The attributes of good character—honesty, compassion, humility, steadfastness—are rarely continuous between times, and the attributes that identify a masterpiece are also dependent upon the vagaries of the often conflicting requirements of style.

In looking at grounds for assessing accomplishment in the arts, the notion of "genius" has historically been brought to bear, not so much as an explanation but as an admission, as in Kant, that in the highest reaches of creativity, explanations must give way to gestures toward the ineffable. (We remember that the reflective judgment is a condition of the self but not the world—although it is supported by the hope that the two will come together in a future synthesis.)

Distinctions between mere talent and genius have long been left to retrospective determinations of how artists, qua genius, have redefined the culture of art. Spotting new talent is a matter of watching the child who prefers crayons to dolls and continues this preference into art school. Genius is another matter: It looks for the art-historical correlation between the exemplary artist and the symbolic needs of a given time. But these are "in-principle" correlations which do not generate hard predictions as to which artist is before-the-fact an exemplary prospect.

II

The question this raises is how there can be valid objective predictions of artistic skill—whether there are, in fact, ways to identify the capacity for artistic activity in an individual—as it ranges from simple talent to exalted genius—in the context of both cultural change and the continuum of brain function. How, in short, can the new formulations that would tell about locating artistic talent in physical conformations of the brain be squared with cultural appraisals of great, good, mediocre, and awful art? (Can there be something, properly deemed art that is also awful art? Does the capacity for making awful art still show up—in some way—as artistic talent in the appropriate sector of the brain?)

It is part of this large question that requires tracing how the sources of art can be codified in non-aesthetic language. Plato was so afraid of the whole aesthetic business—all that suggestive music, and those copies of copies of the real—that he deemed its manifestations a threat to both rationality and the well-ordered state. Interestingly, however, Plato exempted the love of beauty, and the actions of its beautiful lovers, from the negativities of art. But almost two millennia later, just those characteristics that Plato despised: obsessive preoccupation with the senses, a rejection of harmony and balance, disruptive behavior and manipulative social skills, became the characteristics attributed to the creative artist.

Freud, more sympathetic to art, directed the endeavor of art-making—with all its social flotsam—into the early experiences of childhood trauma, and thus liberated a cult of subjectivity that would explain the origins of artistic talent and, by (unspecified) extension, of good art.

Jung, entranced by the mythic antecedents of art, imagined a parallel culture of archetype and racial memory that would offset the opaqueness of bourgeois society and reconnect us, through a psychically liberated art, with our primordial origins. Both these theories found the sources of art in the mind, but the approach was through psycho-analysis rather than brain-analysis.

Psycho-analytic theory as applied to art was discredited by academic disbelief in its claim to a "cure"—that (unreachable) goal which could relieve the artist of the obsessions for making art. It was also vitiated by the growing ubiquity of art and the social ease of assuming the credential of "artist." Art-making in our day no longer requires, for the artist, neurosis or mythic recall; and the cushion of private art-patronage increasingly gives way to a communal sharing of public art and the adventures of art-societies.

So—with art and artists all around us—it makes historical sense that such contemporary largesse (and its social implications) are factors in recent attempts to seek other distinctions between art and non-art—by, for example, looking for evidence of artistic creativity in the workings of the brain. Differences in brain conformations may be indicators of the exclusiveness that "masterpiece" and "genius" once gave us. But however these differences may be codified, they are not, as yet, predictive of what we will appreciate as art in the future.

This conflict btween appreciation and prediction can be seen as part of the broader philosophical debate about the relationship between mind and brain. On the one side, both factors are viewed within a framework of materialism where (so-called) mental phenomena are seen as entirely brain-dependent and thus explainable through neurological analysis, and through the cumulative gradations in species-complexity offered by evolutionary biology. This sits well with theories that consider "masterpiece" and "genius" to be both arcane and outmoded values.

On the other side of the argument, such phenomena as consciousness and self-awareness (as well as such hightened states as genius) are typically relegated to a private "subjective" world, a specifically human world, that is not entirely—if at all—reducible to a physical site. Whether such a reduction could ever occur, or whether there is, in principle, always something left out (thus identifying new forms of subjective experience that require explanation) is a question for adherents of a unified theory.

The general argument for the unified view goes this way: The mind is an empirical entity, and demonstrably is an explanandum of neural function; it can be altered through disease or surgery; it is captive to heredity; and so is susceptible to physical explanation which does not warrant recourse to an exclusive realm of subjectivity and private access.

The opposing view, that which posits a mind-brain duality, holds that (human) consciousness is an individually (and developmentally) privileged phenomenon. While this privilege may itself be a consequence of evolutionary biology, it is an "epi-phenomenon" of evolution, and it surpasses what can be known about the mind through the brain's incursion into its domain. The faculty of langage, the historical transformations of culture, and the expressible or hidden contents of the psyche, all point to a privileged realm—the realm of "mind"—which, for metaphysical reasons, or for reasons of immature science, is not explicable through reference to the brain.

The dualistic theories—which champion the exceptionalism of mind—are usually considered by its adversaries to be merely remnants of an older, now largely discredited, antithesis between realms of spirit and matter. Haven't we had enough, the monists say, of championing the "unknowable" and "unthinkable" as wisdom that is superior to what can be achieved through proper thinking?

The monistic theories, in their turn, are accused by the dualists of reductively excluding from the argument anything they cannot explain—such as the ongoing variability in historical description, the instability of meaning, the persistence of spiritual beliefs, the inscrutability of the self.

III

I am not here inclined to tackle the great white whale of consciousness (others, like Searle) have sharper harpoons. I do believe, however, that the study of consciousness, as historical testimony and developmental conundrum, is better suited than are present solutions of mind-brain duality for developing a unified theory.

Here, I am interested in a smaller but related issue: the experience of art, and its place in the debate—whether the unruly phenomena of art can be included as a proper part of the arguments between mindists and brainiacs, or whether such experience is best taken separately, as an antiphonal issue in the problem of consciousness and its referents.

But why art? Well, art is a paradigm of exemplified feelings, and is generally accepted as a way in which the workings of consciousness are identified. There are, of course, many other ways of exemplifying the stakes at issue—but art-works are particularly succinct in bringing form and matter together into symbols, and are also privy to the creative feelings and their expressions that traverse the range from ecstasy to despair—sometimes tempered by sublimation or recollection in tranquility.

Then there are the feelings associated with appreciating art, which range from the glow of empathy and imagined possession (who would not sympathize with, say, Tintoretto's self-portrait in old age, or not want to have a Titian nude hanging by the bed?) But then we must include the other side—the recent reactions to all this historical tackiness, and so encounter the minimalist "no-feeling feelings"—the cold-shower of distaste for anything but abstract form (as in Judd, and Serra).

These contrasting modes of appreciation can of course be modulated by the mild pleasure of Saturday afternoon gallery walks, and further civilized by their echos in art-talk—criticism, promotion, explanation—all of which give support to the printed word's collusion with the graven image.

Rembrandt's and Vincent's portraits are familiar cases—there is much written about how they must have felt to portray themselves in these deep yet novel ways. But even when we dig our deepest we can never know what it is they felt when they made the self-portraits which we historically have taken as expressing their and the world's feelings—if that, indeed, is what they were doing.

Then too, there are the feelings that are not extracts from portraits, but are expressed by images that are fictions: How do Titian's Venuses and Manet's Olympia feel about their nudity? Have they become discomfited—as we might suppose—by generations of prurient and penetrating looking? Or have they enjoyed—not having been there at-all—the various reasons for their being looked at.

Although feelings found in fictional images refer to our more general feelings—such as those of discovering, rejecting, loving and hating, of dying and being damned or saved—their sources are no more nor less extractable from actual people then are images of actual people. These latter, like the former, are also fictions—It is a stretch from some chubby, red-nosed, skinny-shanked king of, say, Medieval France, to the God-like monarch, astride his noble steed—the pinnacle of Western artistic hagiography. Do you think old-masters always had it easy?

If one is about locating feelings within artistic (or any other) representations, it would be well to consider—as far as we can retrieve them—the contexts in which they were made. This may begin with the putatively non-contextual consideration of "purely aesthetic" feelings (as in Bell). These are more ideals of feeling than particular sources, and have found their nourishment in Kant's "disinterestedness," which is mainly directed towards finding a phenomenal support for "pure reason"—and enlists the non-acquisitive appreciation of (natural) beauty as evidence of the wanted harmony between reason and sensibility.

The necessary purity of Plato's "Forms," has a different strategy in that it requires a separation of contingent characteristics from the portrayal of essences—both of which (unhappily) exist together in the larger world. Plato was tougher than Kant on the imperfection of natural instances of beauty, being willing to philosophically abandon them because of the damage to reason caused by these transient appearances and evident imperfections.

For us, actual feelings—although they may be identified by derivation from generic names: beauty, valor, lust—must also be specified by attached modifiers to their categorical content: Feelings can be intense or feeble, coarse or rarified, appropriate or unwarranted, bizzare or familiar. Some feelings acquire their specific names in a legislative chamber, a graduate seminar, a tavern, a brothel, a battlefield, a deathbed.

Giving feelings a contextual location complicates the experimental strategies that would want to have its subject pure and found first in the brain and only later in specific contexts: Pure love devolves, even when it is traduced or diluted or betrayed, into its manifestations.

I note parenthetically, that the ideal of "feelings-pure" is much the same kind of illusion as the earlier reductionist ideal of the "protocol sentence"—the irrefutable linguistic link to the actual world—"red-spot-here-now"—that, once formulated, is the foundation for the construction of more complex true utterings about the world.

These formulations, and their supporting beliefs, are like the sticking points of the mind-brain debate: What priorities are being given to the primacy (within cognition) of sensation over introspection? Is the point that "introspection" (like "mind") are simply antique terms and should be discarded? Or is the point that the broad context of discussion should be subject to Occam's razor, namely, the need to identify specific levels of discourse that correspond to concrete uses, and then discard everything redundant, ambiguous, or—for our needs—without an empirical referent.

But there may yet be meetings, held each summer in a western resort on a lake, that cater to mindists and brainiacs for the purpose of establishing a central forum in which informed adversaries (hard-headed poets and empathic neuro-scientists) can stress the flexible possibilies in each position.

If we take the historical view, and embed beliefs and feelings within their particular origins, the context that combines normative and historical factors becomes part of the discussion. The feelings we express, say, in making and appreciating art are formed by what we know of and want from the culture of art—and, specifically, how we understand its present and past, in order to distinguish between art and non-art.

Artistic creation and appreciation, we agree, are strong sources of feelings (and feeling-talk). But tracing these to origins within the brain gives rise to difficulties: Is there, in the brain, some specialized configuration (of, say, location-uniqueness-intensity) that identifies significant involvement and aptitude in art? Are there neuronal measures for mapping a scale of feelings that are associated with art-making and not found in other contexts? How do these maps compare with the ones associated with art-appreciating? Do non-artists ever satisfy the criteria that produce these maps?

Further questions: Is there neuronal-anthropological evidence that "arting" is a trans-cultural and, even, trans-historical activity? Are we measuring aptitudes that are acceptably invariant for the broadest parameters of our study—or are they specific to times and places? If the latter—then what else are we measuring? Still further: Can similar measurements be expanded to include aesthetic appreciation of non-artistic beauty or are the feelings mapped for the appreciation of art different from those in the appreciation of natural beauty? There is much history here: How did, say, Kant's feelings about the holistic suggestiveness of nature (in the third critique) differ from those concerned with analyzing the piecemeal fit of objects under the categories of empirical understanding (in the first critique)?

According to reports, Kant did not care much for painting or music—although he was much interested in the geometry of the heavens—a good place, at that time, to experience his wanted harmony.

IV

Theories that favor the exclusiveness of the arts will deny any strict correspondence, whether of identity or causality, between mind and brain—and will also hold the view that consciousness is both mind-specific and ineffable, i.e., that its primary source is unreachable as a theatre for material analysis. Such theories do not hold that nothing can be known about consciousness by looking at the brain, but in their various ways, they place limitations on the posit of correspondences between neuronal functions and particular states of awareness—especially when the latter are embedded in historical judgments about the public play of such awareness—as in art.

How we feel about art—whether in its making or appreciating—depends on how informed feelings about such things are generally characterized. The terms "talent" and "taste" span the feelings identified with each, and with their roots in artistic conventions—in fact, they have little meaning outside such conventions.

I hold that criteria for judgments about art cannot, in practice, if not in principle, depend upon particularized mappings of brain function that would document the capacities of purported artists. "Artistic talent"—has no known markers in the brain. This term when used as a universal is a gloss within art-historical scholarship, where continuity of the discipline, especially in these fragmenting days, might need the additional comfort of an "innate" (neurologically demonstrable) capacity for creativity that is not (at present) stylistically demonstrable.

If it happens that such markers are offered and categorized by similarities in brain activity of a sampling, say, of successful artists, and are then contrasted with similarities (or differences) in non-artists, one must also ask about the criteria of selection for both groups. Are there, perhaps, some in the former group who are merely flashy wisps, and some in the latter group who are hiding their light under a bushel?

More telling on this score would be a long-range study of a large (neutral) sampling of infants who may or may not have histories of talent in their families, to ascertain if any extant markers have a predictive value for the artistic inclination—in later years—of those the markers show to have such talents, and those not.

But, indeed, there can be analyses that move the other way in that they show how unrecognized ability (failing the early "innate capacity" test) can still find correlation after the fact—through comparisons with brain analyses of (recently) dead great artists—which confirm that such undetected talents must have been there all along.

But when one believes that art is a paradigm for aspects of consciousness that are in principle closed to material analysis, this belief may assert nothing more than that the entity whose location is sought is too physically indeterminate, too sociologically diffuse, and too historically variable to sustain any wanted correlation.

V

The abstract schemas of Duccio and Cimabue, formally admirable, did not show anything of examples of daily life, but much about the cloistering of true belief. Piero della Francesca put the saint into a landscape, so emulating the Greek Doryphoros who brought the Archaic into Classic times. With this gesture, Piero brought Greek Classicism into Christian times. Titian, a good while after, turned Christian belief into a marinade suffused with the eros of Classisicm and the lay interests of powerful dukes.

To skip a few eons: According to theories of modern art, freedom from social dependency was the crucial goal for attaining art's autonomy, and for symbolizing the parallel aspirations of the twentieth century. But freedom from Victorian mores and Academic rules required replacing them with other institutions and ideals. Modernism, in this regard, can be characterised as a flowering period of "isms"—programs devoted to the achievement of social progress, personal freedom, and artistic autonomy: Impressionism, Cubism, Futurism, Dada, Surrealism, Fauvism, Constructivism, are some of the familiar names.

Surrealism is of particular interest for my discussion, in that it conflates a content of dreams, chance, spontaneity, with methods that are precise, contrived, and often academic. Dreams are disguised—in both art and life—through their labyrinthian passage from subconscious sources into consciousness—from their origins in sleep to their fleeting memories upon awakening. One can never be sure what a dream refers to, and how much of the reference is lost or distorted in the process of recollection.

There are, however, methods through which the practical mind can be jostled off its causal track and made to face the irrational, absurd, and possibly meaningless nature of dream imagery in daylight. These are the methods associated with psycho-analysis and also with Surrealism. Some Surrealist strategies involve randomness of reference, configurations developed through chance—all obfuscations and denigrations of the "normal." Other strategies offer precise renderings in pictorial space of a reality that, although using the genera of natural properties, are closer to dreams than to representations of the external world.

The overall Surrealist program (despite its florid history of disputes and defections) is one of putting rational methods at the service of the irrational—for the sur-real world invoked is counted as truer than the one we inhabit in our parochial "unexamined" lives: The "frottage" rubbings by Max Ernst are of ordinary surfaces; the "squares arranged according to chance" by Arp are random in process but fixed in the conclusion of their resting place. Earlier, Fuseli had pictured a demon on the breasts of a sensual woman having a nightmare. Dali, using traditional techniques, evokes the images of sexual, and later, religious obsession.

The methods in all these artworks are well-calculated; the resulting images, however, challenge the precepts and goals of rationality, through the narratives that support their irrational origins.

Surrealism sprang from Freudian dream-analysis and the mythic recourse of Jungian theory. However much all this is now discredited—more so as pseudo-science than bad art—the earlier nature of this infatuation between science and art shows (at least) that accounting for art-works requires a made connection between critical and historical contents—so that we know what we're looking at—and why.

The artistic mind seems most transparent when it is located in a strong historical narrative. The individual action, when it is recognized as issuing in art of some consequence, is taken as evidence—both post and propter hoc—of an artistic mind. But the explanatory transition of mind into brain explanation is likewise "rigged," as its subject has already been identified through art-historical criticism.

VI

What would the constants be, over historical and cultural spans, that could consistently be correlated in any experimental measure of artistic talent? For an objective investigator (with a long –life) it would be interesting to see which brain regions are brightest in the artists considered to be the best of their times, and in the artists ignored in those times but considered best in other later times. Is art progressing? Do not historical changes in valuations of artworks mirror this progress? If so, shouldn't brain tests for art activity also correlate with probability indicators to show (predict) that only certain brain-activities will (albeit statistically) produce a valuable product? The art-dealers would love this.

Modernism had a program, along with its other ambitions, of freeing art from dependency on atavistic institutions and ideologies. The targeted idols fell swiftly: First religion, then nationalism, then the academy, followed by bourgeois morality. An interim report about the late (post) stages of Modernism holds that these idols—whether toppled or not—no longer matter, that anyone can make art—ideologues, innocents, and perverts—and that art can be about anything in the world including non-art. All defining art parameters therefore fail (in principle) before they are established in fact as styles.

The sacred dissolves, but does not fully disappear into the secular: Anyone can be an artist, but, for now, most aren't—and anything can be art, but most things still are not. This needs a further weeding out.

All is not bleak for the mind-brain protagonists. After a hundred years of the freedom that modern art has enjoyed within the arms of the secular ineffable, it is disturbing to see that this freedom masks what is perhaps a greater danger for the liberal suburbs of art-culture: Without its other-worldly buttress, art has little but its recently achieved autonomy to ward off other subjugations. Autonomy, we realize, is not part of the definition of art; it is neither intrinsic nor self-evident. Rather, it is part of a historical conceit that is now lacking because the version of history in which it arose is past. The new conceit is for the incorporation of art into non-art, and it depends on the epistemology I noted at the start—the effort to reduce the ineffabilities of mind into the concreteness of brain function. The twinklings of the brain, not the history of style, becomes the uneasy adjudicator between art and non-art.

My question so far has been about what is being measured and which treasures of old and new such measurings are about. But I still wonder about the politics of this new brain epistemology: how its claim to (eventual) explanatory dominance, will effect the entities it purports to explain.

Art is ever promiscuous; suitors are taken on and discarded at a rate and for reasons bewildering even to those who spend their lives monitoring such moves. Some of today's artists have thrown in their lot with social enchantment (Christo); others have turned to manipulating public spaces (Serra). Still others have used historically derived sexual imagery for haute-pornography (Curran). None of these aesthetic preferences has been located in the brain. Yet, younger artists may well want to take a chance, submit to the probing, place a bet on brain-roulette, and hope to foster their dreams with empirical credentials of bona-fide artistic talent.

The hope is that such evidence carries the imprimatur, the certified stamp of a science, to achieve the validation that young artists will need for recognition within the unfolding parameters of the (post-artistic) art-world. Selected brains, when well-fed, produce good art, they say. Why then, with such hard knowledge around, should an ambitious artist fool with the vagaries of conventional recognition? This is a stretch, I know. But highly grounded values, such as "expression" and "purity," once rested on equally stretchy grounds—see how well they've done! Brain-certified talent may do equally well.

The contrary notion of a consciousness immune to external explanation is crucial to poetic conceits that favor inner experience and insist on the privacy of personal sentiment. Whether the concept of "inner experience" is tenable or not, it has produced some good art. This belief in the separateness of thinking from feeling can be enlisted as a defense for the autonomy of an art that glorifies the "thought of feeling." (Yes, this is the inescapable contradiction in the history of art.)

But what we have now (after the end of art) is another contradiction: Affluent patrons have long read the critics to find out where art and arting happens and where it doesn't—and consequently, they get a sense of what to buy. If the test scores of proto-artists on some mind-brain measure become competitive with critical opinion, the younger set of patrons will stop reading art-reviews and pay attention to neurological graphs of art-ability. The younger set of artists, still smarting from art-school grading, may well object to their career choices being subject to the new tests—unless they score well.

Why am I voicing such skepticism? Well, we remember, for example, that Ayer's gambit of relegating normative theory down to mere taste and opinion, didn't amount to his wanted separation between affective nonsense and scientific knowledge. One indication of his failure is that his theoretic distinction is unusable and even irrelevant to decide between specific cases—where the precise dividing line is located between the two.

Ayer's linguistic attempt to minimize the importance of questions about the "good" or the "beautiful" as being examples of confused semantics, perversely contributed to an acceleration of such values within the larger conversation. Who now would avoid talking about the good in beautiful art—or the moral metaphors hidden within abstract art—unless to enjoy the delectable ironies attending any such combination of values?

This issue goes deeper: We, in fact, have not the slightest idea which art will survive historically (if artistic survival indeed remains a value) or which hopefuls will become icons of creativity. It seems to me that public controversy is far better than either historical or neurological analysis in predicting (and is this not a goal of scientific inquiry?) what will be the good art of the future. (Sorry, "good art" should not be dispensed with—"art" is not enough. If you do dispense with the "good," then what are you measuring?)

The ecumenical approach to value—finding art where 'ere you walk—is a way of packaging historically and culturally disparate activities, into a neat container called "art." This approach then raises the question of what characteristics its practitioners: artists, inspired children, and selected animals, constitutively share. The answers would be valuable. They could, in fact, help to develop a new art criticism where only those whose brains, when suitably wired and under the proper stimulus, light up in areas provisionally determined to control aesthetic capacity, are (or should be) artists. And, as the evidence mounts, through multiple chartings, it can be taken as proof that high-performing subjects are to be correspondingly valued as potentially good artists. The theory can be enlarged to account for superior critics and, even, promising patrons.

I dislike both of the scenarios I have sketched above—although to sketch any scenario suggests its possibility. So I present another sketch: I argue that no-one need fit any particular criteria—artistic or aesthetic, sacred or secular—for determining success—immediate or belated—in art-making. I also hold that artistic talent, viewed like other genetic traits, can always be identified as such in some retroactive way—after the fact. The later manifestation, however, does not imply prior possession of any enabling trait—it only implies present possession of a trait (however ascertained) that statistically seems to match what we already have a name for.

Names are unreliable. Some, like "art" and "artist" have now become weasel-words—as will, I believe, "mind" and "brain." These words increasingly refer to wanted modes of social determination—to flights of fashion—rather than to the realities they presume to expose. The art hope is that the velleities of making, will by fiat settle into cognizable "schools" or "styles" that can then be located in the historical parade. The neurological hope is that mechanisms can be established which will predict (not merely confirm) psychological aptitudes and consequent performances for this parade.

VII

The historical parade of style, that multi-stranded hawser through which we have understood the sequence of past art—the logic of "begats"—stretches back as far as we can uncover, and forward (we hope) as far as we can peer. But continuing to pull on this rope may be just an old-fashioned wish for the security that placing the past and future within the judgments of our present can give.

On the other hand, getting rid of both history and prediction is an adventurous but risky market strategy. There is much to be learned by following random fluctuations in the motivations of such beliefs—as investors and art-dealers often do.

The issue of stasis vs. change, which underlays the philosophical arguments of the ancient Greeks (Parmenides of the eternal present, and Heraclitus of the ever-flowing river) is also apparent in the aesthetic controversies of 1950's American art. There are the one-noters: Rothko, Newman, Reinhardt, who brandish the Parmenidean stillness as justification for yearly shows that repeat the same old (good) art. Then there are the others, Dekooning and anguished Pollock who both had to change, despite themselves, for their own and history's sake.

Once informed by these originals, later artists (there are now so many) should have it easy. They could emulate the present and become non-believers, like Warhol, who wallowed in the fleeting "now" without a thought for Kant's sublimity or Hegel's ascendant spirit—much less the anguish of his own antecedents.

Or these later artists could take indeterminacy seriously as say, Cage and Rauschenberg did, and let chance flesh-out the resultant body of a minimal conjecture. Actual change happens in all these ventures, but in only a few does it still have a mandate—either for determinate prediction or normative understanding.

This may be all to the good. The end of art should not be an empty affair—rather, it should be full of everything that aesthetic excess has not (yet) touched. We haven't lost (isn't it so?) our appetite for the stuff around us—and if some gets thrown out tomorrow, or by cultural fiat is swept into the black hole of the foremost galleries, well, no matter—there is endless stuff.

VIII

Imagine with me: my good friend Rasa, who left the life of a dog—a would-be roamer, fierce defender, and some-time pet—in order to translate his ordinary appetites for affection, food, and being walked, into the stuff of artistic being.

Rasa actually was a dog—my dog—an oversize Alsatian, and he had all the qualities one would want in one's dog—he protected me, shed his hair onto my carpets, and licked my face when I was sad. But then he became an artist! Yes, my dog became an artist. His talents showed early-on when he sat near me as I worked, and barked at each dumb stroke. When it all became a mess, he bit me, although gently, on the ankle. He would also step on drawings I had left on the floor, and his paw-prints were invariably in the right place.

After one rebellious moment early in his life when he was taken from a Texas farm and tucked into my armpit for the journey to a new home, Rasa made as one with my life and grew to where he could take on the role as exemplar of my virtues—which then (he learned well) became his virtues too. But being an exceptional dog, he needed more than obedience to do justice to his gifts.

He was a foxy dog—more vulpine than lupine—so it was not hard for him, even before I accepted that my dog might be a better artist than I, to land a show of his own.

Rasa understood appearances. Whatever the weather he always wore a fur coat, and his face was dominated by a pointy luxuriant nose surrounded by a light but bristly stubble. He also had long and sharp white teeth. His barky laugh—sometimes mistaken for just a bark—was deceptive, as it revealed a pleasure in the attention paid him but it was also nested within a more fundamental rage—easily kindled, that rage, by any demeaning of his new ambitions, or by lack of attention to his uniqueness. No artist before him could bite as hard.

The dealers were entranced. Here is a true original! Rasa's first show was of two ducks, one alive one dead, placed together side by side in a simulacrum whose antecedents were surely of a Pre-Christian age, in which the God could be both worshipped and eaten in the ceremony of belief. The live duck quacked and quacked, pining for its river home where, safely away from art, it had a chance against predators. The dead duck, which had been partially cooked in a Chinese

Restaurant, hung by its head from a hook, slowly dripping its fat onto a plate. Rasa, in his performances, usually growled at the live duck—for he liked the smell of fear as an appetizer—but then he ate the dead duck, cooked in the manner of Peking Duck—for he was not, given his ambitions, immune to the tastes of the more advanced of human artists.

The critics were astonished: Life and death, belief and blasphemy, cruelty and sacrifice, miscegenation of the species, all brought together in a gala mid-town opening. Rasa did not have to kill animals to fill the daily needs of the show—this was done by a service for conceptual artists. Instead of chasing prey, Rasa was stroked and admired by the professional great-artist-spotters; he posed with fashion models in the nude; and there was even an offer—which he refused—to replace his dog-fur coat wth sable. Great fun for a super-canine, pseudo-lupine, aspiring vulpine in the middle of Manhattan. He had become a successful artist.

Yet, there were few calls for lectures—Rasa looked too risky with his easy snarl—what if he leapt upon the dignitaries and their ladies in the first few rows, especially if they laughed too loud? Remember what happened when King-Kong broke his shackles in New York? Oh my. Still, there were other appearances, more intimate and well subscribed to, in which Rasa's hairy coat and his repertoire of snarls and whines provided the wanted image of a really feral yet wholly sensitive artist—a genuine beast at one with his vulnerable psyche, and yet, attuned to his audience.

All this however, whatever the enticements, was fol-de-rol for divided Rasa, and it did not last—although there were ducks a'plenty and the collectors continued to line up. The reason it did not last (only I know) is that Rasa, in his growing mistrust of non-feral ambition, and his dislike of cheap white wine, decided to go back to where his fur coat would be used for its intrinsic properties—to keep out the cold and wet and hide him in the woods. He wanted his needs to again become the ones he knew as a pup—prowling in search of content that did not interfere with food. Now, he could no longer accept theatric slaughter of subjects suitable for public performance—uncivilized and unfeeling pseudo-art! Back I go, said he, to where "red in tooth and claw" is the only way!

Rasa's need to leave became increasingly evident (mostly to me) with every performance of his increasingly expensive duck-shows. His growls grew weaker, he began to drink, ate less, and he would leave before the audience was entirely satisfied with what he was doing to the ducks.

In the City of Cities, the contrast between wants and obligations is intoned thrice-daily by the angelic choir of Radio City Music Hall. Rasa was taken there many times by his agents. The choir sang, and the lyrics intoned—even there in mid-town Sodom—that the longer one sits with his nose in a martini and the more one puts his cleaned-up nails into willing apertures, the less one will be fitted for a life in the western forests. Rasa, as it turns out, was the only one in all of Sodom who wanted to return to the forest.

Another voice, a less friendly one but familiar to those who live in the mean streets, began to replace the angelic hymns and invade his (Rasa's) morning quiet. It was a deep voice, alternately threatening and cajoling, and it seemed to come from the Hellish regions abutting the tunnels underneath Manhattan—the places where the homeless live in perpetual warmth, inhaling the smell of ozone, and braving the risk of drinking the dribbling waters. (Why is the Devil always sung by a basso—and never a counter-tenor?) Whatever—this was the voice that woke Rasa in the early hours: "Why are you dissatisfied now with what you have—when you were once only a simple undivided animal?"

The Devil's needs have traditionally been antithetical to celestial purposes, but in this case the Devil joined with the Heavenly Host in singing the cajoling song of Rasa's return to the feral side of life. Why? Because—of the conjecture (shared by both Heaven and Hell)—that beasts, even artistic ones, are best suited to a non-normative existence—where they have drives rather than choices—and so face, upon demise, neither Heaven nor Hell. This upholds the necessary difference angels, devils, saints or sinners—and the lower ones, who are mere beasts. It is this difference that supports the eternal conflict between Heaven and Hell. Who would worry, given these high stakes, about the soul of a dog?

But this animal-art-thing is a curve-ball! Consider what would happen, asked both sides (the representatives of heaven and hell) if beasts were to become recognized as artists? Come on! Even after the new permissiveness, and the Formaldehide Shark, this would be too much! Think again, my friends, about the famous Rasa—you know, the dog that (who?) became a performance artist—and about what he will face when he is about to die.

But now—he's a real beast, he is. Here he comes! Be careful! He might bite! As indeed he should, given his acquired taste for the moisty upscale prey (not only ducks, you know) that used to circle around him. Real saints and sinners they were, and tasty too.

One early morning, tired of listening to the droning Demon, over-stuffed with last night's Caneton a l'Orange, and gagging on all that pudendal perfume, Rasa decided to drop out—now, not later. He began to trot, lope, and then run as fast as he could, while leaving his droppings behind as a warning to art-lovers who invariably (that's what they do) smell out the path of the dying artist. Rasa, dead and famous, is worth more than Rasa alive, still biting, and having nothing more to say.

IX

What does this have to do with artistic talent and its origins? Everything! Time changes these questions! Now that Rasa is a pure predator again—somewhat bruised by his skirmish with the difficulties of artistic status—he no longer has to distinguish between physical happiness and cerebral content; he's already done that—although nobody really got it—except me, of course.

Rasa was a friend of mine, and we have often talked about such matters. I once told him that I would transcribe his thoughts (Did Rasa have thoughts like mine—or was it just my attempt to think like him?) into a story about the artist's life and its leaving—or ending, as the case may be—for him and for me. He demurred at first; he said that he and and his beasty friends used to think that writing, especially about art, was sissy-stuff—only fit for critics, curators, art-historians—but not for beasts or artists.

The conversations in the market place happened long ago—and Socrates the garrulous hero who did not write his profundities is now long dead. Is non-writing, then, for our Rasa-artist, to be taken as an emulation of the philosopher whose literary muteness was often seen as an ingredient of artistry-in-philosophy? Was Socrates a performance piece played by Plato?

Eventually, Rasa had to bare his teeth at all those denigrators of the word (his early friends, after all, were only dumb animals) and he began to write—a hard choice what with the history of his origins, not to say his lack of an opposing thumb. But he was able to use his longest claw to press the keys of his computer, and he really started to write when both he and I no longer cared whether writing diminishes or enhances the status of being an artist.

Rasa still prefers to search the wild woods for prey, but he has gotten somewhat stiff in the lower joints and the prey would get away—or simply trot around his furthest reach, making light (those kids can be vicious) of his best attempts. But he had alternatives when he was forced to rest from hunting: Supermarkets are now very competitive, and so they tolerate drifters, nay-sayers, the great unwashed—and even hungry carnivores. Rasa, who had wisely invested his art-money and had obtained a credit-card, did not starve—as long as he behaved himself during trips from the vegetable isles to the meat counter. The cheese display on the way posed a problem—for the customers who buy good cheeses, being both salivative and indecisive—were very much to his feral tastes.

There you go—Rasa-pet-friend-artist-writer—a first theme: Write about the contrary needs of taste and nourishment provided by the haunches of Caribou and the thighs of wealthy matrons. Tell us what the killings feel like, and whether the eating of hot raw flesh can be fashioned into an occasion for both food and art. I'm sure you can—just think and eat before you eat and shit—and then write—or tell it to me and I'll write it for you.

But what are the post-prandial questions that would get us closer to your art? Are there two areas in the brain—fairly far from each other—one area controlling eating and the other arting? On the chance that there are, I will call the one "carnivoris" and the other "artisticus." Having been encouraged by recent theories of interchange, they (the areas themselves) may well be pushing tendrils toward each other (neurons become social pathways before we know it) hoping, for developmental reasons, to form an alliance that is sturdy and regulative at bottom and light and quicksilver on top.

I realize that it will no longer do to repeat the sins of the past and relegate carnivoris to the brain and artisticus to the mind (or soul). Even with the distance between them, they will find pathways which have long been clogged with the rubble of Scholasticism and Humanism, but which now, given the advanced design of our conceptual roto-rooters, are ripe for open-minded, mutual incursion. What would the progeny of carnivoris and artisticus, if we could get them together, be like? Why—heavy on bottom and light on top!

X

Rasa, you once told me a story about an ungulate you saw at the edge of your territory. She (it was a she; you noticed the nipples) ran out of the forest and into the desert that has no trees—her natural home, not yours. But you followed her, you did, loping along despite burning paws and a growing thirst, hoping to run her down and slowly eat her moist innards, so conquering both the desert heat and the fires inside you.

But you did not catch her—you said you really did not think you could—and it is to your credit, dear boy, that you gave up the chase in time to drag yourself back to the forgiving forest and the cool pools where you live. Yet, for many years after, you berated yourself for cowardice: The burning sands were really not that hot, you said; she ran fast but not that fast. I would have caught her could I have separated my lupine desires from my vulpine caution. I still imagine being astride her, chewing slowly on her neck. But there, happy in my work, I was vulnerable to her horns (yes, although they were largely decorative, she did have horns as pointy as my teeth).

Bleeding and unsatiated, needing to rest, I could only watch her rise up on those skinny shapely legs, shake off my saliva, and with the smallest backward glance, trot off to where she was sure I could not follow. You know me; I did not go after her beyond the range of my sensible Carnivoris. Its competitor, Artisticus, on the other hand, asked something else of me—more running on the burning sands—wailing in ecstasy like a saint when it became really bad.

I refused. It would have been the life of me, but had I continued, it could have been the death of me. Had I survived it for a bit- although I could not catch her, my lovely ungulate—and assuming she did not return to see what was up with me or offer me a moist nipple to ward off my extremis—it (my eventual death in the indifferent desert) might well have become a marker on my previously unnoticed attempts at artistic immortality.

XI

Freud's famous compendium of artistic desires: money, fame, love—is enjoyable only by an intact (integrated is too strong) self. There are obstacles: Money invokes the demands and jealousies of fame; fame confounds the private space of creativity; love raises the suspicion that it is offered because of fame and money.

This is much like our childhood game of paper-rock-and scissors—the spread hand of paper covering the rock; the forked fingers of the scissors cutting the paper; and the clenched fist of the rock breaking the scissors. A lesson for our adolescence: The weak and the strong are forever changing places.

To where must we retreat, then, we who want the stability to find our artistic center? Is nostalgia the answer? Do we return to the studios of the Renaissance—with their rediscovery of classical geometry; or to the ateliers of the French Academy—where prurience and fame combine to make the stew; or to the bohemian garrets—where poverty is said to help art; or to the class-rooms of the Bauhaus—where early reachings into science and philosophy must result in and for the betterment of art.

But in all of this, how will we see our three ancient antagonists—Rock scissors and paper—finally brought into a coherent order? Well, we can choose between them: "Rocks" say the hard-heads; "scissors" say the sleek-ones; "paper" say the mystics. But is choosing one at the expense of the other two a cogent response to the present climate of fragmentation, or is it just an old-fashioned affectation—a need to get it (the art) right before its time gets too late?

Self-knowing, until recently, was seen as a prime ingredient of artistic success, but much else soon crowded in. Self-knowing is now in serious competition with: not-knowing, non-knowing, social disobedience, personal naughtiness, stony indifference, just-us-folks, fuck-you-all—as attitudinal signposts of success. Yet, to be noticed at all, each such strategy needs to achieve some public face or other—to become known as a prime exemplar of rock, or paper, or scissors.

Feeding these fractious ambitions may be the face of art today. This is more a matter of praxis than of ideology, and may show the failings of today's art viewed as constituting a new "style." Whether the accumulations of art-works appear in gallery shows or in Biennales, there is no mode of art-talk that underlies and directs the ambitions of future art.

But do we want such talk–this decadent need for historical winnowing-in-our-time? What is so bad with being left with the democratic uncertainties of Rock, Paper, and Scissors in eternal conflict?

Well, there are always brain-scans lurking around when critics fail. There may indeed be a stylistic equivalent of the Higgs boson in the brain that, even though it itself has no substance, would give common substance to all the dissimilar practices of past, present, and future art.

XII

Rasa and I left the arena of art-making—not just from defeat but from boredom. Rasa was interested in eating his artworks and fucking their inspirations. I did not put my needs so bluntly (although I had them too) but I somewhat disagreed with his sequence.

In the forest-primeval where Rasa returned to chase his prey, there had existed, from time immemorial, an ancient order situated within a Grovian Temple that practiced the murmorial (as in "forest murmors") rite of ruling through annual choosing between paper, rock, and scissors. This is the site we have often celebrated as the "Sylvan Groves." Soon after Rasa arrived, however, civil strife occurred: A band of younger murmorers revolted; the ancient order of Grovites was disbanded; the old murmorers were cooked and eaten; and playing the traditional PRS game was forbidden: The new head murmorer stated that all three aspects should have equal value in the new forest community, and so there is no reason—indeed, no right—for them to be in conflict.

After the rebellion against the Grovian elders, it turned out that large parts of the forest were leased to developers. We, Rasa and I, had to move from our cave by the river to a trailer at the edge of a growing suburb. Rasa was by now reduced to chasing neighborhood kids when they tried to vandalize my car. He did not bite them hard, for their taste was super-market sweet—not at all like the pungent blood his free prey once offered. Rasa (he is older in dog-years now than I) had in his later years graduated from arting and eating to reminiscing. Grudgingly, he accepted the diminishing of both his carniveris and artisticus, and he tried to supplant them with his need for returning to a single-species identity. But, as he had already gone through the miracle of being both an animal and an artist, the return to simplicity could not be simple. We remember, back then, that even Rasa's prey recognized him as the newest model of the predator-cum-artist in the ripping-slashing sequence that gave content to the aesthetics of their dying.

"So it is you, the famous Rasa, who will end my life. I'm glad it's you and not those callow jackels that don't know how to do it right: We will make art, you and I—for my only life cannot be replicated, nor can your killing of me ever happen again. So, in all the bloody chewing, your snarls and my screams, the smell of dying, my silence when finally dead—all this will make a new art. Isn't that what you said when you asked me to slow down?"

Rasa's patrons, unlike his prey, did not understand: "OMIGOD, they cried, This Work Is So Strong! The Best You've Done So Far!" But the sweet deer gave him her love and her blood; the art got him some shows and a few bucks.

Rasa was an exemplary dog. He was able to hunt and eat and make it art—all at the same time. I am not like that: I don't like to hunt; I enjoy eating (mostly) dead food; but I am irritated when being watched while eating—or making art—or making love. I can't bring them all together—as Rasa could.

XIII

The Rasa-talent that brings all these aspects together may hold the secret to the off and on affair between mind and brain: We can pretend they don't know each other, but when the Carniveris and the Artisticus sound their mating calls in separate rooms, we must wave a benevolent arm, pour a stiff drink, and invite them into the third room where they must (doesn't it seem that way?) evolve together.

Oh, there will be Idealist mutterings about playing fast and loose with eternal categories, and there also will be Empiricist shruggings that such Neo-Hegelisms are not scientific. Scientists seldom read Hegel; but some who do are led to say that evolutionary optimism—the historical inevitability of transcendence—while it may be covert theology, is an issue that science may again need to examine: Don't look only at the things themselves, look at their sequence, their coupling, their projections—even in our lousy times.

This remains difficult. We know that concepts and the territories they map both change, particularly in a young dispute—as in the relationship between mind and brain. It may be the case here—as it was with ether and phlogiston—that the terms themselves are impediments. New terminology is not always generated by new findings; it comes about through criticism of tenured descriptions that have become patently inadequate to account for what we have come to know about their referents. Language, in this regard, is both conservative and protective—particularly systematic language. It takes a lot to abandon descriptions that have been useful in accounting for what we think we know, and around which we have built an elaborate scheme of reference and meaning.

The mind-brain separation seems intuitively to accord with our experiences; it also bolsters much psychological and normative doctrine: Where else could the coupling of free-will and moral-obligation rest but on referring causally generated behavior to the brain, and unregimented choice to the mind? The uneasy march of history and our intimations of mortality also require this separation.

But all this assumes that there are distinct entities for which these terms are determinants: It seems easier now to refer to the entity that is "brain," than to the conjecture that is "mind." One recent solution is to discard the more opaque term—to substitute "brain-talk" for "mind-talk." This solution has a more general philosophical counterpart in the proposal to substitute "extensional" for "intensional" language. But such a solution also acts to widen the gulf between accounts of what matters—to create separate tiers for language, with the one limited to what is "empirically verifiable," and the other left to poetry, eternity, dying, and the like. This reduction and purification gambit is somewhat like a Western Movie scenario of first rounding-up and then stringing-up the rascals—while the town-folks watch.

Wittgenstein could not have thought, concerning his conclusion in the Tractatus that we must be silent about what cannot be said—that it (silence) is either a possible or, indeed, a desirable consequence of the logical parsing of language. His conclusion smacks instead, of a despair (much like Pascal's "Horror Vacui") that the blooming and buzzing of the world cannot be caught within a regimented language—and of Wittgenstein's own uncertainty as to whether it is the world or language that should be changed.

This uncertainty may also be the case with the concepts of mind and brain: I am conscious of what I think—and this (as I think it) occurs in my mind—for this (I know) is where I think that I think. But then, where is my mind—which I so-far have known as a child knows its nipple? The rough boys outside say it is nowhere else but in your head. My brain, also being in my head, then becomes an adversary—indicating, through its growing power, that there is no room for the both of me—brain and mind—unless I agree that my thoughts, dreams, reveries, desires and fears, are consequent on neural quivers over which my so-called mind has no awareness or control.

Yet, I have little desire to relinquish my mind's claim over my private experience—however much it can be represented (although never fully, I hope) in the synaptic language of on-off, or however much it can be altered by surgical (or other, e.g. drug induced) invasions of my brain. In this former case, I plead disinterest; in the latter case, the resultant changes in my sense of "myself" will be for others (not me) to understand.

But can I deny that this semantic worm of change, once introduced into the conceptual blood-stream, will not undermine the old school of thought—now become the historical enemy—that asks whether where we come from (as physical entities) dictates what we (as free agents) must do?

The separation of mind and brain has old roots: There are the basic and recurring questions of body and soul, and of determinism and free will: Taken to a theological level, the separation questions the decision-making of an all-powerful God when He deems it best to lose control (if indeed, He ever had control) of the wayward actions—often brutal, salacious, and self-defeating—of His created beings. (The problem of evil). Misfortunes can always be blamed on the formal necessity of autonomy (free will) in those created in God's image. As Decartes said, we are like God in that we have infinite will, but unlike Him in that we have but little knowledge. This rests uneasily, however, with the notion of God's omnipotence in both will and knowledge relative to the fortunes of his creation. Does what God freely gives include evil? Unthinkable! Unless evil –with all it attendant sufferings—is an ingredient, like the hot-pepper in the chile, for the purposes of the ultimate good?

XIV

Some cultures have become used to the pragmatics of such antinomies, and have fashioned edifices that allow unwanted practices to go their separate ways without censure. Those most vulnerable to deviance, in our enlightened times, may be understood through a scrim of early abuse, bad heredity, and other conditions over which they had no control. Consequently no blame is assigned to their aberrations—as these certainly originate in the embattled brain. Bad art can become good art that way.

Statesmen and other Divines, however, are required to live a life determined by mind's free will, which does not posit a physical standard of credibility for the tasks assigned them—no neurological excuses here for blunders. The sins of public figures cannot be excused by the workings of their brains: It is the errant mind of leaders that brings them down.

Are those of us, then, who are not leaders, free (another contradiction) to take on the brain defence for all-our-sins? "It was not "my" fault; it was something in "my brain" that made me do it." This is a potent legal strategy which, in practice, confirms the division between the "conditioned" brain and the "free" mind.

Given this conundrum, we may be facing another separation of cultures: "brain-behavior" vs. "mind behavior"—each reflecting its own social sphere. This new description, however, is not between the private world of "inside" and the public world of "outside," but between political parameters and practices in which the one or the other description is used for strategic purposes.

The worlds of inside and outside, having sensed the battle ahead have mounted their strategies. The inside world, according, say, to Derrida, levels a semantic attack on the outside through a demonstrated subtilization of language that enhances its autonomy and the infinite variability of reference, but eludes the possiblity of corrigible description of actual events—including life, history, and eternity.

The outside world, in contrast, with its manipulations of animal brains, and tests of afflicted human brains, seeks to show that there is nothing in the interior (if indeed there is such) that cannot be changed by external methods—and yet, by some strategy (as yet obscure) indicates that life and love will continue.

To resolve this conflict, it seems inadequate to only go half-way, and hold that some of our actions—the extensional ones—the empirical findings—are a consequence of brain-determination, while the intensional ones—ethical, religious and aesthetic judgments—are an issue of free will. That split has been around for a good while, and now bothers mostly philosophers and lawyers; but it is not as important in its theory as in its use as weaponry in socially adversarial contexts—as in the legal question of guilt, or the aesthetic question of artistic value.

It might now be well to reject the "mind-body" duality altogether, and pursue the question through the notion of consciousness. This has the benefit of replacing the "inside-outside" impasse with the more flexible interchange of developmental thinking where anthropology, sociology, and biology can trace simple irritability into grades of awareness and into self-awareness—thereby conjoining time, organism, and culture in a description of the development of consciousness.

In as much, therefore, as there can be no psychic state without a physical framework so there is no physical state without its psychic recognition: The cat on the mat, and the unheard tree falling in the forest must both be accounted for. This interchange in the long term is anthropological; in the mediate term it is historical; and in the near term it is sociological.

Notice, in this sketch, how the categorical two's and three's play off each other. I do believe (without arguing here) that two is the form of being and that three is the form of becoming. Arguments about the stability of being are broken down by the volatility of becoming, which indeed—as dialectic suggests—again seeks a new being. Mind and brain are both located along this cycle.

XV

Plato, in the Phaedrus, portrays the journey toward wisdom as a chariot driven by the soul, that wanting charioteer who has to contend with mismatched horses—which exemplify the conflict between desire and purity. Why these horses are mismatched is Plato's gift to us as a metaphor for the human condition.

The one horse, as we imagine, is powerful, thick, and hairy, insatiable in its lust for the pleasures of the body. After a dull day climbing, he (certainly male) is inclined to drag the chariot to the outside of the road, so that he can graze in the bottom-lands of actuality. The grasses are green and tasty in the meadows, and the buzzing of the bumblebees flying in and out of blossoms is cacaphonal to the music of the celestial spheres he had been hired to reach.

The other horse, finely boned, pale with a soft coat (probably female) and wanting above all to obey her mandate, tries to stay on the righteous road, and so struggles with all her might—despite having to pull more than her share—to reach the wanted destination: the place where the Gods reside, that semi-circle of the heavens from which one can glimpse, through the appertures that pierce heaven's roof, the region of the eternal forms.

The Gods, although they have the best view, take only sporadic looks at what lies beyond the heavens, for they are preoccupied with perfecting the best of earthly appetites: incense and myrrh for scent, nectar and ambrosia for food and drink, and dancing younger nymphs vying with old satyrs for after dinner frolics.

But the philosophical mandate for the charioteer is to journey further, and transport the earthly soul to just that point beyond the heavens—past the need for food and the fear of death—to where the forms are sequentially arrayed in their non-sensate splendor, and arranged according to their eternal place in the scheme of true being.

Well and good. But the problem, says the hairy horse, is that our driver—our soul-cathected charioteer—is uneasy (he's just human) about going to the heavens. It's awfully far, he says, the road gets icy at the first sign of disbelief, and the food is really better here on earth. Of course, my skinny harness-mate might very well prefer going right on to the forms. But she, as I suspect, is both anorexic and ascetic—why, she would have passed the Godly array of satyrs and the tables laden with heavenly nourishment with barely a whinny or a glance! She is well suited, she is, to the rituals of non-objective belief.

I know full-well, said hairy, that I shall always be considered by my charioteer (and his philosopher friends) as an early impediment to rationality. He needs someone to blame—poor soul. He thinks that by getting to the center of the Good he will live forever. So be it—the Olympian Gods don't care; their time, as his and mine, is ending soon.

Plato is not big on "becoming"—his thing is "being." It is no wonder then, that his stand-in for the soul—his charioteer—should have such trouble in getting his warring selves into line for that all-important journey. It does not say in the Phaedrus, how the poor soul expiated for the failure to reach his goal (more prayer? More discipline?). Limited souls should be satisfied with the interim pleasures offered by the transient Gods—but this is not the way of philosophy.

Plato does not say much about the Olympians' own limitations—that even with perfectly harmonious, heaven-bred steeds, they could only catch a "glimpse" of the forms. Perhaps this was a premonition of their decline. They did not think to take on the larger journey: to descend into Hell then rise again on the third day.

XVI

It may be time that Rasa and I become one and effect a synthesis between our appetitive and reflective selves. But in doing this we will have to, much as we hate to, relinquish the extreme pleasures enjoyed in the sanctuaries on either side. After this albeit admirable gesture of denial, we may end up supping morosely on the vapid cuisine of the middle—warmed over hamburgers with soggy french-fries—not a proper reward for hairy-brainy explorers of new categories. Yet we have learned to know that taking sides—worshipping two as opposed to running with three—is a hindrance to the new explanation that promises, if little else, that there is nothing about which we must remain silent.

7

The Crooked and the Straight

I

Snake-heads emerge cautiously from the mouths of long-dead birds

Light wiggles into day like a rivulet that first shows itself as a stain on the brown mud of night

Then the gathering waters reflect their origins in the sun and by late morning the light spills over everything that likes darkness

We who are happy in the daylight avoid those who prefer the night and we do not care to recognize the next coming of the waiting gloom

Snakes at twilight like to lie on desert sands and also on concrete patches for these retain the heat of day after the sun goes down

The late-day city runners that snakes will bite are not like rodents for they do not provide a balanced meal

Minerva's owl (she's no fool) takes wing at dusk just when the snakes are getting better at their biting

I wake with the morning light and my slanting shadow falls upon the bright fangs that encourage history's bird to fly again in search of the night that has no day

II

We are all children of the crookeds and the straights, although the battles between us show no signs of abating. The prophets of progress-in-our-time separately sing that the dialectic resolution of all such conflicts is just around the corner. But such prophetic chants cannot long remain in plain-song. Young curiosity will soon fold simple opposition into the complexities of counter-point.

After living eighty years or so, I hold that straight roads are best avoided. But, wouldn't you know it—few of my friends will listen. I suspect that as they age each gravitates toward the comforts of the other side. I know a club of adamantly ecumenical older folk—they call themselves "The "Crooked Straights." What other ways are there to go, they sing, but to play crooked and stand straight—what with life so short, and worthwhile goals so near in mind but yet so far away at hand?

Do you not see the hills without valleys and the ponds that are neither deep nor shallow? Look both ways. There, lurking in the twilight just behind the prickle bushes are the lions and tigers and bears of olden days. But they are welcome even when they bite, for fleshly blood is a way to pass beyond its seepage of becoming into the clotted realm of being. When the snake bites, what will you do with your remaining time? Deny, deny that there are reasons for which you live.

You should, at any rate, avoid the irrationality of snakes, as well as slanted shadows, inchoate whisperings, the fleeting glimpse of thigh, and non-Euclidian geometry. These are the seductive signposts of evil. Your slightest sign of interest in one or more will open the chasm, alert the internet, and cause the demons to pull you down before your time. And they will surely choose that moment when you have stepped off the straightaway onto some beguiling patch of dewy grass that wets between the toes, or that leisured time when you are wading through the softly swaying reeds in the summer sun—and you see the swaying as limbs of wantons moving in the wind.

Such visions, whether by the shore or in your bed, have potent ingredients. They are contributions from the demons of infernal theatre to the recipe that mixes your essence with your appetites. If you let them, these demons will bake a cassoulet so fully fashioned that, when finally you are stuffed, you will be content to just rest there, farting among friends. But then, after the last gas has passed, and all friends are dead and gone, you will be alone again, emptier than before, in the moonlight that now shows only a coruscation of dead leaves.

Consider the recent Sunday sermons by our new minister who says he dwells upon the practices of evil so as to fix them as negatives in our minds. (He is much taken, as he admitted at Friday's cocktail hour, by the spectacle of Bosch's sinners rent and rendered by fearsome lizards—and also by the torments of Saint Agatha). Some parishioners object—they say his principle is priapic. Representations of evil, I admit, can themselves be evil, for they cast a too-revealing light on what should remain forever hidden.

My oldest and most suspicious friends in the Straight agree. The enticements of evil feed upon the pictured punishments meted out to sinners. The writhings of the damned, however artfully conceived and beautifully rendered, will bring us nothing but obsession with new evil. Away! As the clear crow flies, so will I—avoiding the pricks and poesies of pious pornography—and with me on my journey I will take only those who fit into the small-sack of straightforward belief.

Someday you will see, beneath the rictus of my dead once deadly face, the spare contentment of attained achievement. I got there, I did, and before the others—those mostly crooked souls who say they also journey straight up, but hit every motel en route. My way, in contrast, is calumniated by them as narrow- straight; but I assure you that its direction follows the real history of eternity. So, dear my kiddies, you must be clear about which way you want to go. It's getting to be past time now—you are older—and you must proceed at once to the starting point what with your scrubby shiny faces and firm impassioned tread.

What is it I hear you say? After all my teachings, you're not quite ready? Speak louder and come here into the brighter light. Yes, yes, I can see the quivering of too-fat cheeks, the unfocussed blinking bloodshot eyes, the flaccid pudgy limbs—none of which promises well for a commitment to direct ascent. Well, you are not too wrong to be afraid, my kiddies; neither the world nor I (I admit this to you in strict confidence) really knows the true direction of the Straight-and-Narrow. Self-satisfied belief on this score has been the very devil of our club, making a muddle of our attempts to pin down the self-evident path of righteousness. But times do change—although true belief should not. Rather than seeing you succumb to the greater evil of non-belief, I will inform you, (you are now old enough for this) that if you just can't stand it here (sometimes I can't either) there is a different club which in its unseemly way, claims the same rights of origin and goal as we do. We call them the Crooked-Straights. In return they call us the Straight-and-Narrows. Although the distinction is more a difference of nuance than epistemology, you can spot them easily. They are less steadfast in bearing than we (being mostly fat and easily winded) and they are secretly pragmatic in politics (not a categorical dogma anywhere in their heads).

In fairness I must admit that despite their flat feet, and the sweet-and-sour smell of their ambivalence about the right direction, they too are bona-fide members of our most-comprehensive club of aging oldies that, for various ideological and prudential reasons, has named itself "The Straights." When pressed, The faction to which I once belonged calls itself the "Narrows," thereby claiming directness, clarity, abstemiousness, in our claim to the best seats in heaven. The other faction, which we derisively used to call the "Crookeds"—until its members took the label as an advertisement for their inclusiveness. The Crookeds do not see themselves as irretrievably (or even slightly) deviant—certainly not as is sometimes claimed by the straightest of the Straights. Remember—the crooked (was made) straight and the rough places plain.

Crookeds react to accusations of their waywardness by insisting that they seek a middle ground between doctrinal inflexibility and directionless relativism. They (and there seem to be more and more of them) insist that they be counted as members of the loyal opposition which, while not agreeing with all decisions, yet did once in younger days contribute to the choral cadences of the Long March.

You can find the dwelling place of Crookeds by crossing the big street directly in front of the inn, and then turning the first corner to the left. They have a new and shiny temple, whose outer courtyard functions as a coffee-shop that serves all the European blends and exotic pastries; further back, sweet-smelling smoke identifies a barbeque emporium which, they insist, provides the best ribs to be found this side of non-belief.

But my advice to seek them out—I must tell you—has generated trouble for me at the old temple. Listen to the comments of my peers:

"balderdash, poppycock, blasphemy and bullshit" is the cry—even from my dearest friends among the narrow Straights. These Crooked leftist rascals, they say to me, to which you would so blithely send our children, will soft-sell their hedonistic ways and promote a no-sweat path to get to where we, the narrows, through our saintly efforts to make the crooked straight, are surely headed.

Here, I argue with my colleagues. A needed reformulation of ancient verities always brings criticism—particularly from the old and skinny folks of worn belief. But just look up the road, I tell them, there are no narrow Straights to be seen out in the suburbs—except for those still living near the dusty road that starts behind the outhouse and heads toward the stagnant bogs. If you are a fledgling poet, it's worth a trip to talk with those forlorn creatures. But after days of dry and musty natter, you may ask yourselve why anyone can find it holy to face the mosquitoes and the muck and mire of narrow choice?

In contrast, the Crookeds offer alternatives (such being their stock-in-trade) that are flexible and up-to-date. The main exit from the Krooked-Klub Motel is well paved—not like the gravelly-gritty originary path the narrow ones still insist on taking. The upscale road, if you decide to go that way, merges, yes it does, with a cross-country superhighway. You must consider, my children, that if you want to get somewhere—to where, for example, the aftermath of a crooked party can lead—the soft-curve is better than the gravel path as a way to get to where your someone is waiting. This remains true even when you can no longer remember, the following day, who that one was.

But let's pull back a bit. I may, for fairness' sake, have over-vilified the enemy. It doesn't matter which road you take to get to where you really want to go. Careful, now. Take note of the friction factor in your decisions on both love and travel. The Narrows seek out roads that go on interminably up-hill, and they are undeterred by the painful rubbings of dry penance. The better lubricated Crookeds will raise their hands for roadside help most anytime, especially if things get too bumpy between sighs and thighs. But roads do cross. Caravans coming from opposite directions find convergence in a place where mostly strangers come to meet. So it is with bands of Straights and Crookeds who have reached the juncture where the originary roads are now the super highway. They have come there many times to sit and eat together. When challenged, both will attribute such meetings to a cosmic coincidence. But if shown the old films—mostly 8 mm—they will remember the sharing of beds and memories with each other. For are not we and they—the wise ones on both sides say—members of the same persuasion? Not quite, not really—but it could be so with a little work.

III

You see, my friends, it's an old story. The Straights are dualists: For them, there is a never-ending war between good and evil. Evil, even in disguise, has no access to true belief, because the musky smell that identifies the source of evil (despite all the new detergents and perfumes) has remained unchanged throughout eternity. Evil, the narrowest of the Straights insist, is the other to everything that should be, and it fills its eternal time by chewing on the out-lying shoulders of the narrow way so as to make it dangerous. Like the snowy ridge that stretches from where you stand to a distant peak, that way may no longer be substantial enough to hold you when you are only halfway across. One misstep and down you go through the footless powder—without even a scream or the jolt of a rope held by the good Swiss guide you were too cheap to hire.

No problem, say the Straights (they are familiar with the geography of evil) we always lose a few, but it doesn't happen often. Now that we again are coming into money, we will send up the teams we've hired—all illegal immigrants with high-country experience. They have instructions to widen and make smooth the true high path, reinforcing the drop-offs with imported shoring, and placing warning signs where the snow-puffs on the shoulders are most seductive.

The Crookeds, while they do not deny the presence of evil, yet do not regard it as absolutely other (they also are not fond of snowy peaks). The spiral is their alternative to the straight and narrow way, for unlike its single-minded competitor, the spiral has expanding latitude within which to envelop others' interests as well as one's own.

Evil was once considered absolute, but when it is caught within the wider swing, it can be shunted forward into the more malleable context of the merely unpleasant, and once there, it can be further nudged in normative stages so that, sooner or later, when caught in the cosmic tides, evil will be swept into the outermost rings—the exurbs of the good.

But this comes slowly, mind you, as in the digestion of a big snake's catch. Evil can fulfill the needs of a new world-view by diminishing its contrast with the good. In this transformation, evil divides into positions of varying, even contradictory, schools of malfeasance.

But with evil willing to so divide its once immaculate self, this leaves the good (as believers still call it) without a clear-cut enemy.

According to the grand plan of the Crookeds, when evil is brought into the subtleties of social discourse about right and wrong, and exposed to pedicures and steam baths, it will (never completely but increasingly) shed the scaly skin of dependence on its Satanic source. In time (admittedly much time) the plan of the Crooked Straights is to make evil into an energizing variant—a gadfly of the stolid stationary good. This way makes evil, however unwittingly, a participant in the next stage of forming a better good.

Goodness knows where the good resides. Kant hypothesizes only a good will—as documented through a self-examining measure that provides, but cannot mandate, a universal for moral action. Schopenhauer holds instead that will is all-pervasive, but must in any case be overcome—in order to achieve an a-historical goodness. If you are still morally inclined, he says, listen to music. Hegel thinks that good comes out best in the end—when it corresponds to the final achievements of spirit.

For uncommitted travelers, the road to follow that gets you to goodness presents a real conundrum. There are the dark trails in the forest, with Dorothy's demons tittering in the bushes. These can lead to enervating wallows, full of biting snakes and suffocating slime—not to mention unsettling glimpses of aging showgirls who their bosses found too greedy and sequestered them in trailers perched on precarious patches of dry ground in the South. Some of these saggy beauties can still give a good semblance of kicking up their heels, but they will not leave the swamp (even with you) because they prefer the warmth it gives—especially in winter. After all they've been through, snakes are no problem, and they even have come to like the smell of rotting plants—better, they say, than unwashed crotches.

A few, however, will rebel and turn before their time toward the higher ground where the path leads inexorably to the primitive ridge that traces across the mountains and silently offers itself as an access to distant peaks. But when the weather worsens—as it always does—one can slowly freeze to death, or retreat in desperation to find lower ground, only to fall and be buried in the clear-smelling snow without a trace. Crinkly beauty frozen in the virgin snow is indeed an image that will survive.

Yet, all these ways, when considered from a third vantage are still straight, that is, they each offer their own best way of arriving at the same destination—that most comprehensive goal of getting: Where? Why there! So, for all the centuries of across-the-aisle scowling, the Straights and the Crookeds might agree that both are end-directed. They share the objective of getting (to the) good as the only way to release them from not-going (bad). But why, ask some, shouldn't we, like those show-girls, just stay put?

Well, going is going-somewhere—better to the good than elsewhere. Oh, we know the way is long, and as we grow older, the legs tend to give-way first. But going requires an admixture of crookidity and straightitude—for without the two there is no movement (although it doesn't have to be a 50/50 split). There are, as with martinis, many styles of mixing, generated by great debates over due proportion. But a martini is not simply gin and ice—there must be the civilizing presence of vermouth (just a few drops) to encourage our having more than one.

There have been many clashes between the factions along the way—but don't you remember those times, mostly saturday nights—when skinny scarred and smelly straights would wander through the outside dark sniffing at the chic and fatty effluence that emolliates the limbs of their crooked adversaries? There were other nights—you might also remember—when the coiffed and softly rounded, reliant on an all-volunteer army, and suffocating from their pent-up need for penetration without words, turn on the front-hall lights—at which time the spare and bony, attracted like moths to the zapper, will forego violence and mutely acquiesce to a four-hand massage.

At journey's end, all such frolics are forgiven. Now that the journey's over, each side, without penalty, can inhale the vapors that identify the other side. The young and curious who were conceived along the way, might even want to mingle the distaff fragrances and arrive at a scent that increases their itch to grow together.

This ecumenical scent, centuries in the making, is not only an admixture of prurience and penitence. It also exemplifies the irresistible waft and promise of barbeque. Oh, how those pork-tips, first dry-rubbed and then well-mopped, can smell after hours of slow smoking. Let us view this new-time celebration of the loaves and fishes as a practice in ecumenicity. We begin by stretching the privileged plump, brushed slightly with a red-wine marinade, upon the rack of abstinence. Heavy groans and sub-rosa pleadings to do us 'til we're done already. What fun! Then we throw in the rinsed-off Straights, slathered with honey and hot pepper, and brought together with the chubbies in a comprehensive fricassie: Breathless squeals and diminishing denials; hands-on congestion negotiating with no-touch shyness—more fun! The caterwaulings that ensue are joined together through the contrapuntal logic that reveals the inadequacies of the separate voices, which, if left to sing only their own lines, would miss out on what can be done when the girdle falls.

If you are still concerned with missing-out, consider that the standpoint of eternity is not always critical of a dumb campaign. Failure in a good cause is typically due to overreaching, but the debris of failure need not be discarded—but can be sorted through for valuable artifacts. The shards of great failures are, after all, testimonials of trying. Eternity is quite benevolent, even though ecumenicity is a practical not a formal art and does not flourish without some historical gestures toward completeness. There is much secondary literature about the wars between the lean and fat, stroked or scraped, wet and dry, raw or cooked, hip and square, easy come or corked-up tight, and the less quick if not-quite dead.

Slow-smoked barbeque assiduously basted, is where we all come together at road's end. All conflicts about the Greater Good, whether they start in the head or gut, and however much they are meant to reveal the better way for all of us, are, when pressed, like pomegranates giving forth their seeds—too many to count and no good way to choose between them.

So the philosophical attempt to create certainty continues without fail, to fail. What would adjudicating between the appetites and beliefs of straights and crookeds come to? Is it the dry rub, the slow smoker, and the winy marinade that give the best taste when the rib is well tended before its eating? Or do we falter and reach too impatiently for the secondary sausage, the sides of cole slaw and potato salad, and, yes, the corn.

IV

The ideas of a road and a destination can be separated, a move which may someday be celebrated as part of the consequential history of the "end of progress." Roads that have destinations are forever strewn with corpses. Times do not change in time of war. After the caudal kiss, there is little left for us to do but watch the killing, and help the dying die.

The only road that resists the bloodshed and teleology of our past is the one in front of the house that circles the barn and comes back out again to rejoin itself—it has no destination. It is the sufficient and blameless road one takes when going to where one already is. You need not believe me—but look down there: A new Highway 99 is being laid atop the dusty road that goes to town. Someone's grandfather said of that road that it was originally dirt and then became gravel during the war. It was later lengthened and covered with asphalt, which lasted until the good times came when they made it all concrete, exhibiting its twists and turns in brand-new overpasses that take us from the south end of Restoration City to the junction of the rivers up north.

The road that is intermittently straight and crooked is the one most of us travel. It is not a road of choice; it is a road of circumstance—of having learned not to choose other roads because of what such choosing might entail. Our road is now well-marked and dotted with competing super-centers, those cornucopias which offer more than before of all we are learning to want. Oh, it truly is a hubbub in those isles, a trampling under foot of both underage crookeds and aging straights. But, at this late date, any other direction—one that that would lead for example, to a neighborhood fresh-made sausage shop, or to a local artisan of austere pots, or a single-mother winemaker—does not match our map.

After all these years of separation, and having finally arrived at the joining of the roads, both Crookeds and Straights need not revert to the path of early discord. So let us, the elders say, declare an ideological holiday. Let us begin at the far-left and far-right of the bazaar; these are the traditional place-marks of discord. From there we will erect walkways filled with promises of full satisfaction, which then further divide into small winding paths dotted by faux-grottos with blown-up bathing beauties in six-inch heels tempting you to buy what you only recently said you did not want.

Then, if you turn again to the right, further up the uphill road, there is a continuous drone of chants inveighing against the flesh—whether eaten for sustenance or for pleasure; there are also free handouts of veggie recipes. Here one finds pre-school cautionary tales, and lectures directed to the old folks about how to avoid the last temptation.

The new wave, just down the up-hill road, has a different program. Felafel and egg-rolls abut offerings of jerked goat and all-beef hot-dogs, and in the center, there is a large inviting sit-down place with a full menu of couscous, garlic, lamb and, from 6 to 10 pm, tattoed belly dancers. On the far left, hidden somewhat by bushes, is the area frequented by the flower-children, as well as veterans of the wild times of social disobedience.

But there are other roads that lead to nowhere anyone would want to go. These are the scary roads, far away from the forward looking highways of both left and right. It may be (I have lately come to think) that the persistence of such roads into our privileged times, signals an end to the very notion of direction. For why should one take a road that goes to no particular where—except that going nowhere might (just might) be more interesting than the crowded road to somewhere. Reason's imperative these days is so enmeshed in destination that it generates few wondrous findings—such as the Form of being-lost. Wonder, which over centuries has been the devoted companion of unformed thinking, is now in danger of dilution. Like a single-malt scotch, wonder, when watered, goes down with nostalgia but only little bite. Wonder should not, I pray you, be diluted.

When taken straight, wonder deposits us in peculiar places—like the place where the old folks lived and, without an unseemly murmur, died. It was a small apartment on the second floor of a four-story walkup with views onto a side street, a quiet place except when, twice a day, children came in and out of school. It was a place of small grace that housed common things of unaffected modesty—a place as good as any for keeping memories of what is worth remembering.

A considered life, as it is known by connoisseurs of living, is not complete without the spectre of punishment at its end. Dying is punishment enough; going to hell is punishment of another kind. Some of us like to stoke the wonder required to play the agony game: What would it be like to be a living cinder, to burn in hell for all eternity without a moment's rest to even think about the pain?

Other conjectures, less wondrous, satisfy post-life concerns through homey rituals—burials consecrations and memorials—that bode well for salvation, offer less pain, and are designed to make death seem more life-like than life.

In suburban split-levels and tenement walkups, in coffee houses beery bars and stuffy parlors, living and dying continues being remade in aromatic shapes, and wafted out to join the smells of other end-term occupations. Such smells are easy enough to live with when you have passed the years hunkering down every night in an ancient bed that, when the weather gets warm again, releases the accumulated funk of winter abstinence. The crotch, when given no romantic reason to be washed, can become especially funky—worse than the backsides of herbivores for sure—approaching the impact of a ripe Limburger. But like the smell of strong cheese, continuing exposure changes the first whiff's shock into the possibility that, after time, the aura of unwashed and aging flesh might actually transmute into wonder. As we all or will all know, it is hard to avoid the smell of getting old—even when one keeps remembering to wash.

But the interests of the young in sexual funk are not simply a counter-cultural celebration of what you kids are not supposed to like. It goes back further, to the smells of mothers and fathers who, during a particularly cold night, will insist on your coming into bed with them so that we all keep warm together. Smelling is also central to the myth of creation. Think of it: Adam and Eve did not begin to smell until after they were cast out, and their recriminations (echoing Lucifer's malodorous pique at his failed coupe) are the first discords we know that crack eternal order. These are exemplified by the offal offerings with which the two, once naked but now concealed by goat-skins, strew the dusty downward road they had to take after heaven's gates slammed shut.

Memories of seduction are impoverished unless imbued with the smells that guide each special evening–the antique musk of sexual fluids mingling with the scent of flowers, perfume, and fine wine. Neither should the assertive odors of gin and garlic be regarded as always contrary to desire, for they provide a different correlation between temptation and smell, and thereby become popular sign-posts in the search for optimal ways of having sex. Recall the odors encountered that gala evening when, overfed and looking for the bathroom, you stumble instead into the host's master bedroom which despite daily cleaning, retains the mix of excretory and sexual juices. But this mingling of desires does not accord with the rules we encountered, just seconds after we are born, when we found that we must choose between this or that—between staying on the breast or shitting in a piece of cloth. This was not a choice, if I remember, we had to make in the womb.

The murder of crown-princes by courtesans, and the rape of wives and daughters by marauders are examples of not choosing but being chosen. Sex and violence are not easy to separate: Rape is a concomitant of warfare; more rapes occur in war than in peace. Enemy women (or is it women of the enemy?) are more likely victims of rape than of killing; this grant of life makes them useful for further raping. Stench is certainly more present in war than peace—soldiers have little opportunity to bathe, and women little chance to complain. Otherwise, sex in both war and peace employs practices that also have been associated with the delights of avant-garde society.

But then, the avant-garde often attempts to make art out of dicey social practices. The differences between advanced art and ordinary life, are hard to keep distinct. The non-fictional rape victim (mostly but not always a woman) has an ancient obligation to not enjoy the act. However, in order to avoid being killed, there is the parallel obligation to pretend, at least minimally, to show enjoyment and thus avoid the degeneration of sex into killing. Once accepting the obligation of life, there is also the need to find a rhythm with which to accommodate the many assaults—much the kind that prostitutes use to accommodate their tricks for the long day. The matter of a rape-victim's assenting to rape is certainly not part of the definition of rape, although in practical terms, assent can be necessary for continuing to live—which is the advantage a rape victim has over the dead soldier. Women who are raped and then escape back to their families face different responses in different cultures, ranging from a death inflicted by stoning or servitude in local brothels, or an enticing offer from a traveling Russian to join a girlie-show in Istanbul.

If you have a choice, I say go with the Russian—it's easier to escape in Turkey, and once you get to Greece, the smells are better and it's half-way to America. If you are really lucky and get to the promised land, you will have options that range between the Columbia School of Social Work, to gigs in Las Vegas, to marrying some jerk in Queens.

V

Recently, much philosophical attention has been paid to the epistemological import of the senses. The non-sense epistemologies (faith, pure reason, meditative intuition, revelation) are historically early in claiming primacy for true knowing. The epistemic amalgam of faith and reason does not depend on seeing, hearing, smelling, tasting, in providing knowledge of reality. Latter-day empiricists bridle at such a-priori pomp and offer instead, sensory evidence and constant conjunction.

But even within the offerings and orderings of sensibility, evident distinctions remain: Vision ranges farthest and is most inclusive—a vision of the infinite. Telescope and microscope, as you see, are but natural extensions of this sainted sense. Hearing is more immediate, containing whispered wishes and car-horns, kinds of music, and the approaching rumble of stormy weather. Touch is a ubiquitous sense—providing signs of distance or intimacy—which ranges from "don't touch me" to "a touch of class." Smell is mostly about social distinctions—our concerns with presentations of our own bodies, and with the places and people we want to embrace or avoid. Taste is the lowest sense in the hierarchy of sensibility; it is arbiter of the food you eat and the fleshly places you are drawn to.

But 'taste' has another dimension: it can be a potent metaphor. There is good taste and bad taste, and this distinction applies equally to the artistic issue of all the senses. Indeed, having (good) taste is the hallmark of an aesthetic disposition, and this generates judgments that are outside the verifiability asked of sensory information in the sciences. Quixotically, this, the least of our senses, is here given the function of judging between some of the most valued of our social products. Judgments about the respective values of literary, musical, and visual arts, in this turn of language, are called judgments of taste. These are not empirical judgments—which entail adequacy of representation, nor are they of the normative kind that demand universality of application. They are, as Kant indicated, merely "reflective" judgments, which rest on a hope that the world conforms to our experiences. So, to justify their use—given their undoubted social power—we up the ante and garland "taste" with modifiers: "advanced taste" "educated taste" "provincial taste" "poor taste" "no taste." We erect hierarchies of taste: art-historical, sociological, anthropological, ethical, political, religious. All of these have different, and often obscure criteria, and we argue interminably, without any real hope of (or perhaps desire for) consensus about the comparative merits of these judgments, or whether they can (or should—if indeed they could) be brought together under one encompassing "meta" judgment that adjudicates between all possible cases where taste applies.

The choice by the Straight and Narrows of the path they take is largely immune to internal disagreements about matters of individual taste. There is the integrity of the community to be maintained, and the clarity of traditional practices to be exhibited. Objects that decorate home and town are inherited between generations, although the lot is constantly diminished as grandpa's sofa eventually become too threadbare for even antique dealers. The objects that replace them are chosen for various reasons: nostalgia, parsimony, familiarity, among them. But all, in turn, will be discarded in their time, and their memories replaced with new objects.

Once upon a time, it must be said, Straights took artists seriously—back then before the days of revolution and the triumph of the bourgeoisie. Artists (by definition) had taste—in paintings and music and dancing; they knew about rarity in objects and subtlety in the play of fiction, and they had the skills for making the likenesses that would stir the senses.

But later, art took on a foreign mode and artists began to act like revolutionaries. It turned out, however, that the revolutionaries didn't trust artists either—artists don't pay dues and they're not predictable. Revolutionaries, in their way, are also Straights; they want to win—to get ahead. Straights of all persuasions have historically become uneasy when artists emerge from studios or garrets and signal they want to be reasonable. These sentiments have been described by Freud as the trivialization of art—primarily by the desire of artists for fame, money, and love. Such rewards, after all, are what most of us have always wanted—which is why we are now all artists.

But in the meantime, Straights still need designated enemies. Artists, from time to time (less so now) play the confrontational roles they first took on during early revolutions. They once presented themselves as defenders of the oppressed, advocates for the disenfranchised, champions of pure love and the redistribution of income. But after revolution fell out of fashion, art changed. Artists once idealized naked bodies by plucking them out of myth to have them stand erect in the village square, or sprawl about on velvet throws. Later, following Picasso, artists fragmented nudes through dissecting lines and occluding splashes, and so changed their special subservience into the ordinary one of common objects—nude as still-life. Some artists ignored them entirely—for the sake of purity.

Crookeds are not shocked by changes in art as easily as are the Straights. They will remind wayward artists that although their civic skills are wanting, they are good decorators none-the-less. With the revolution a distant memory, and free markets providing the economic rule for the world, artists, as with other entrepreneurs, want in. So, the Crookeds will say (building upon their historic compromise between good and evil) that we must conjoin the extremes of social protest and tasteful decoration into a center where art both astonishes and behaves. For such a center to hold, it has to move discreetly in and out and back and forth between competing interests. But the main presumption of post-polemic art is that contending ideologies are to be accommodated rather than selected. In this scenario, we leave the high and sparse terrain of the Straight and Narrows, and come to the lush and artsy wet-lands of the Crooked Straights.

The Straight-and-Crooked-Center-for-the-Arts has no particular shape; its compromise is formed by moveable modules on unstable soil. This instability provides for changing densities between buildings and grounds that are symbolized by the play of colors in the lagoon water and the seasonal changes in vegetation.

These markers do the job of retaining minimal stability within conflicting tastes. As well as sensitivity to nuance, they have a clear gradient, and are thus effective in locating the emergence of conflicts—uncivil disagreements that would encourage extremists to go beyond boundaries and trash the grounds.

Once strife is localized, resolution is simple: Decrease the flow of water, and thin out the overgrowth a bit—so that polemics and their bodies will all dry out in the mid-day sun. Or, if that doesn't work, increase the flow of water and make opposing factions swim around and past each other. Ideally, in the domain of Crooked-Straights, no such conflict is publically aired. Conflicts show themselves as currents that are too fast for sailing because of frisky winds—although the skies are clear. Or, sometimes, they appear as a fetid stench emanating from the backed up creek that reaches to where those tear-down shacks, used by hunters for god-knows-what, still stand. The winds across the sound will slow down soon; the smells in the back-waters take longer to clear.

Notwithstanding the contrasts between them, both versions of the Straights—the Narrows and the Crookeds—have surprisingly similar concerns. They are both afraid of other enemies with deeper strategies—hidden ones that do not roil the waters or have a smell. A scant century ago, all but the dull-pates agreed that things are bound to get better. What things? How better? When?—No matter. Aristotle's causes had been rescued by one Hegel and turned into spirit, the evolution of which, given constant expansion and selective inclusion (necessary functions of teleological process) is bound to make bespoke things better sooner or later.

There are historical disagreements, of course, about how spirit's evolution goes and shows. The Straights want to empty out the showing so that, peering past the debris, they can come to see the anorexic beauty of only that which must endure. The Crookeds, in contrast, are for plenitude, for the inundation of the world with all that can be rescued to provide the swift gratifications which should replace the slow and grudging pleasures of yester-year. The best of crooked pleasures is not to be found by reduction. The hedonism of Crookeds is satisfied through the interplay of individual pleasures, each by its nature being receptive to merger (or at least, some sharing) with the others. Such communal arrangements may need political finessing—the Straight-and-Narrow backlash from the outlands, with dire warnings of schism, is a recurrent threat. But Straight-and-Narrows, as a rule, do not disdain all pleasure; they fully enjoy the residue of their reductions. These mostly meatless bones they gnaw on are after all the symbols of success in achieving a balance between wants and beliefs. But, according to these beliefs, they must reach the final merger of thought and world without an ounce of excess weight. Imagine those Crookeds, they say, puffing up the slope towards total synthesis with an overflowing waistline!

VI

You are still anxious, Lucian, about the rescheduling of the parade that was planned in your honor—the one, remember, in which you were to be hoisted on the shoulders of acolytes, whirled about by sky-high maidens, carried in triumph through the main streets as the unwashed multitudes resound with hosannas for the savior (you) of the union between art and life.

Alas, although I do hear drumming around the corner, it's not for you. It's not coming, that parade, not a chance—but of course you knew that when you were young and watched parades pass by. Still, for now, there is no other fruit of the imagination—not even a free pass to Farouk's harem—that would better fill the space of a tepid afternoon. But supposing that it did happen—your parade—tell me what you think would happen.

Well, when we round the corner of Broadway and nineteenth street- on the way uptown, I get dumped, yes, just dropped by those cheerful acolytes onto a pile of lumpy garbage, which even for New York, is remarkably smelly on a cold late-winter afternoon. Why did I get dumped? Because my worthies had received word of a weightier hero to carry—a champion, not of art's penetration into life, but of decontrolling trade with deserving third-world nations. I never did meet the chap. I presume, because of the subject, that it was a man—for had it been a woman, I would have put the right arm of art onto her left breast.

We men, you know, lie on the left side of the bed, so that our right (dexter) hand is free to reach over for the roaming that traditionally precedes the act of making love. Left (sinister) hands, except for violin-playing virtuosos, never do the job as well. I myself, however, am philosophically ambidextrous, more a pianist at heart (although I do play the fiddle), and I admit that I prefer roaming with both hands to the disequilibrium of preparing with just one. Using both hands lasts longer, covers more terrain, and importantly, it provides space and time for conversation—yes, between the squeaks and squeals, a civilized account of progress achieved thus far can be voiced and alternatives offered for a more generous, geographical appreciation.

Some don't enjoy this indirection. It differs from sex as they know it, for it lasts too long, and as I said, it involves a lot of talk. No ordinary talk this; it is a focused rather than escapist kind in that it concerns the prime variants of ecstasy and how they can be coerced without succumbing to the parsimony of immediate orgasm. The more modern ideals of coitus have moved beyond the "beast with two backs" scenario, and the variety is now recognized in both the first and third worlds. But the pundits of the sheltered second world theorize that the sanctioned practice was first introduced into the colonies through the bravery of missionaries from the first world who dared to forsake the dangerous delights of top-rear-tongue and toe, and such other forms of address then practiced by the locals. These straights (for so they were) insisted, disregarding danger to themselves, on the sole propriety of the above-mentioned "two-backs" position. Some were killed, it is noted in the chronicles, for the crime of abetting boredom.

Eventually, we of the second world found that the direct way (the Missionary position as it was then called) was too paternalistic for extended conversation, and further, that chatting with one's partner about the goings-on is not restricted by a language barrier between natives and their liberators. Enthusiasm and simple gesture combined with heart-felt gutturals often bridge distrust between both peoples and nations. Squeaks and squeals, for example, can be made part of erotic conversation if they are understood as a form of talk. It is important for world peace that people talk while having sex, and so affirm the portent of their actions to themselves and to each other. Such talk can be heard in the sounds that whales make, and will coalesce, if we are diligent and persevere, into a version of the music of the spheres. All those who have contributed, can listen in.

To return, now, to the parade in my honor that was never completed—the time when I was dumped into the rubbish to make way for the new parade in honor of the successful candidate. I wish everyone well (me included)—but you know, parades, when viewed from sidewalks, are often dismal affairs. What's the big deal? So we won a war or you won an election; or they celebrate a saint who maybe never was.

I do remember a parade going uptown on Seventh Avenue, commemorating some or other pride-day. A friend cautioned me, when we got into the press of the crowd, to put my wallet into an inner pocket. I looked around but could find no one resembling a dip—but I had been away from New York for some time. The cohorts of the march—ugly, uncoordinated, and mostly hairy exhibitionist pigs—were propelled from behind by the standard oom-pah, and the floats were dull and ordinary.

But on one—behold—sitting astride a beer keg, was a most beautiful girl wearing only pasties and a necklace above the waist which permitted her to flaunt her substantial breasts in a side-to-side movement. It was getting cold by then, and I had to wonder whether goose-pimples or chilblains would soon be part of her performance—also whether there was anything I could do to help. That parade passed too, as had mine, and as with mine, some pieces fell away—although I'll bet that my transient love, my jiggling chimera, would not be discarded as I once was. She, I'm sure, is still in demand—although the ribald cheers that washed her movements lacked the earnestness, depth, and intensity of the greeting I would have met her with.

Let us call her Sheila. Goodby Sheila; sorry, I hardly knew ya. True, I could have broken through the barricades and leapt upon the lady, but only to be dragged back before I could get to talk to her—about her breasts and all they portend, which, as I would describe them to her while suckling, are iconic of a proper union between flesh and spirit. I did, in a moment of rhapsody, articulate this value, but the police were unimpressed—just another codger with loose marbles. Yet I insisted, as I was bundled back to the sidewalk, that this thrashing about of mine was not personal; my attempt at ingesting this girl's charms was meant as a tutorial for the folks who are inclined to hide behind their better selves. Before the cops grabbed me and said now-now and come along, I was trying to sing "O Tutto Amore" to the Sheila on the float; and I do remember, even though it did not happen, that she sang something like "Per-Che No" in return. I'll never know. Discombobulated and diminished, I was trundled back to the sidewalk and deposited at the place between the building walls and the rear end of the throngs—yes, by the garbage cans. The parade continued uptown with Sheila's jigglings becoming more congealed and schematic as the cold increased and the blocks went by. Sheila! Watch out for scaly skin! I tried to follow, running through the small space between mute walls and noisy vulgarians, but someone tripped me up—or I took a wrong turn—nothing in New York is by accident. So I never got to the place where Sheila stopped her jiggling and put on her jacket. Pity.

Parades start from a convenient spot and stop at a prescribed place. Rarely does a parade end where it begins—too metaphysical, that, for New York. However, nothing about either spot or place, beginning or end, indicates that one is better than the other. It would, of course, be a contamination of well-considered purpose if a parade were to start at the end and end at the beginning. Ends surely are derived from their beginnings—and as such are beholden to them. The journey from beginning to end is both a theological and evolutionary march and also patriotic. So considered, its import is that ends are more advanced, more inclusive—yes, better—than beginnings. There are some, in both popular and academic circles, who believe the opposite—although proponents of the higher value of beginnings are reluctant to join battle with the champions of the end.

What do you say, then, to the marchers, to Sheila with her chilblains, and to the hairy-raggedy dancers, who were full of hope about getting to the end, but once there are tired and hungry, and no longer care about the beginning promise of endless wine and all-night revelry that will await them at the end? Gullibles, I say. Yes, you are all gullibles—and now, even worse, you are victims. What should you do, you ask? You can of course blame your parents and your teachers, or to not hearing what your country has been asking you to do for it. But you can also blame yourself for being so dumb—for believing that the end of a parade is truly better than its beginning. Ask cold frozen Sheila with her puckered breasts who, at the end, after all that freebee jiggling, was offered only sympathy and a luke-warm hot coffee she had to pay for herself.

VII

The difficulties with "where" is often a fault of words: Words are usually clearer than the world is. Distinctions that words provide, package the murk of experience into bundles that are extracted from the sensible morass—a process that, in effect, makes sense of sense. Yet, it is not altogether clear that sense need be tied to words—how about songs without words (Hegel didn't like those) and pictures without representations (we moderns like them too much). Notwithstanding, we should not mind distinctions between the paths taken by "Crookeds" and the "Straights" as long as we accept that following either path goes to a place where all such distinctions converge.

It is gratifying to know, despite the above, that life can be composed of circles, not merely of straight lines. The straightaway takes us to a "there"—a "somewhere" that was there from the beginning, but no-one who just goes can know where the "real there" is. The rondalay way leads to a "somewhere" that may be here or there but cannot be placed anywhere for, in principle, it lies everywhere—in the before and after, top and bottom, inside-out, sooner or later, now and then.

"Wheres" that we know to be somewhere can still be difficult to locate, but they are indubitably within the present that separates past from future. "Wheres" that are everywhere are even more difficult, for they are where past and future, and all accessories of the present, merge in a way that excludes location in both space and time.

There is also a "where" that is nowhere, so "nowhere" both is and is not a state of affairs. "Nowhere" is more compatible with circles than with straight lines. Circles go nowhere—although they can spin, while straight lines have a beginning and an end, and therefore do go somewhere—although, because straight lines do have widths, the wheres they go through vary. The conceptual straight is clearer than the actual straight—as all the varieties of "straights" we have discussed are aware.

"Somewhere" is compatible with "elsewhere"—but not with "nowhere." "Somewhere" can be found if we look up the path or retrace our steps. But, be warned, "somewhere" is locatable anywhere.

"Everywhere" is the where of transcendence—as in Leibnitz where God is the external arbiter of intersection between monads. Or it is the where of immanence—as in Spinoza where God "just is" the whole plurality of nature. "Everywhere" is compatible with circles, but not with straight lines—for the reason that one cannot square a circle.

Circles, given their history of achievement, are only modestly ambitious, for despite their repetition they grow more interesting each time around—not because anything has changed, but because there is always something missed last time by those who stay on for another turn of the cosmic carousel.

Straight lines are more ambitious but less duplicitous. For those who have suffered an unhappy childhood, straight lines provide a better ride than do circles, because the beneficent end-to-come of a straight line is already firm in the hopeful and believing mind—even when approaching death—as inculcated there by the purveyors of progress.

The divigations of a dream-filled night do not follow the logic of a straightaway day. Yet, they do not either exhibit the continuity of circles. Dreams suggest, in their uncertain turns of hopes and fears, the schema of a spiral. For the ecumenical planner, the contrast between hope and fear suggests the spiral as a compromise between circle and straight line—a way of getting to a there that is "somewhere" rather than "nowhere"—even if it is not, upon reflection, to where you thought to go.

With spirals, as with all such compromises between good and evil, there are vacillations—foreign to the straight line and the circle—to be suffered through. Slinky-toys are better at going downstairs than up, and they never do stand straight. True skeptics, who believe in neither good nor evil, prefer that each dark and light is a singularity which affirms infinity's independence from any scheme of action. In this view, no directions—whether "forward by all means," or "remain by all means in place," or "let's follow the slinky way," are any different.

Sceptics have a point here—for survivors remember how each choice of the way to go was favored at its time of choosing, and how each would lose credence, despite negotiations, when faced with the armored presentations of the others.

Nevertheless, it is important, what with our imbedded anxieties about the good life, for all of us to anticipate the mix between straight ascents and crooked byways within any passage to our preferred "somewhere." Let others decide, then, whether the straight line, under a strict definition, must never bend, or if the circle, within a communal view, can straighten out a bit, and become a spiral.

VIII

"Going somewhere" is a phrase to watch; the "going" is clear, but the "somewhere" needs skeptical attention. Going is the age-old condition of a simple being in time. Somewhere speaks to where the going goes. Here we see the strain. When there and where come into conflict, then the imposition of the value somewhere on the passage of time rekindles the debate about how and why the world continues to go. We can take the notion of progress as an explanation for going somewhere other than where we are; and that somewhere, as identified by progressives, is, in principle, better than our present where. And so progress reveals the necessity (not demonstrable but undeniable) that the direction of time, both human and—if one wants to stretch it—cosmic, is good.

The circular scheme, in contrast—time as neither passing nor going—shuns the somewhere. Time, Parmenides says, is an illusion. In this view, time's duration gives us no way of discerning, much less believing, that the future will be better or worse than now—or even that such charged words as "better" or "worse" have meaning much less necessity, when applied to time. So, if we care about such things, about the way the world will likely be becoming, we return to the debate between skinny transcendent hope and plump obdurate skepticism.

In the country, road-signs marking the travel that charts the way of days are not very good; they have lost access to the central map that once gave them authority to actually point to somewhere rather than elsewhere. Nevertheless, one can still find out how to get from here to there by asking directions of local folk. The folks who live there know where that is but won't tell you much unless you present them with an open face. a robust if slightly awkward manner. and a hint that you are much in need of a somewhere they might approve of.

But if your shanks have grown flabby, your gray beard might become a talisman for the younger folks who know no better. Then you might still get to that place where you can actually enjoy the shrinkage of your once large life. This may not square with the ambitions you had in your early-feisty days, but late in life and deep in brooding, there is no longer any reason to repeat the historical mistake by traveling to one place rather than another. Geist, reacting to recent slander, has shrouded itself within a cave that, yes, has shadows on its walls.

If you are willing to look at shadows rather than the prancing figures in the outside light, go into the cave. Stay awhile—a longer while than you planned—and your sojourn will give you reasons for not trying other ways to go.

The very notion of a way to go is scary. "Way to go" cried the hoodlum from his passing convertible, when he saw me doing what, with all his badness, he could only dream about: kissing the tall blond with the willowy legs and somewhere husband, in the middle of Times Square with nowhere else to go. We kissed and kissed but eventually did go back to reconstitute the foursome at the restaurant to which we, all good friends, had gone for a Saturday night-out expensive dinner. It seemed to me then—although it doesn't now—that the latest echoes of geist required our continuing to kiss, and while still kissing to walk along the public way—that broadest of all progressive ways which go uptown. But we didn't. She married someone else and I went to the mid-west.

What if progress is simply the small space within which the episodes that affirm us are joined, a space that divides time between the remembered moments of our lives, and the blank passages that we, even as we pass through them, are not aware of. Progress, if one really prefers it to other modes of passing time, does require an austere itinerary: Get rid of the detritus of insignificance your life has strewn across the path; and cut back the obfuscating vegetation that presents a hindrance to the understanding of your worth—vegetation no doubt planted decades ago by your future enemies. Engage in prescient plastic surgery—put on a future-face.

There is, however, the other way. If we were, tout-court, to deny the notion of progress, then all this accumulated debris could stay around. Detritus, viewed from a sitting position, changes into homey clutter; facial creases and a pot-belly are signs of achieved character; and predatory vines and prickly bushes become safeguards of privacy. Having come around to this, we can join the folks who spend their time choosing the memories they can remember.

Those of us who are finally willing to sit, can choose our memories. The times I best remember, given my proclivities, are sometimes juicy and noisy, at other times stark and quiet. I do not much remember paydays, or promotions, but I do remember figures moving in gymnastic flings that slowly dissolve into twitches come resting-time.

I once asked a model to keep moving while I drew—a nice idea, but I didn't know enough to bring the scratching of my chalk together with a celebration of her movements—but how that girl did move I still remember. Such memories, were I not browbeaten by time's impatience, should be lingered over longer.

But, hey, we still have time. With an ample bit of wine and the earthy company of others who are willing to gab the night away, we can ignore the drum-beat of the coming of tomorrow, and remember the sight and sound and taste and smell of lingering in the dark.

Not so fast—antediluvian hippie! If you are really saying that the alternative to future-fright is to wallow shamelessly in the past and turn it into juicy memory, your choice is—as the waiter said when I ordered mussels in black-bean sauce—a good choice. But you may be, probably are, a nervous skitterer, and you want to hedge your present through a historical reconstruction program. You will be caught—if you don't watch out—between the late-night phone calls from the past (most are worse-off than you) and the opaque faces of the present (they are still concerned about themselves) and the antique-laced seductions of the future (they should be—but are not—celebrating you).

You say you have a plan: You will discard your past (most all of it) as a passel of youthful mistakes, criticize your present (despite all your smarts) as a weakness for exotic moments, and estimate that your future, (despite all you've done) is more grey than golden. You will then retire and move to the far country and watch sunrise and sunset play on the red-rock cliffs. It's a flawed plan, you must admit. Before you finish with the filling-in of what should have happened, and the weeding-out of what didn't happen—there is always death. Death does not provide answers for the dead—but perhaps it can give some answers to the living left behind who might be curious as to why, that time, despite the blandishments of Lobster- Cantonese, you chose the mussels.

IX

There are now new attitudes toward progress that transcend dilemmas of personal choice. They are not based on the older understandings of post-dying realms of death—for such realms are mostly theological. These new attitudes conceive of death as less a realm than an unsolved problem which, trivially, remains physically instantiated by an indefeasible rotting, but which, substantially, is an occasion to subsume the physical individual within a concept of culture as a teleologically-receptive organism that requires the juices of its historical members to develop. You, dear boy, can be part of that.

But even in our latter-day neo-mystical times, such new understandings have not penetrated academic circles. Imagine, for example, a young and eager soul, a just-out PhD newly hired by Middle-States University to teach introductory ethics, who is surrounded from the moment of arrival by aged rhinoceri deeply committed to the physicalist interpretation of the mind-body problem—to wit: the mind is the brain, the brain is a proper part of the body, the body inevitably dies and disintegrates and that's all. Immortality is merely a matter of remaining in print. Could this wounded soul profess in class—or, more dangerously, in writings—such absurd conceits as a "post-dying realm" in which dying need not lead to death? Even the hoary tenured ones cannot risk such atavisms—unless there is some mitigating theological cocoon attached.

Yet there are a happy few, come-lately renegades from the realm of clear thought, who want now to stand on their heads—despite all linguistic seductions to straightness—and so get on with their re-mystified lives. We (although I am not yet sure I am one) plan to live and think (the two, they insist, should co-habit) in the new style of presentness, where we are entitled to laugh (following Nietzsche) at the official hope that there is a single material description for everything worth mentioning that exists. What should not be mentioned, they say, deserves disdain and silence. But the silence only excludes what—given present parameters—is not worth talking about; it cannot exclude all that exists.

"Presentness" is a recent neo-way—a ploy that seeks to omit the old guilt about adequate reference by getting on with street-smart versions of how anything can be talked about. We might—we shaven or shaggy heads, lolling of an afternoon in the best disreputable places, dressed to the nines in wife-beater shirts and washable tattoos—be able to separate the notion of progress from its metaphysics. Instead of being strung-up on the rack of final causes, or the cross of spirit's evolution, we could view the continuum of past to present as being composed of the stories we tell each other. These stories (they are best told by those who have known each other in the days and nights of hate and love) are a good way of protecting ourselves from those who say that living is simply what we go through to reach our dying.

I am one who is a raconteur of living. I do so partly because of the ordinary fear of dying, and partly for polemical reasons—to debunk the notion that dying always leads to the non-narrative happenstance of death. Historically, I am a late-comer to these considerations, and yet, being late gives me access to the latest ways that life goes on even as it ends in death.

Wait! (It's Wladyslaw again) You are a literary opportunist, dear Lucian, stooping to feed feel-good advice to the fear-of-dying crowd. The TV shrinks make money doing that; you just want recognition. So I must, at this point, sorry, separate myself from you. But before I go, let me tell you this: What can be extracted from birth to death is only the value that is generated within that little time-bound arc. Admittedly, it is a value hard to pin-down, for it is nothing and is yet eternal—as you are, together with rocks, seas, trees and sky—an instance of what transpires. And yet, it is stable, your personal sense of the duration of your existence within this other. Aquinas calls it the "habitus." You—moribund hulk, prime-time sybarite, once moist babe—must acknowledge your habitus through a last hard act of understanding before you die. Why? Well, is there anything better to do? Nothing for it but to go through the last itches of existence that, however much you hopefully scratch your dick, will soon stop.

Through the wiles achieved by learning to survive in post-depression Brooklyn, sharpened by the ethnic mix of high-immigrant ideology and special local pleadings, I moved away from imperatives of obedience and sublimation. I could then recommend—but only to myself and susceptible others—the earthly, fleshy, ways of growing up—all this before I had any idea of what, in fact, we had to do when they fail.

It seems a hundred or so years ago, but—as the song says—I remember it well. No need now to relinquish fond memories for any new imperative that would have me disavow the juices that marinated me in those days. See! They drip a little, still.

So I must say to you before you leave, my critic and one-time me, that you too are a hypocrite. Why do you not understand that my swerves and pseudo-offerings were in fact, only modes and manners of solicitation that would help my ambitions to be praised. The deeper metaphysics that support such ambitions are not new, nor are they particularly mine; they have been better voiced by more subtle contestants over centuries.

Why then, you ask, did you not reach for the deeper ones? Well, only to keep Lucian in the running—I was afraid of disappearing. But I see that this excuse falls beneath your critical floor. I understand: For critics to judge well, they need a historical cipher, a sense of what gets up high enough to attract attention. Lucian is not there, you say. But he does want to be judged fairly; if not that—to be idolized (which is fair, no?) for doing everything that—if ever read or seen—could still blow the minds of those out there.

X

I now go on to other issues which, unlike art, are independent of taste, and so have nothing much to tell us about how our collective preferences will tumble out in later life. These issues are the ones with which I began this writing, namely, the perpetual conflict between two schools of Straights; the Crookeds and the Narrows.

Both Crookeds and Narrows, despite their differences, are committed to going straight—that is, to believing that their chosen path will get them, or their loved ones, or those the loved ones love, to the better future place. The choice between the two comes down to how much latitude—wiggle room (the gift that Sheila gave us)—in the realm of straightness each version allows its followers.

"Wiggling" for the non-believer is its own justification; it not only feels good, but is both ground and reason for consuming all the nectar and ambrosia you can swallow along the way. These are the same condiments, so agnostics say, that nourish the optimism lubricating the best minds—which includes those late Hegelians who have abandoned the belief that Geist is programmed to make life better—but that nevertheless life can be made better. So they feel free to wiggle as they wish before and after work each day. For the committed Straight, however, wiggling is a conundrum. Straights of all persuasions wiggle some. But how much wiggling is enough and how much is the too-much that strains the conscience and the back? There can also be too little wiggle in a lifetime. The memories of how much one wiggles intrude at most any time—whether one is sitting on the pot or cooking the books or slicing the roast.

Does the wiggling in our future, ask the elders of both persuasions, make our ascent to true belief less rather than more certain? This question is simply answered by the Narrow-Straights, whose general program is to tuck in fledgling flappers and sit on them until they are bespoke adherents of the narrow faith. When asked of the Crookeds, the answer is that letting their fledglings out into treacherous reaches strengthens their and our belief that they can be reeled in, only slightly bruised but much the wiser, just before the serpent snaps its jaws.

But what if both are wrong? What if there is nothing to be gained by either prudence or profligacy? What if it all comes to the same old death after which there is no questioning—no agent of post-life beaurocracy to tell the freshly dead whether their life was good or bad? The Narrows believe that the specification of what counts as virtue, buttressed by incessant reiteration, will win favor even with a truculent and censorious God. In contrast, Crookeds envision a God of empathy (it may be the same God) who excludes from grace only those that fail to request early permission for later deviance or those who overdo it.

Both ways quite destroy my hope for an unencumbered moment with Sheila. (Remember her?) A thoughtful skeptic would view this as a welcome happenstance—for what nerdy septuagenarian would want to subject a girl like that to a slow and creaky loving when her pressing need is to find directions for a fast and lubricated living. Older folks, those who can no longer come up to speed, celebrate the weariness of slower living by insisting that their day are neither slow nor dull—they exemplify a more subtle, if gesturally diminished, form of life. And don't forget! A grand catastrophe may be waiting for us all—young or old, pretty or puckered—as early as tomorrow. Large sequences of unremarked time usually include catastrophe: the giant meteor, having done the dinosours, comes again for us; mutually assured destruction flies overhead. Both of which at any rate are better than a slowly spreading disfiguring and incurable plague: "Believe me if all those endearing young charms." So wiggle to the end, my Sheila.

Through many nights, I have wrestled with my dreams; they do not follow the directions I set down while nodding-off. Instead of cuddling willing Sheila, I am alone and on a journey whose destination keeps changing; and after days on high windy paths I wander down through neighborhoods which are familiar, but the people (maybe relatives of Sheila) threaten me because of something terrible I have done.

Some dreams are not like that, and I wake to find, especially on Sunday mornings, that the coffee is better, and on the table there is cream cheese and freshly-toasted bagels which can also be adorned with lox or smoked white-fish.

Sheila should join me here; I'm sure she would love the food. She could also tell me—what with her breasts now demurely covered in the slather of lox and cream-cheese, and pieces of white-fish between her toes—why she needs to seduce all the world of seventh avenue, from Bleeker Street to Times Square, when the greatest of septuagenarian lovers is running, in fact and mind, right there between the crowds, trying his hippety-hoppety best to keep up with her. He has the talent (I have testimonials) to stroke her daily needs and sometime fears into a howling communion, ever and forever. A good proposal that, but I couldn't present it to her because of, you know, the crowds—and anyway, Sheila was hoping to enjoy, after her frigid wigglings, the warm and steamy clouds of young concupiscence instead of my sincere and selfless offer.

But there are still other possibilities: As often happens in the movies, Sheila and I could be selected by the powers, plucked out of the grunge and floated above the roiling celebrants, well beyond their gibes and gestures of lasciviousness. These calls of brutish mating (which Sheila admits once heated her) would then sound like distant bird-songs beneath the clouds where we lay in intercalate privilege. Suspended by celestial tenterhooks, we could watch the grungers and then glimpse the geometry of ideal things.

My way of living, however, is not in keeping with the ambitions of Sheila's circle. Those glassy girls are accustomed to swift encounters with priapic elders who can finess their contributions to the enterprise of a January- June relationship. Does money figure in that smarmy pact? Yes, of course. But I have to offer only the belated wisdom that shows how to recognize the illusions that make for wasted time. I am a good example of wasted time. I would confess to Sheila that I, a sometime artist and one-time professor, have no knowledge of the money-making world. But I do have a fertile—some say febrile—imagination which, even now, is of some value. For example: I can expound on subjects of mutual interest until everyone is exhausted; and I like to pontificate on matters I am just learning about.

I sometimes think of poor Anna-Nicole, who had gotten the big bag of gold, but was screwed-up enough to stay high and die. But maybe she preferred dying to the rehashing that marks the criss-cross of generations: Old men mask their waning powers with sleight-of-hand techniques that gull the innocent and untried into the belief that these are more civilized, certainly less exhausting than those other ways—and there is still time to enjoy a late dinner. Such techniques are said to result in a high number of early orgasms and in this sense are true to the age-old covenant of passing down wisdom between old and young. But this covenant does not address young needs for fumbling and failure—which I say are the preludes necessary to living and loving. These are not satisfied by the clever play of creaky appendages, nor are they mollified by the sojourns in upscale restaurants (more champagne my dear?) that form the atavistic joy of elder creepers.

Sheila, you never knew me—nor I you. I only saw you from the middle distance of your brave and waving tits, and you never noticed me at all. So I should not hope—although I do, despite my well-developed logic that countermands serious hope for the actuality of miniscule possibilities—that we will be together. I continue hoping that you will appear (soon-soon) within the narrative of my life. I imagine (I am adept at telling myself stories) that my construction of your breasts into the finest poesy, and your re-casting of my reduced body into what is tolerable, will provide a feasible representation of our future. What might kids born of Sheila's wagging mammaries and my long old bones be like? (Note: "tits" are here and now; "breasts" are now and then; "mammaries" are found in books). Well, the kids will be long-boned, big breasted, or both.

Snakes that bite are good subjects for late narrative: If the poison is countered by an antidote, then we have another travel story that tells of miraculous survival. Even if the poison is severe—say, that of a Boomslang encountered by straying off the prescribed path in the Australian outback—then the drama of primordial death in this day and age, would undoubtedly generate a successful book—much like Ms. Pomperduff's best seller "The Asp and I." She did get her pampered ass bit by the worst of the worst—but as she then died, she didn't write the book.

I do not notice snakes even when they're there where'ere I walk. Pomperduff believed that the world has guaranteed her immunity from venomous intrusions. I, much poorer and more metaphysically minded, think that in some world it is possible I should get spat upon by a cobra. But I fear that my present road, as it is more a ramble through the woods than intrepid ascent, does not show the good-old rugged strength—the fervor of fusing self with universe—that would bring a celebrated adversary—a champion reptile—into my path.

Sheila had never thought about snakes—except in idle phallic day-dreams. But those complaiscent reptiles only served to dull her daily life and so do not compare to other snakes which, did she accept their biting, would lead her to a last fleeting sense of things—venom often shows a temporary kindness—through which she might recognize her uniqueness before she disappears. This is not a sense she knew she had, but it is one that you and I, Wladyslaw, we ancient and insatiable voyeurs, are free to imagine how, did she know how fine she is, would not flaunt her charms in front of all those red-rimmed mid-town eyes.

So, old serpent, confess: You slithered, didn't you, through the crowds, braving the stomping heels (you were faster in those days) and then you bit her, yes, did bite her in the heel. Were you thinking then that you are young and flexible enough to eat her whole? Now, alas, as you did not eat what you bit, you are forever Sheila-less, and you must endure the coming years knowing that she, now dead, will never, no not ever, demonstrate her trademark twist and turn—known to us as the wiggle.

X

Snake-heads yawn when they meet dawn's first light. Their tongues, which have been flickering moistly through the darkest hours, are now dry; the nightly task of separating food from foe is almost done.

The catch last night has been good: five straights—two crooked—and one tasty girl who insisted as she died that she was in the wrong time and place because the old man, that one squatting on the rise above the concrete walk, told her it's the way to go.

The snakes each took a tiny bite of her—no more than one—in deference to her beauty. The straights they ate up whole, knowing that bones and sinews are easy to pass through—although the fatty crookeds give more nourishment. But between rumps and thighs, nose and toes, whether succulent or stringy—and the superb flavor of the still wiggling appetizer—it was a good night.

Minerva's owl—you remember her ambitions and her fear of snakes—has now become a fat old bird who confines her hooting to Friday dinners on the upper west side where believers come to sing the old-time songs of progress. Then the dawn greets the revelers with its glimmer of irrelevance and sends them to their creased and seasoned beds.

The owl can only sit—for flying has become too difficult—as she waits for the night that is not followed by day.

www.ingramcontent.com/pod-product-compliance
Lightning Source LLC
Chambersburg PA
CBHW050340230426
43663CB00010B/1933